# CORE ISSUES IN EUROPEAN ECONOMIC INTEGRATION

*Edited by*
Eamon O'Shea
Michael Keane

Oak Tree Press

Dublin

Oak Tree Press
Merrion Building
Lower Merrion Street
Dublin 2, Ireland

A catalogue record of this book is
available from the British Library.

ISBN 1-86076-111-9

Printed in Ireland by Colour Books Ltd., Dublin

# CONTENTS

# LIST OF TABLES AND FIGURES

# ABOUT THE CONTRIBUTORS

**Michael Cuddy** is Professor of Economics at the National University of Ireland, Galway. He obtained his primary and masters degrees from the National University of Ireland and his PhD from North Carolina State University. His teaching interests are regional and rural development and transition economics. His research interests have been primarily in regional and rural development and his present focus is regional development in transition economies.

**Stilianos Fountas** obtained his BA and MA from the Athens University of Economics and Business and continued his postgraduate studies at Ohio State University where he received his PhD. He teaches monetary economics and econometrics at the National University of Ireland, Galway. He has published in the areas of international finance, European monetary integration and open-economy macroeconomics.

**David Jacobson** obtained his undergraduate education at Hebrew University of Jerusalem, his masters degree at Sussex University in England and his PhD at Trinity College, Dublin. He currently teaches at Dublin City University Business School, mainly in the area of industrial economics. His research has focused on various aspects of industrial subsectors, but he has also published work on European integration, multinationals, and the political economy of innovation. A current project, among others, is on the evolution of networks around the subsidiaries of software multinationals in Ireland.

**Michael Keane** holds a BA and an MSc degree from the National University of Ireland and a PhD degree in economics from Simon Fraser University, Canada. He teaches courses in microeconomics, spatial economics, regional and urban economics and development and his research interests also cover these fields. He has published widely in the area of spatial economic analysis, tourism economics and regional and local development. Current research projects include the economics of tourism, territorial economic dynamics and social entrepreneurship.

**Terrence McDonough** holds a PhD from the University of Massachusetts at Amherst and teaches economics at the National University of Ireland, Galway. He is co-editor of *Social Structures of Accumulation* (CUP). He is currently interested in theories of economic crisis and recovery and the economy of nineteenth-century Ireland.

**Eithne Murphy** is a graduate of University College Dublin, Kiel Institute for World Economics, and the European University Institute, Florence. She teaches European Economics and international trade theory at the National University of Ireland, Galway. Her research interests include agricultural trade, international economics and agriculture, and the environment. Her current research relates to international trade, growth and multinationals and their effect on host country welfare.

**Dan O'Flaherty** is associate professor of economics and director of the graduate programme in public policy at Columbia University. His book, *Making Room: The Economics of Homelessness*, was selected by the Association of American Publishers as the best economics book of 1996. He has also been employed by the City of Newark and the New Jersey State Senate.

**Eamon O'Shea** is a graduate of University College Dublin, the University of York and the University of Leicester, where he received his PhD. He teaches welfare economics, health economics and public finance at the National University of Ireland, Galway. His main research interests are the economics of ageing, health economics, the welfare state and social policy. He has published widely in each of these areas. Current research interests include the economics of dementia, the economics of parasuicide, and social entrepreneurship.

# INTRODUCTION

The idea for this book developed as a result of frustration at the absence of a suitable text for the teaching of an inter-disciplinary course in European Economy at the National University of Ireland, Galway. There are, of course, many texts dealing with the issue of European integration, but none seem to capture all of what we wanted to say on the subject. In addition, the vast majority of conventional textbooks are too narrowly focused on economics and very often are too technical for those not majoring in economics. There was a need for a text which would deal in a substantive, but not overly technical, manner with the economics material, while at the same time acknowledging the broader social and philosophical framework within which the economic analysis is necessarily embedded.

Over the years, the European Economy course at NUI, Galway has evolved into a treatment of the main core issues of integration, namely: the single market; economic and monetary union; fiscal federalism; regional issues; and social issues. Two years ago, we decided that if a suitable text did not exist for this course, the solution was to produce course material ourselves, in the form of a reader that covered the major issues in a way that would be interesting and attractive to students of various backgrounds taking courses in European integration. The book takes advantage of the range of expertise available within the Department of Economics at NUI, Galway on European issues, but does not seek to impose any particular view with respect to the desirability, or otherwise, of existing or future European integration.

The basic aim of the reader is to provide a comprehensive, mainly non-technical account of the core areas of economic and social integration in the European Union. The book covers seven areas in the following order: the values framework for integration; the single market; economic and monetary union; regional issues; enlargement issues; social issues and federal relationships. The discussion in each chapter draws on theoretical material, but there is a strong effort made to link the theory to public policy issues emanating from consideration of each topic. The book is about European integration, and not directly about how Ireland will fare in the process of integration. However, given the location of the authors, Ireland does feature quite a lot in the text. The material is, nevertheless, intended to be of relevance and interest to students taking multi-disciplinary courses in European Studies in other countries of the European Union.

The past ten years have seen enormous progress made in the drive towards European integration, which as a concept is now more than forty years old. The momentum towards final economic and monetary integration has been so impressive that we are now a matter of months rather than years from probably the most significant change in European economic and social policy-making ever recorded. Sovereign governments are about to hand over considerable decision-making powers in the sphere of monetary and economic affairs to a centralised non-elected Central Bank of Europe. They are doing this largely on an act of faith, because there is uncertainty about the full dynamic consequences for the citizens of Europe of such a transfer of power. We can, of course, make predictions about what will happen to interest rates, unemployment and the like, but even here the signals are contradictory some positive, others negative. Moreover, while the monetary issues tend to dominate the policy process at present, other equally important issues, such as regional and social policy, enlargement, and federal decision-making structures, are debated less, even though they are very important elements of the overall integration process. This text deals comprehensively with all of these issues.

The book begins with an extended discussion of the principal features, and underlying values, of a market economy. Almost all of the recent progress towards integration has been based on the desirability of creating a single market in Europe, linked to a single currency, and supported by conservative and tightly controlled fiscal policies. Chapter 1 explores the implications of the market process, and deals with the positive and negative consequences arising from the elevation of efficiency as the primary motivation of integration. The chapter sets the scene for the issues covered later in the text, and is an important framework and integrating instrument for the project as a whole.

Chapter 2 deals with issues in international trade and European integration, with particular reference to Ireland. The main concern of this chapter is to provide an explanation for the tendency for economic activity to concentrate spatially. Both traditional and new trade theories are used to explore trade patterns in the Community. Ireland is an interesting case study on which to test these theories given its now well-documented "tiger" economy, despite its peripheral location. The chapter concludes with a warning that, even in the face of substantial success, economic prosperity will be unevenly spread. The implication is that, even with buoyant markets, government intervention will be necessary to spread the benefits of economic growth to all citizens.

Chapter 3 examines macroeconomic policy-making in the context of monetary union, and is the most technical chapter in the book. The objective of the chapter is to examine the broad welfare effects of monetary integration. The theories of Optimum Currency Areas are used to address the various costs and benefits of integration. The issue of optimal path or transition towards full monetary union is also considered. There is a review of the conflicting accounts of the potential gains to Ireland of a single currency. The chapter acknowledges the uncertainties associated with the whole unification process, and the absence of a theoretical basis for many of the so-called rules of engagement for monetary union. What is clear, however, is that despite the warnings of many economists, monetary union will soon become a reality because the political will exists for it to happen.

Chapter 4 deals with regional issues for existing members of the Union. Regional disparities are currently dealt with in the EU through the Structural Funds. The operation and impact of the Structural Funds are covered in this chapter. Theories of regional development are also explored with a view to saying something about the optimal approach to dealing with the problems of uneven development. The discussion on regional issues is continued in Chapter 5 where the costs and benefits of the proposed eastern enlargement of the EU are examined in some detail. There are significant labour market, trade, investment, agriculture and budgetary dimensions associated with enlargement. The new Eastern-bloc countries will have a greater claim on the structural resources of the EU due to their poor economic status. The less developed and peripheral regions of the current EU member states are particularly sensitive to these effects.

Chapter 6 covers social issues and is concerned with the development, evolution and future prospects of social policy and the welfare state in the EU. The chapter sets out the typologies that have been used to characterise the welfare states of Europe. It discusses the relationship between the labour market and social protection and argues for equal primacy between efficiency and equity in analysing issues concerning integration. The current status of EU social policy is considered, along with some discussion of how progress might be made in developing this policy. The main conclusion is that participation-enhancing and potential-enhancing models may be the key to a more expanded role for the EU in social policy-making in the future.

Federal relationships are considered in the final chapter. Traditionally, the concept of subsidiarity has been central to the debate about policy integration and competencies in the European Union. There are grounds for the belief that the principle of subsidiarity is now used in a negative way to keep awkward issues off the Community agenda, without much concern about the validity of this approach. The principle of subsidiarity could equally be interpreted in a different way to place the onus on the EU to become more involved in issues which can reasonably be shown to be beyond the capability of a lower authority. But this raises an even more fundamental point about whether a principle that is so open to interpretation is a principle at all, and whether it offers much by way of guidance in respect of the allocation of policy functions and competencies in the new Europe.

The approach taken in this chapter is that special districts are the key to an alternative view of how the emerging federal structure in the EU might operate. The chapter explains the concept of special districts, within the context of the modern economic theory of organisation. Generally, a special district is a unit of government that is organised for a single function, and separate from other units of government. The chapter is exploratory in approach, but does point the way to the potential of new forms of organisation within the EU.

This book concentrates on the key elements of European economic and social integration. It provides a solid theoretical and conceptual framework for the analysis of the on-going process of integration. The material is primarily aimed at students taking courses in European economy within a European studies, or public administration, programme. These students will likely have taken a principles course in economics but will, most probably, not have taken higher level theoretical courses in the subject. For such students, the book can be used as a stand-alone text, particularly if only the major elements of economic and social integration are being examined. The text covers the integration material in an accessible way, drawing on a rich set of ideas and possibilities which are not normally included in conventional economics textbooks. The student is exposed to a wide-ranging literature, and there is an extensive set of references with each chapter which point the reader to the original sources for many of the ideas discussed in the text. For students majoring in economics and taking courses in European economy within conventional economics programmes, the book should be used in conjunction with a more technically specific economics textbook. The book will also be accessible to the general reader who is interested in

European issues, and who is willing to accept the challenge posed by the more technical parts of the material.

# 1

## MARKET, STATE AND COMMUNITY

*Eithne Murphy*

### 1. INTRODUCTION

An economically integrated area, in an institutional sense, is one without internal legal and administrative barriers that impede the free flow of goods, services, capital and people. The term *economic integration* is to some extent a misnomer, since the process by which countries agree to dismantle the legal barriers that impede commerce, and construct new common rules governing economic activity is essentially a political process. There are degrees of integration ranging from preferential trade agreements at one end of the spectrum through economic and monetary union and, ultimately, political union. The defining aspect of the process of ever closer integration between countries is the increasing curtailment of national policymaking autonomy in the different spheres of civic and economic life.

Given the political and cultural diversity of European nations, integration is an ambitious project. As we head for the next millennium, the European Union (EU) is evolving through a process of widening and deepening. New countries are being admitted to membership and the rules governing conduct and co-operation between member states are changing. It is important to address the objectives of national governments as they continue the process of constraining their own political autonomy. What is the end goal, the ideal for which national governments are willing to circumscribe their own power?

One possible answer is that economic and political independence in the modern world is an illusion and that political structures are merely designed to dispel the myth of national autonomy and reflect the reality of our inter-dependence. Two major wars in Europe this century clearly illustrate the human cost of nationalism and international rivalry. The new route of co-operation is recognition of our interdependence and common destiny.

European Union is also an economic experiment.[1] It reflects an ideological commitment to the view that markets, when unimpeded by excessive administrative and institutionally created obstacles, are the surest route to economic prosperity. By facilitating international commerce and the free mobility of capital and people, it is assumed that:

- Resources will be more productive;

- Material output will increase and;

- Welfare will improve.

Any analysis of the integration process must address the presumed causal links between the new institutional arrangement and more output and between more output and increased welfare. This raises inevitable ethical issues about welfare and its determination.

The objective of this chapter is to provide a framework for what follows in the book. There is a lacuna in the literature on European Union on ethical issues. This doubtless reflects a common tendency to define welfare in narrow economic terms and a belief that economic prosperity must first be achieved before other social problems can be tackled. The interaction of economics and ethics and the role of economic man in society need to be addressed. For example, the presumed identity between material

---

[1] I use the word "experiment" deliberately, since no one can predict with certainty the economic consequences of the proposed economic and social arrangement.

well being and individual welfare should not be taken as axio-
matic. It is also opportune to question the unit of analysis or level
at which welfare is evaluated; that is to say, whether the focus
should be on the individual, family, region, state or supranational
state.

The following are examples of some issues that could arise (or
indeed, some might argue, have already arisen) in the EU at some
time in the future, and which can be evaluated from different
moral perspectives. Economic growth could create *unexpected* social bads, such as adverse affects on the physical and social environment. If this does occur and have adverse affects on the welfare of some or all groups in society, would the political will exist
to tackle the unexpected social bads? This begs a subsequent
question as to the factors that determine social solidarity. Is economic prosperity a necessary prerequisite for social solidarity or
does the extension of the market into all areas of civic life undermine our capacity for altruism and commitment to equity? Is solidarity less likely among the electorates of different nation states
than among the citizens of a single country?

The extended discussion on values that follows is an attempt to
highlight the diversity of ideologies which exist on normative issues. This is necessary in order to have some standard against
which to evaluate the past and prospective evolution of the European Union. The objective (admittedly an ambitious one) is to
show that economic prosperity, as conventionally measured in
terms of output in the EU, is one very limited moral standard for
judging the performance of this political and social experiment
and does not in itself guarantee either the success or stability of
Europe.

Section 2 looks at society and materialism and the contribution
of private consumption to societal welfare. This is followed in
section 3 by a discussion on individual liberty and the extent to
which it can be realised in a market-dominated society. A central
issue in the debate is the limits that societies place on individual
autonomy in the interests of other social objectives, such as order,
justice and cohesion. Equality and social justice are the focus of

section 4. Of interest here are the various arguments (ethical and functional) used to defend existing social inequalities or to justify their abolition or diminution. In sections 5 and 6, we turn our attention to the actual process of European integration in its microeconomic and macroeconomic manifestations. The microeconomic aspects of integration deal with the single market and these are analysed in section 5, while the macroeconomic aspects (which are intimately connected with the imminent introduction of the single currency), are the focus of attention in section 6. In both sections, the implications of market integration for economic efficiency, spatial equity and social justice, are evaluated. Section 7 addresses directly redistribution issues and the structures that exist within the EU to ensure that no regions or social groups are marginalised or left behind in the quest to create a dynamic single market. Section 8 contains concluding remarks on the future direction of the EU. Emphasis is given to the need for imaginative structures both to strengthen civic society and redress the democratic deficit which is a by-product of economic integration.

## 2. SOCIETY AND MATERIALISM

Contemporary society is dominated by market capitalism. As a social system, capitalism has been incredibly successful in harnessing the productive potential of the resources necessary for human existence. The growth in output this century in societies dominated by market capitalism has been phenomenal and without historical precedent. This raises the question of the centrality of material well-being to human and societal welfare and whether the elevation of material goods, as the primary objective of all human endeavours, can have negative consequences for society.

Orthodox economics considers utility maximisation to be the motor that drives human behaviour. The more we satisfy our preferences, the greater is our utility. Furthermore, a central assumption of economic theory is that human preferences are monotonic; that is to say, the more goods we have, the better off we are (the greater our individual utility). In fact, our desire for goods is so strong that the problem of scarcity will never be resolved. The human desire for material goods is considered to be infinite. If one accepts this materialistic view of societal welfare, then market capitalism has been amazingly successful in terms of *producing the goods* that can enhance societal welfare.

Cynic, Stoic and Christian philosophies, with their emphasis on ascetic and spiritual values, have always challenged the centrality of materialism to human self-realisation. More recently, Communitarians (Etzioni, 1988, 1993) have taken up the gauntlet with their emphasis on the social nature of individuals. According to the Communitarian thesis, individual well-being comes from a combination of self-advancement with investment in one's community. Once basic needs are satisfied, higher levels of personal income will not guarantee higher levels of personal happiness. The equation of preference satisfaction with human well being, a philosophy first expounded by the eighteenth-century philosophical radical Jeremy Bentham (Bentham, Burns and Hart, 1990) has been challenged by, among others, Sen (1973). What people prefer may not be good for them, because in a world of uncertainty, people make mistakes. Preferences are not necessarily as complete and rational as economists assume.[2]

Poole (1991) makes the point that the survival of capitalism as a social system depends on its success in generating wants. (The extent of marketing and advertising in capitalist societies would add credence to his assertion.) Since capitalism *creates* wants, as well as producing the goods that *satisfy* wants, utility will have increased only if the ratio of satisfied wants to unsatisfied wants has increased. Notwithstanding the undoubted capacity of capitalism to produce goods, there is no proof that it has succeeded in making us better off in the subjective psychological sense just described; that is, in its capacity to satisfy our ever increasing wants.

---

[2] To say that preferences are complete is to assume that individuals know their own minds best and can rank actions and outcomes in terms of their contribution to their own well being. Rationality presupposes consistency in the exercise of individual choice. Both assumptions assume that choices that an individual makes are the *best* given the constraints of their situation.

In addition, capitalism, with its emphasis on material consumption, has been responsible for the production of bads; that is to say, consequences that impact negatively on human welfare. Our physical and social environments have been altered as a result of the production and consumption of goods and services. Clean air, unpolluted water and an unpunctured ozone layer are as essential to human existence (not to mention welfare) as material consumption. Other bads, such as congestion and noise pollution, while not life threatening, do affect the quality of our existence. The spread of the market economy and the growth in production and consumption has been positively correlated with increased environmental degradation.

Growing inequality (among countries and individuals) has also been associated with the spread of the market and increased globalisation. Historically, market capitalism has succeeded in simultaneously raising average material living standards and reducing inequality in countries with strong state regulation of the market and active redistribution policies from wealthier to poorer citizens. However, in the last three decades, there has been a global movement towards rolling back the state and deregulating the market. This trend has been particularly evident in the United Kingdom and the United States since 1980. Increased inequality has been greatest in countries where the rule of the market has been most dominant. In some countries inequality is associated with unemployment, while in others it is associated with low paid or insecure employment. The less equal (or relatively disadvantaged) are, regardless of how inequality manifests itself, less capable of participating in the principal activities of society.

Research by the British Medical Association (BMA) has shown that life expectancy for those at the bottom of the income scale has fallen. The more unequal income, the greater the loss in the self-esteem of the less equal and the greater the manifestations of socio-psychological stress (Hutton, 1996: p. 224). Thus, inequality is a bad for those experiencing the status of being less equal. The negative consequences of inequality extend beyond the ranks of the relatively less well-off. The need to protect our persons and property is a need that increases with growing inequality. It is not always instrumentally rational for the disenfranchised to respect the social norms that justify inequality. Inequality has negative resonances for us all, regardless of steps that we may take to enhance our own security.

Free market advocates consider inequality to be the necessary price to be paid for increased efficiency ensured by free markets. The market rewards hard work and entrepreneurship (as well as penalising the less able, the lazy and the risk-averse) and ensures that the national cake is larger as a result. Moreover, incentives created by the market system will result in a trickle down effect, whereby everybody will be better off. Personal material prosperity is considered more essential to the good life than reduced inequality. The dominant value of the market capitalist system is the necessity of private consumption in order to realise the good life. The most important activity that capitalism endorses is paid work, not as an end, but as a means to increased consumption. Work-sharing, which would remove inequality of access to work, resources and leisure, is not a popular solution to the problem of unemployment. Those currently in work are resistant to any reduction in their capacity to purchase private goods, which work sharing would imply. Those not working would prefer a level of work that would allow them to experience the level of private consumption of those in work. The predominance of paid work, as the principal and central activity of most people's lives, has reinforced an individualistic conception of self.

Rectifying the bads that capitalism has generated will only be possible if private consumption is no longer seen as the ultimate good. Public goods, such as a clean physical environment and a secure social environment may, or may not, require the diversion of resources away from private consumption. Their provision will, however, require a *willingness* to divert such resources if necessary. This willingness to forgo private goods for public goods will only exist if our conception of the good life changes. Moreover, when evaluating society, levels of personal consumption and preference satisfaction are not the only issues of moral concern.

There are other standards by which societies are judged, such as their contribution to individual liberty and the realisation of justice.

## 3. ECONOMIC MATERIALISM AND INDIVIDUAL LIBERTY

Economic materialism and free markets have regularly been defended on the basis of liberal individualism. Politically, this means that the individual is the appropriate focus of social analysis and that the broader social and political community does not have an identity independent of the individuals of which it is composed. The purpose of society is to serve individual interests and concerns. Economically, liberal individualism has been used to justify free markets and the politics of laissez-faire. This view owes much to the political philosophy of John Locke, as expressed in two essays which he published in 1690 (Locke and Wooten, 1993). For Locke, society and government agencies exist to protect life, liberty and property, since these are considered to be inalienable natural rights. The common good and the protection of private rights, he viewed as synonymous.

### Liberty as an End or as a Means to an End?

Individual liberty is almost always equated with freedom. It implies an absence of constraints on individual actions, thus affording the individual greater autonomy, in the sense of a greater range of possible actions. If individual liberty is a value of moral concern, it is important to put this value in context. Is individual freedom important as an end in itself or is it important as a means to an end? In other words, is a life rendered valuable by the mere exercise of choice, or is it valuable because the exercise of choice allows us to pursue other ends, which we, as rational self-determining individuals, have deemed to be important to our sense of a valuable life.

The classical economist John Stuart Mill falls into the first category, in that he considered the mere exercise of choice to be of intrinsic value. For Mill, individual choice is a fundamental expression of our humanity, even if the choices we make have undesirable consequences. He argued that finality was not only impossible, it was also undesirable, since human lives are subject to perpetual incompleteness, self-transformation and novelty. Therefore, all solutions must be tentative, notwithstanding which, a valuable life is one where we make choices, accepting as we do the possibility of error (Mill, 1969).

Catholic social teaching also subscribes to the view that man fulfils himself by using his intelligence and his freedom (John Paul II, 1991; Scaperlanda, 1993). Likewise, libertarians view liberty to be of fundamental value; they have a commitment to liberty independent of its consequences for individual welfare or society (Hausman and McPherson, 1994).

Others are more consequentialist in their defence of individual liberty. Utilitarians, liberals and even some schools of Marxism subscribe to the idea of individual liberty as a means of achieving unique and differing human ends. People must be allowed to make choices and the greater the range of choices, the more likely it is that they will choose an action or object that will yield self-realisation. For the latter, the value we seek in our activities is not freedom but the value internal to the activity itself which freedom of choice allows us to pursue (Kymlicka, 1990).

## Market Capitalism and Individual Liberty

The unencumbered market is often considered to be one of the best defences of individual liberty against excessive coercive state interference. A market society is one in which individuals have a right to own property and engage in voluntary market exchange. The free market is considered non-coercive; individuals are free to choose how to allocate their time and their resources. Yet the free market is not a natural organism, it is a social institution protected by the laws of the state. Market capitalism functions within a legal framework that protects private property and contract.

Fundamental ideological differences exist among political parties as to the appropriate role of the state in the civic and economic affairs of citizens.

Libertarian philosophy asserts that the role of the state should be minimal; that is to say, it should be confined to measures such as policing and defence, which are necessary in order to protect private property and individual liberty. Libertarians object to laws such as: the compulsory wearing of seatbelts and motorcycle helmets; airport screening; gun controls; sobriety checkpoints; to name but a few of their *bête noires*. They object to the very concept of the welfare state. This is not to say that they are indifferent to the consequences of drink-driving, or to poverty, or that they do not value charity. For Libertarians, it is a question of deciding on the lesser evil, which, for them, is always minimal state interference. Poverty is unfortunate, and charity is morally worthy, but charity should not be compulsory. It should not involve appropriation of that which belongs to another (which is what taxation is considered to be). The philosophical basis for their position is self-ownership; that is to say, people have an absolute right to objects that they have appropriated from the external world, provided that no one is made worse off by the appropriation (Nozick, 1974).

The libertarian perspective assumes that the only constraint on individual liberty is the law. Liberals, for whom individual freedom and choice are also social values of primary importance, tend to take a more benign view of state activity. John Stuart Mill, an avowed liberal, welcomed state intervention in education and labour legislation because he thought that, without it, the weakest would be enslaved or crushed, whereas its existence would increase the range of choices for the vast majority of men, even if it restrained choices for a minority. The nineteenth-century Oxford idealist T.H. Green defended state intervention, on the basis of what he called positive freedom, that is, actual capacity to make a choice. For him, freedom of contract was an example of negative freedom; that is to say, a legal right. However, a contract between very unequal parties, such as a powerful and rich employer and an indigent job searcher with limited alternatives could be classified as coercive. state interference to protect and empower the weaker party (for example, labour legislation and minimum wages) is an example of a positive liberal policy (Sabine and Thorson, 1973).

Unfettered capitalism might claim to be a form of social organisation that best protects individual liberties, but the liberties that it protects best are the rights of those with property and resources, as opposed to those without property and resources. More contemporary liberals, such as Rawls (1973) and Dworkin (1977, 1981), in their respective systems of justice, describe their ideal societies where inequalities, which are not a product of choice, are eliminated. However, they too emphasise the importance of effective choice. Individuals must be allowed to choose their version of the good life. State interference, in the form of redistribution from the wealthy to the poor, is only justified if the economic position of the latter group is as a consequence of factors beyond their control.

## Critique of the Libertarian and Liberal Positions

The common ground between the libertarian and various liberal social philosophies is the emphasis on the individual and individual rights. The liberal view was first criticised by Hegel for its incorrect reading of human psychology and its failure to recognise the individual as a social being.

According to Hegel, the highest of all human needs is the need for participation, to be part of a purpose higher than private wants and satisfactions (Hegel, Knox and Pelczynski, 1964.).

Communitarianism represents the major contemporary critique of the liberal position. While communitarian philosophy rejects the extreme position taken by Hegel (for whom individual liberty consisted of submission to the state), the Hegelian influence is evident in their conception of the individual. For Taylor (1979, 1985), the liberal idea of freedom as choice is without moral value, since true freedom is situated. In a liberal world, nothing would be worth doing, as nothing would count for anything. For liberals, the good life requires us to discover what it is we want to be or do, whereas for communitarians, it is to discover who we are. For the liberal, the self is prior to its ends, whereas for the communitarian, the self is constituted by its ends, many of which we do not choose but discover by virtue of being embedded in some shared social context (Sandel, 1982).

Any critique of liberal atomism is also a critique of orthodox economics and the intellectual sustenance that it gives to unfettered markets. Economics, as a discipline, is based on a narrow view of human nature: that is to say, all individuals are assumed to be greedy and rational. While it is undoubtedly true that individuals often manifest greed and sometimes behave rationally, it is quite a simplistic, albeit understandable, view of a more complex reality. Moreover, by exalting individual greed into a social virtue, it has served to validate individual greed.[3] For economic theorists, the attraction of focusing on rational self-interest is obvious. It gives them a methodological tool, with which to analyse situations and policies.

It is only in more recent times that a broader view of human behaviour has filtered its way down to economic textbooks, in the form of chapters on altruism, bounded rationality and decision making under conditions of uncertainty. Moreover, work in game theory has shown that competitive behaviour is not always efficient and that co-operative behaviour (which usually requires an element of trust), in many situations, yields a more socially benign outcome for all the parties involved.[4] According to Etzioni (1993), rampant individualism has not only made Western market societies more conflictual, it has also had negative effects on their economies. The social atomism that capitalist society promotes is leading to individual alienation and social breakdown. He states that no economy can thrive if greed is overpowering and that no

---

[3] The idea that greed is good was first expressed by Adam Smith and has its contemporary formal expression in the First Welfare Theorem of Economics. Individually egotistical, rational behaviour, if contained within the context of competitive markets, results in an outcome that is socially benign.

[4] This is also known as the Prisoner's Dilemma, whereby the outcome of two parties acting egotistically, rationally but non-co-operatively under imperfect information is inferior to the outcome which could have been attained if both parties had co-operated.

society can function unless most of its members most of the time heed their moral commitments and social responsibilities. He criticises the individualism of the liberal position, which has given rise to a society of too many declared rights, too few responsibilities and too many polarised positions.

Communitarians stress the need to protect what they perceive as the fragile social architecture of society. In other words, social and economic policies need to be more encompassing and less guided by a narrow financial cost benefit ideology. Social institutions, that encourage civic participation, need to be maintained and fostered, be they the local school, the local post office or the local community centre. Living in society requires an awareness of our interdependence and common ends. Many of our contemporary social ills, such as drug addiction, crime, inequality, social breakdown, even environmental degradation, are a manifestation of the extent to which living has become privatised. They are a more extreme expression of lack of civic engagement. This phenomenon of disengagement is apparent in all countries of the western hemisphere. Studies in the US have revealed that, compared to the 1960s, in the 1990s less people vote in elections, there is a lower level of both trade-union membership and church membership, and fewer parents attend parent teachers association meetings (Putnam, 1995). The US has also become a much less equal society since the 1960s. For the first time in US history, the children of recent immigrants are not expected to do better economically and socially than their parents.

Many of the values that are dear to liberal hearts, such as tolerance, pluralism and social justice are not operational in an over-individualised society. Individual liberty requires the active maintenance of the institutions of civil society. Self-respect must be balanced with respect for others. An over-individualised society is one that lacks the social solidarity necessary to help the less fortunate, tackle common problems and resolve differences in a non-conflictual way. Society has to place limits on individual liberty and self-determination if it is wishes to preserve the social conditions necessary for self-determination.

## 4. SOCIETY AND EQUALITY

Equality is a central and controversial notion in social philosophy. When we talk of equality of people, do we mean that all individuals are equal as a matter of fact, or that all people should be treated equally? Moreover, if all people should be treated equally, what does that mean? Does it imply equal treatment in terms of civil and political rights, or equal chances in life, or equal shares of the earth's bounty? Probably the greatest area of dissent in any discussion on equity and justice is the extent to which economic and social inequality is a product of individual choice as opposed to factors beyond individual control. The latter problem is fundamentally an empirical one, although shifting the debate from one of value to one of facts does not necessarily make it easier to reach a consensus.

### Why Does Inequality Exist?

If, according to Natural Law or the Law of God, men are equal, why does inequality exist and is it contrary to nature? According to Rousseau, men in a state of nature are equal and inequality is as a result of the social contrivance of private property (Rousseau, Ritter and Bondanella, 1988). This idea inspired Marx and inevitably led to the demand for the abolition of private property, if society was ever to be established on egalitarian grounds.

If private property is the cause of unnatural social inequality between people, then Communism should have eliminated inequality in the societies where social organisation involved, *inter alia*, the abolition of private property. Dahrendorf (1972) rejected the Marxist argument on the basis of empirical evidence, but he also rejected the human inequality thesis. Every society has its norms; that is to say, a moral character, and operates a system of rewards and sanctions based on compliance and non-compliance with its moral code. These social norms regulate individual behaviour and the highest stratum in each society will contain those individuals who most identify with and comply with its social norms. Moral deviants, in the sense of those who do not, or cannot, comply completely with the social norms, will be part of the lower strata of society. As Dahrendorf says "all men are equal before the law but they are no longer equal after it". For him, a society where all distinctions of rank between people are abolished is a sociological impossibility. On the other hand, social inequality is also the cause of the instability of society, as those less favoured seek to realise a set of social norms that will favour them. Thus, all societies are inherently self-destructive.

The other principal defence of inequality is that it is necessary for the smooth functioning of society. According to the functionalists, in every society there are different social positions with different characteristics. Some are more pleasant than others, some are more important and some are more difficult. The only way to fill these positions adequately is to attach different social and economic rewards to them. This results in social stratification and social inequality. Inequality is a product of functional necessity (Davis and Moore, 1945). The inequalities generated by capitalism and the free market are justified in a similar way; they are necessary for the greater good of maximising national productivity and efficiency. The principal weakness of the functionalist argument is that it denies the extent to which social and economic inequality makes society dysfunctional.

The central issue in the debate on inequality is not whether social inequality can be completely eliminated, but the extent of inequality that is acceptable in a free and civilised society.

## How Much Inequality is Acceptable?

A minimalist view on equality is the endorsement of civil and political equality. Libertarians subscribe to this view, since for them, individual liberty is the overwhelming good, and hence, the state should not engage in the appropriation and transfer of resources from the better off to the less well off.

Utilitarians believe that public policy should be directed towards the greatest good for the greatest number. The policy implications of the utilitarian perspective are not clear. It could be an endorsement of an active state role in redistributing resources to the less well off (justified on the basis of diminishing marginal utility of income) or it could be an endorsement of laissez-faire, if non-interference increases output and, hence, utility for most individuals (Kymlicka, 1990).

The liberal position is that *only* inequalities, which are a product of factors beyond the control of the individual, merit redress by the state, in the interests of equity (Cohen, 1993). Individual choice has to be respected. The difficulty for liberals is in defining a social system that can distinguish between unmerited inequalities and merited inequalities. Rawls's *A Theory of Justice* (1973) is considered to be the seminal work on the issue of necessary rights and liberties if people are to be treated as moral equals. He is generally credited with having regenerated normative political philosophy. His system of justice advocates complete equality of basic civil and political liberties, and social and economic inequalities to be so arranged that they are to the benefit of the least well off in society. Hence, in comparing two forms of social organisation, A and B, where average income is higher in social form A compared to B, but the income of the poorest person in social form B is greater than that of the poorest person in social form A, social organisation type B is to be preferred in the interests of justice. The innovative aspect of Rawls's theory is the view that natural talent (just like social circumstances) is a matter of luck, and is, therefore, morally neutral. Consequently, no one deserves a higher income just because he has been lucky in the distribution of talents. A system of justice that endorses *equality of opportunity* (as normally defined) would be lacking according to this view of unmerited inequality.

Dworkin (1981) criticised Rawls's system of justice, firstly, for not going far enough to remedy inequalities that are a product of morally neutral factors and, secondly, for not respecting inequalities that are the product of individual choice and hence meritorious. Rawls defines the worst off position too narrowly; that is to say, in terms of economic and social goods. Two people could be equally well off in a Rawlsian sense, yet one may be in a worse position due to, for example, a physical handicap. The less advantaged individual clearly needs and merits more resources than their physically able counterpart, in order to have equal chances in life. Dworkin refined Rawls's system, first by financially compensating people for natural inequalities and then by dividing what remained (in terms of resources) equally among individuals. Thus, those naturally disadvantaged through no fault of their own would be given the resources necessary to allow them to pursue their conception of the good life. Equal division of remaining resources represented a mechanism for respecting individual diversity and the subsequent inequality that could result from individual choices as to how to use their resources.

Another criticism which could be levelled at the Rawlsian system of justice is that his philosophy is more efficiency oriented than equality-driven. Economic well-being is considered more important to the well-being of the individual than reduced inequality. Social and economic inequalities are acceptable, if they lead to the greatest benefit for the least advantaged. So, in a choice between two types of social organisation, one of which allows for more inequality but greater material well-being for the least advantaged and the other, where there is less inequality but also a lower level of economic well-being for the least advantaged, he opts for the former. Rawls's system of justice sanctions inequality, to the extent that it is functional in assisting his objectives.

Other philosophers, such as Sen (1992) and Le Grand (1991), also attempted to define what constitutes true equality of opportunity. For Sen, justice requires equality of capability sets. The latter are personal characteristics which determine our choice sets; that is to say, the *range* of things that we can do, given our capability sets. For Le Grand, equity requires equality of choice sets, where the latter defines the set of possibilities. The common factor in the theories of all the aforementioned liberals is that they are choicists. The common problem that they all face is empirical: how to determine the extent to which one's economic position is determined by factors beyond individual control. The problem is compounded when the whole question of preferences is addressed. To what extent are preferences socially determined, and hence beyond individual control, as opposed to an object of individual choice?

For Marxists the answer is straightforward. All choices are socially determined, so that the individual is not responsible for the consequences of his choices. In such a determinate world of no free will, justice and equity demand equality of outcomes. In the more complex world of some free will and many constraints, including those of some socially determined preferences, the outcome will always be second best, due to imperfect information. This is not a justification for social apathy, since (as pointed out by Le Grand, 1991) consensus may be reached on *some* of the factors that may constitute a constraint on the individual situation and therefore be deemed inequitable and subject to redress.

### Social Organisation and Equality

Capitalist societies (that is to say, societies where the law protects private property and enforces contracts and where the government is not an active player in the allocation of resources) usually exhibit widespread economic inequality. The principal defences of the inequality that capitalism generates are merit and functional necessity. Defenders of the market mechanism usually tend to assume that economic success is merited, in other words, it is a product of individual effort. The other defence is functional; in other words, it is claimed that capitalism leads to an efficient use of resources and maximises output.

Countries where governments have been more interventionist in economic affairs have generally exhibited less inequality. The standard criticism of government interference in the economy is that equality is achieved at the expense of efficiency and growth. The empirical evidence is varied. Government intervention takes different forms. Social democracy in the different countries of Western Europe is not homogenous. Yet most countries with social democratic systems had relatively high levels of growth and average living standards in the post-war period. The economic problems that they faced in the 1980s and 1990s are not problems confined exclusively to countries with interventionist governments, they are more global. On the other hand, state intervention in the socialist economies of the former Soviet Union and countries of Eastern Europe, with their socialised production and central control, was considered to be a contributory cause to inefficiency and economic stagnation in these economies.

A society may have many aspirations, not all of them necessarily mutually compatible but not necessarily incompatible either. There is no conclusive proof that economic efficiency requires inequality. Likewise, de Tocqueville's thesis that liberty and equality are mutually incompatible can be challenged (de Tocqueville and Reeve, 1961). Rendering society more equal may interfere with some liberties but it will also enhance the positive liberties of others, in particular, those whose liberties are very limited due to economic circumstances. The philosophy of nineteenth-century Toryism was that social distress and economic depressions were evils divorced from politics (Thomson, 1974). The philosophy that led to the creation of the welfare state was the right of individuals to protection by the state from social and economic misfortune, a right derived from citizenship. It was an expression of solidarity among citizens of the nation state. It was the culmination of a process that began with the ideas of the French Revolution, whose protagonists did not perceive the objectives of liberty, equality and economic well-being to be incompatible. Defending economic privilege on the basis of natural rights, such as individual liberty, is ultimately a very self-serving argument. Individual liberty is not an absolute right in a society where others may have competing rights. Moreover, the right to choose is not just a right that is defined over a set of private, excludable goods and services, it is also the right to make an informed choice as to the type of society in which one would wish to live.

We have seen in the previous sections the different standards by which societies can be judged. It is therefore opportune to turn our attention to the European Union and its historical evolution from a small union of relatively homogenous member states to its present form, as a much larger union of heterogeneous countries.

The various transformations of the EU since its original inception and the *raison d'être* underlying the different legal and institutional initiatives that have been taken, can then be evaluated against the broader framework of values just elucidated. This involves looking at the microeconomic, macroeconomic and redistributive aspects of the market integration process as well as other institutional developments that enhance or constrain market forces. These are all issues that are investigated in much greater detail in subsequent chapters, so some degree of overlap is inevitable. The purpose of briefly analysing them in this chapter is to link the analysis on normative issues with the reality of developments in the EU, and to introduce the reader to some of the material that will be explored in much greater depth in the rest of the book.

## 5. EUROPEAN UNION AND THE SINGLE MARKET

### Process

The Treaty of Rome (1957), which launched the European Economic Community (EEC), represented the first step on the road to European Union. Since then, the size of the association has increased from its six original member countries to the present 15 and the process has needed the stimulus of re-invention and re-invigoration which the reforms contained in the Single European Act (SEA) in 1987, the Maastricht Treaty in 1991 and more recently the Amsterdam Treaty in 1997 have variously provided. While the political objective has always been the closer union of the peoples of Europe, the economic objective (which it is assumed will facilitate the political objective) has been the creation of a genuine common market. A common market is an economic space in which goods, services, capital and people can move freely without having to overcome artificially created barriers.

The process of welding national markets into a single common market has not been without its complications. The Treaty of Rome provided the basis for the removal of all visible barriers to internal trade (such as tariffs and import quotas) and the adoption of a common external tariff. These measures were not sufficient to ensure that international trade among participant countries was as unimpeded as internal (or inter-regional) trade in any member state. Less visible barriers to trade still existed and these ranged from the use (or abuse) of domestic health and safety legislation to protect national markets, to a distinct national bias in the public procurement policies of national agencies. Customs barriers at points of entry into countries remained a very visible manifestation of the extent to which the countries of Europe were still divided. The economic objective of the Single European Act was to ensure the completion of the internal market by December 1992. From that date, all customs frontiers between member states of the European Community (EC as it was known after the signing of the SEA) were dismantled. Other institutional reforms were also adopted to remove non-tariff barriers to trade and facilitate the single unified market.

A genuine common market requires the creation of a level playing field, so that the only factors determining the extent of economic activity and the direction of trade and factor flows are market considerations. National economic policy should not distort the process. Hence, industrial policy, competition policy and taxation policy of national governments are all subject to scrutiny to ensure that they do not interfere with the market process. Capital controls were removed in July 1990 and the major economic innovation contained in the Maastricht Treaty was an agreement to create an economic and monetary union (EMU) by 1999; that is to say, a single currency, which is an important step towards the creation of a genuine common market. The Maastricht Treaty incorporated the European Community into a European Union (EU).

## Theoretical Basis

The creation of a single market through the harmonisation and centralisation of national economic policies is the dominant element of the European experiment. This political act reflects a liberal economic philosophy; that is to say, a belief in market capitalism as the best form of social organisation to guarantee growth and prosperity. The ideology is a materialistic one, as output is seen as the source of welfare (the key to the good life). The role of government is to ensure that all obstacles which interfere with the effective functioning of the market be removed. EMU is the culmination of the market integration process.

Economic theory tells us that when perfectly competitive markets unite in a larger common market, then all regions and countries should gain economically from the process (Samuelson, 1939, 1962; Kemp, 1962). According to the First Theorem of Welfare Economics, if markets are perfectly competitive, then the resulting consequences, in terms of production and allocation of output, will be characterised by an absence of waste. No economic actor (individual or group) has economic power when markets are perfectly competitive, in the sense of being able to dictate market outcomes. The latter are determined by the impersonal forces of supply and demand. All resources (labour, capital and land) receive a return that equals their *opportunity cost*, i.e. they get paid the minimum amount necessary to secure their services (which is what they would have earned in their next best alternative). This renders the market outcome harmonious, since no other return to resources is practicable. If resources are paid less than their opportunity cost, then the services of that resource will be withdrawn from the particular activity in question. There is no scope to pay resources more than their opportunity cost, as that would push the unit cost of production above the market price and render it unsaleable. When markets are perfectly competitive, it makes no difference to the outcome, whether capital hires labour or labour hires capital (Samuelson, 1957).

A perfectly competitive market results in an efficient use of resources to satisfy the pre-existing wants of individuals. The goods and services produced are those that individuals want (where preferences are backed by effective purchasing power) and competition ensures that all goods are sold at the lowest possible price. Furthermore, prices are the mechanism by which markets are regulated and this mechanism is assumed to operate in such a way, that markets will always clear in the long run (demand and supply will be equal). Optimal government policy in this context is *laissez faire*, or non-intervention. This assertion as to the efficiency of unregulated markets was first expressed by Adam Smith in 1776 (Smith and Skinner, 1986).

Economic integration is simply an extension of the politics of laissez faire over a wider geographical space. Theory tells us that, to the extent that integration represents a movement towards free international trade and free international mobility of resources, then it enhances the efficient use of resources. The increased force of competition, which is consequent on the removal of trade barriers, compels all countries (and regions within countries) to specialise according to the Law of Comparative Advantage. In other words, each region will specialise in the production of what it does relatively well. Determinants of comparative advantage (what it is that each region does best) are resource endowments, productivity of resources and pre-existing preferences of individuals. An important assumption is that, since regions differ, every region must have a comparative advantage in some line of economic activity. The outcome of the specialisation process, induced by enlarging the common economic space, is that the overall level of economic activity increases in the integrated area as a whole and, moreover, all regions and countries gain, in the sense of being able to afford increased levels of aggregate consumption (Ricardo, 1963; Ohlin, 1933).

Removal of legal impediments to resource mobility will permit resources to go where the returns for their services are greatest. Since the return that resources earn is presumed to reflect their marginal productivity, this means that resources go to where they are most productive. An important assumption that props up the edifice of perfect competition is that of diminishing marginal productivity of resources. All other things being equal, it is assumed that the greater the abundance of a resource, the lower the productivity of that resource at the margin. This assumption leads to the conclusion that, all other things being equal, the return to capital will be lower in capital abundant countries than in countries where capital is relatively scarce. The same holds for labour. Hence, when resources are freely mobile, the theory of perfect competition would lead us to expect that capital will flow to labour abundant, capital scarce regions and that labour will move to capital abundant, labour scarce regions. The net effect of these resource flows should be to enhance the effects of free trade and result in higher overall levels of output for all regions and countries (Meade, 1953).

A single currency gives added impetus to trade and resource mobility by removing the transactions cost of international trade and investment and by neutralising the inhibiting and costly effects that exchange rate uncertainty has on international transactions. In other words, if markets are perfectly competitive, a single currency is necessary in order to fully realise the efficiency gains of a common market (Scitovsky, 1958).

The ideal of a perfectly competitive integrated European market is an attractive objective for all national policymakers and one that could justify the abrogation of national autonomy in the area of economic policy. While the theory of perfectly competitive markets does not assist us in determining whether countries and regions within the EU will converge, it does (if realisable) hold out the promise of higher levels of material prosperity for all countries. This promise rests on the very fragile assumption that the operation of markets can approximate to the ideal of perfect competition.

### Market Failure

If markets are not perfectly competitive, then they lose their claim to efficiency. Imperfectly competitive markets do not satisfy individual preferences in an efficient manner. Laissez-faire is no longer the optimal policy when markets are imperfectly competitive. Intervention is required, either to render the market more competitive, or to counter the effects of market forces. The less competitive markets are, the greater the possibility of asymmetric gains and losses across countries and regions consequent to the creation of a genuine single market.

Theories that reject the perfectly competitive stylised view of the world are wide-ranging. At one end of the spectrum is an acknowledgement of market imperfections but a belief that these imperfections (the noun is revealing) are not wide-ranging and that, where they exist, they can be rectified. The appropriate role of government is to intervene where such intervention is necessary to assist markets. At the other end of the spectrum is the view that markets cannot be separated from the political and legal framework and that political culture reflects market power. This more radical perspective views markets as a source of social ills, which can only be eliminated through the severe curtailment of the role and scope of the market in social and economic existence. In between these two extremes are Keynesians and Social Democrats who, while accepting that market failures are not just of a micro nature but rather of a macro nature, nevertheless endorse government intervention in order to defend the market and ensure its survival. Rather than give an exhaustive account of market failure, this section will highlight those market failures about which consensus exists (a consensus that does not, however, extend to political solutions).

If there are *barriers to entry* in markets, then incumbents are in a position to control price. This is a form of market power, that can result in the exploitation of the consumer through high prices and which generally generates economics rents for the firms operating in that market. Conflict is endemic in such markets, as the different groups involved in the production process bargain over the distribution of the rent or surplus. Wages and profit are no longer uniquely determined. They can range from a minimum opportunity cost level to a maximum level, where all the rent has been appropriated by one side or the other. The outcome will be determined by the relative bargaining strength of each side. The source of the barriers to entry into markets may be legal or technological. The former can be removed without creating efficiency losses, if the political will exists to remove them. The latter are more troublesome, since they are a product of what drives that particular market.

*Economies of scale* in production and distribution mean that larger enterprises are more cost efficient than smaller enterprises. This inevitably leads to the domination of a market by a few large firms. Market domination means market power, which can be used against all adversaries, be they consumers, competitors, workers or even politicians. Another technological feature that can be associated with production in some sectors is *economies of agglomeration*. The greater the concentration of economic activity in an area, the greater the cost savings to the individual firms who are located in that region if economies of agglomeration exist. Conversely, enterprises in areas that lose firms and resources become less competitive as a consequence. When the price or cost of a good does not reflect its true social value or cost, we say that the consumption or production of the good in question creates *external effects*. When external effects exist, the market either produces too much or too little of the goods in question, since economic actors are only responding to price signals, not to the true social value or cost of the activity in question.

If markets are imperfect in the ways described above, then the effects of economic integration are much less determinate. The existence of economies of scale and economies of agglomeration creates a predisposition, in a unified market, towards unbalanced growth, unless countervailing tendencies are also present. Unlike trade based on comparative advantage, trade flows based on economies of scale are less conducive to *ex-ante* prediction. It is also theoretically possible that countries (and regions) could be worse off after free trade, if the restructuring effects of freer trade results in a loss of increasing-returns industries. Mobility of resources could widen the economic gap between richer and poorer regions, if agglomeration economies are a feature of the economic landscape of the single market. Moreover, the scope that a large single market affords firms to exploit economies of scale, may result in industry becoming increasingly dominated by a few large firms, thus rendering the market structure even less competitive. Such market domination could impact negatively on the welfare of consumers and workers, since dominant firms have the potential to control prices in both product and factor markets. If the creation of a single market leads to very unbalanced economic growth, then there could be other unexpected negative external effects, which are a consequence of spatial asymmetry in levels of economic activity. For example, when economic activity is highly concentrated in certain areas, undue degradation of the natural environment is almost inevitable. Declining economic areas create their own negative external effects on the social environment through depopulation and poverty (Graham, 1923; Myrdal, 1957).

Of course, none of the above scenarios may be realised in an economically integrated area. Countervailing tendencies, which tend to enhance the competitive features of markets, may dominate. Trade based on comparative advantage may be more important than trade based on economies of scale. Spread effects may ensure that growth is not confined to a certain country or region but spread over the commercially unified area. Diseconomies of agglomeration may hold in check economies of agglomeration and halt the monotonic expansion and decline of regions. The reality is that we do not know what will be the effect of the completion of the process of market unification. While there is a strong probability that the EU as an entity will exhibit stronger growth (since economies of scale and economies of agglomeration facilitate such growth), it is much more difficult to make a prediction as to the spatial and social effects of a genuine common market that comprises all of Western Europe. Theory does not help in this respect, when markets are characterised by imperfections and failures.

## 6. MACROECONOMIC ASPECTS OF EUROPEAN UNION

### Process

The Treaty of Rome makes little reference to economic and monetary union (EMU) but according to O'Donnell (1992), it is probable that EMU was the ultimate objective of the founders of the original common market. A single currency is a necessary corollary to a common market, in order to fully exploit the microeconomic benefits of trade and resource mobility. Currency exchange renders an international transaction more costly than a similar domestic transaction. This is due to transactions costs and hedging costs (trading currency either in the forward or in the options market, in order to insure against the risk of an adverse movement in the exchange rate).

The macroeconomic benefits of a single currency (or exchange rate stability) are considered to be low inflation and economic growth if the system is dominated by the currency of a low inflation country, such as Germany. This was the logic that led to the establishment of the European Monetary System (EMS) in 1979, where the range of fluctuation that the system permitted was ± 2.25 per cent for most countries. Flexibility was preserved by allowing periodic realignments when the value of a national currency was deemed to be out of line with the country's relative competitiveness. The disadvantages of this system of fixed but adjustable exchange rates were all too clearly highlighted during the currency crisis of autumn 1992. The system allowed for speculative, self-fulfilling attacks against certain currencies (most notably, the lira, sterling and the Irish pound), creating private fortunes as a consequence. The impotence of individual central banks to defend their currencies against the might of private capital was clearly exposed.

The most important economic element of the Maastricht Treaty was the decision to create a single currency by 1999. Member states eligible for membership will be those who satisfy the convergence criteria with regard to inflation, interest rates, exchange rates and public finances. The new currency, the euro, will be issued by a new supranational institution, the European Central Bank (ECB). At that date, member states who sign up to the single currency will cast off the last vestiges of national autonomy as far as monetary and exchange rate policy are concerned.

### Theoretical Basis

The Maastricht Treaty did not alter the objectives of the Community, namely, growth, high employment, economic convergence, economic and social cohesion and price stability. Yet, the criteria for membership of the single currency focus exclusively on nominal variables and public finances. The eligibility criteria are devoid of theoretical justification. The objective is to ensure that applicant countries, in the run up to membership, follow relatively similar restrictive fiscal and monetary policies.[5]

The theoretical basis for a single currency is the classical and neo-classical assumption that unimpeded markets are efficient allocators of resources. When the price mechanism functions properly, markets always clear: that is to say, excess demand or excess supply do not exist. According to the logic of market clearance, a country could link its currency with any global currency, without fearing macroeconomic disruption.[6] If domestic prices are flexible, then the real exchange rate is flexible. The macroeconomic expression of this microeconomic creed is that national output (GDP) is determined by supply-side factors, not demand-side factors. For Classical economists, the long run aggregate supply curve (AS) is vertical. For New Classical economists, the full information aggregate supply curve is vertical. National output depends on: national resources (including how hard people work); technology; and functioning markets (Mankiw, 1990).

In this world of price flexibility and market clearance, aggregate demand (AD) merely determines the general level of prices. Expansionary monetary or fiscal policy will not change output, it will only result in inflation. The focus of macroeconomic policy in a classical and new classical world is on nominal variables (such as inflation and nominal interest rates), since these are the only variables that are determined by macroeconomic policy. Therefore, the loss of autonomous monetary and exchange rate policy,

---

[5] The fiscal requirements are, first, that government deficit should not exceed 3 per cent of GDP and, second, that total public debt should not exceed 60 per cent of GDP.

[6] This rather extreme assertion should not be interpreted as meaning that the choice of partner country in a currency union is a matter of complete economic indifference. Obviously, it makes economic sense to link the national currency (when feasible) with the currencies of countries with which there are strong trading relationships.

that countries must accept on entering a currency union, is not a real loss and the only concern should be that the common monetary policy is oriented towards low inflation. Money may only be a veil in the classical and new classical world, but undisciplined and permissive monetary policy is capable of disrupting the real economy through its effect on inflation. Inflation inhibits the proper functioning of the price mechanism as an efficient allocator of resources (Driffil, Mizon and Alph, 1990).

The principal distinction between the Keynesian school of economics and its predecessors (classical school) and successors (new classical school and real business cycle theorists) is that the Keynesians believe that market failure on a macroeconomic scale can exist. In a Keynesian world of uncertainty, expectations drive markets, money can have real effects, and prices are not sufficiently flexible to ensure market clearance. In this world, adjustment to adverse demand shocks takes the form of a fall in output and increased unemployment. Expansionary macroeconomic policy (monetary, fiscal or exchange rate) can increase output in the real economy by stimulating aggregate demand, since national output is determined by both demand- and supply-side factors. The loss of monetary and exchange rate policy, as instruments of national macroeconomic policy, can have real effects in an economy whose domestic prices are insufficiently flexible to ensure market clearance (Mankiw, 1990).

The theory of optimum currency areas (OCAs), which highlights the suitability criteria for countries contemplating monetary union, is only of relevance in a Keynesian world of sticky prices and non-clearing markets. In such a world, asymmetric shocks could result in a fall in output and employment in some regions and excess demand and inflation in other regions. No monetary or exchange rate policy is consistent with the economic needs of all regions. Only if countries have relatively similar economic structures are asymmetric shocks unlikely. Moreover, the more diversified a country's economic structure, the less likely it is that it will be subject to asymmetric shocks of any significant magnitude. Symmetric shocks, which impact on all countries and regions in a similar way, do not pose problems for a monetary union with in-flexible prices, since adverse effects can always be counteracted by appropriate monetary and exchange rate policy, which is consistent with the economic exigencies of all regions. The greater the degree of labour mobility within a monetary union, the less grave are the social consequences of asymmetric shocks, since labour can migrate from areas of excess supply to areas of excess demand (Mundell, 1961; McKinnon, 1963; Kenen, 1969).

Whether the integrated market of the EU approximates more to a classical or Keynesian framework and whether, in the latter instance, it is an optimum currency area, are issues that will be discussed in greater detail in chapters 2 and 3.

## The Consequences for Efficiency and Equity of a Single Currency

If national markets of member states of the EU function better in a monetary union than they have to date, then efficiency of the union will be enhanced. A low inflation macroeconomic environment, combined with flexible markets, will also contribute to increased output and growth in all countries and regions. This will aid cohesion only if poorer regions grow faster than more prosperous regions, but even competitive markets cannot guarantee cohesion in the sense of reduced spatial inequality. Moreover, the prerequisite of market clearance is price flexibility, which may not aid the cause of social cohesion, if it means more wage flexibility.

If national markets of the EU do not function any better in a monetary union than at present, then the straitjacket of a single currency could exacerbate economic problems of certain countries and regions, especially if they are not competitive at the new common exchange rate.[7] The only palliative for increased unemployment and reduced output are emigration or capital inflows. The former is not a popular option in today's political climate as it is viewed as an admission of economic failure. There are no guarantees that private capital will flow into depressed regions or that

---

[7] The effect of currency union on the economy of the former German Democratic Republic is a case in point.

such flows, if they do occur, will be of sufficient magnitude to off-set unemployment and economic depression. Public capital in-flows, via the Structural Funds, are subject to political negotiation.

The policy options of national governments in an EMU are quite limited. The only area of macroeconomic policy which has some national autonomy is fiscal policy, and that has been quite severely circumscribed by the Maastricht criteria and the subse-quent stability pact agreed in Dublin in December 1996. Also, the constraining effects of budget deficits on any pump-priming ini-tiatives are more keenly felt in a monetary union with mobile re-sources, since it is harder to raise taxes. Indeed for small open economies, such as Ireland, fiscal policy is not even an effective instrument of aggregate demand management, due to the low multiplier effect. Budgetary constraints also make it more difficult for national governments to realise their own internal equity ob-jectives. National governments will be required to respond to the challenges of a single currency through supply-side measures, that is, through facilitating price flexibility and market clearance. The situation becomes serious if market imperfections and market non-clearance are endogenous aspects of the economy. If, for ex-ample, economies of scale are a technological fact of life, then there are efficiency costs associated with trying to make such markets more competitive. Recent theories on sticky prices have shown that price rigidities (and consequently market non-clearance) may be endogenous, thus rendering them immune to supply-side policy initiatives.[8]

The missing link in the unification process, which started with the formation of the common market, is the absence of a federal fiscal system, where central government has sufficient taxation powers to allow for redistribution throughout the union. A fed-

---

[8] Examples are efficiency wage theories and the literature on menu cost. The effi-ciency wage literature focuses on situations where it is not profit maximising for employers to lower wages, even if there is excess supply of labour. The menu cost literature shows that price flexibility is not always the best strategy for a firm, even when the economic environment changes, since there are costs associ-ated with changing prices.

eral fiscal system which automatically increases transfers to depressed countries/regions and increases the level of taxes that it levies on booming countries/regions, has the in-built flexibility to respond to the differing economic needs of heterogeneous countries/regions. It also institutionalises inter-country solidarity, since transfers to economically depressed regions are non-discretionary. In its absence, inter-country solidarity is expressed through the Structural Funds. The extent of such solidarity depends on the overall size of the Structural Funds, which in turn depends on the extent to which the more prosperous members of the EU are willing to continue to finance the more economically disadvantaged member states. Assistance is not guaranteed, it is discretionary and finite.

## 7. REDISTRIBUTION AND EUROPEAN UNION

### Process

There was no provision in the Treaty of Rome for either regional policy or social policy. Yet, economic and social cohesion have always been a declared Community objective. Subsequently, in an attempt to formalise this commitment, the Regional Fund, the Social Fund and the structural element to the Agricultural Fund (now collectively known as the Structural Funds) were set up. The Single European Act in 1987 confirmed the commitment to regional equity, and backed this commitment by increased budgetary allocations for the Structural Funds. The Social Charter was also signed by all member states, with the exception of the UK, in 1989. The Maastricht Treaty contains references to cohesion, and there are protocols attached to the treaty on:

- Economic and social cohesion;

- Social policy; and

- A committee of the regions.

Gradually, redistribution issues in a spatial and social sense have become more important and this is reflected in the legal framework of the EU and in the ever-increasing importance of the Structural Funds in the EU budget. It has been estimated that by 1999, structural elements will account for 36 per cent of the EU budget.

While the Structural Funds remain discretionary, in the sense that their size and destination are subject to the political process, at least their importance to the Community objective of cohesion has now been explicitly acknowledged in the Maastricht Treaty. The Commission is also obliged to report every three years on progress made towards cohesion. There is increased scope to fund a wider range of projects and the provision on equal co-financing (where national governments match structural funding) can be relaxed, if deemed necessary to the budgetary health of the government of the recipient nation. The Committee on the Regions allows representatives of regional and local authorities an advisory role on issues relating to, *inter alia*, economic and social cohesion. The actual powers of the Committee are negligible at present, but it represents a first step towards more democratic accountability.

The most serious criticism of the Structural Funds relates to their operational mechanics and size. The EU will have almost all the features of a federal state (customs union, free movement of people and capital, a single currency), with the exception of a federal budget of sufficient size and scope. One of the features of national governments and federal states is the existence of an automatic tax and transfer mechanism. A large percentage of taxation goes to central coffers and much public spending and many social transfers are financed by central government. Hence, if a region suffers economic decline, it will automatically pay less tax and receive more transfers, whereas the reverse should happen in booming regions. Such transfers are not discretionary or subject to negotiation and the political process, they are an in-built part of the welfare state and they serve the cause of spatial and social equity. (Of course their existence does not preclude the possibility of special aid packages, along the lines of the structural funds, to regions in need). The overall Community budget is less than 1.5

per cent of Community GDP, while the Structural Funds are less than two-thirds of 1 per cent of Community GDP. This falls far short of the level of transfers that one would expect to see in a federal state, or in a union of nations committed to economic and social cohesion.

The Social Charter is in effect a workers' charter. Although its provisions have been criticised for not going far enough to support the rights of workers, it represents, for the first time, a recognition at EU level of the need for legislative protection of workers rights. The objectives of the Community with respect to social policy are: the promotion of employment, improved working and living conditions, improved social protection, dialogue between management and labour and the combating of exclusion. The UK refused to sign the Agreement on Social Policy, on the grounds that it represented undue interference in the operation of labour markets. In 1997 the Labour Government in the UK decided to join the Social Protocol, and as a consequence, it has now been incorporated into the Amsterdam Treaty's provisions on social policy, education, training and youth.

**Theoretical Basis**

The absence of provision for regional and social policy in the Treaty of Rome does not necessarily indicate the primacy of the value of efficiency over equity, or a lack of regard for distributive justice. The objectives of efficiency and equity were, simply, not perceived to be incompatible at the time. This is understandable in the context of the ideological foundations upon which the European Economic Community was constructed. Markets were the solution to poverty and other social ills. Perfectly competitive markets were the ideal and, according to mainstream economic theory, free trade and resource mobility would guarantee increased material well-being for all regions and countries. Redistribution was acceptable, provided that it did not interfere with market signals.

Encouraging economic activity, through the use of financial inducements, in regions where it would not otherwise occur, was considered to be an inefficient use of resources and ultimately self-defeating. If market forces did not lead to the economic development of a region, then no amount of regional aid would make it autonomously competitive. Moreover, overall output in the Community would be lower as a result of such interference with the market mechanism. Regional policy had no role to play in this perfectly competitive nirvana populated by fully informed, rational economic agents.

The same logic applied to social policy. In a perfectly competitive market, relations between labour and capital are envisaged as simple exchange relations between equals. The need to empower and protect workers does not exist. In fact, legislative interference of the kind envisaged in the Social Charter is inimical to the interests of workers, since it places unnecessary restrictions on the operation of the labour market and will only result in increased unemployment.

In this context, the emergence (and ever-increasing importance) of regional and social policy in the Community scheme of affairs is interesting. It is a tacit admission of the need for active financial and legal initiatives if the objectives of economic and social cohesion are to be realised. It is a recognition that markets may not be the panacea for all economic and social ills. It is the realisation that markets are not perfect, and maybe even that the ideal of perfect markets is not realisable. This realisation may be a product of the experience of the Community to date but it has been reinforced by the emergence, in the 1980s, of new theories of international trade based on imperfect competition. The liberalisation of imperfect markets does not guarantee efficiency and, more particularly, it does not guarantee either spatial or social equity. In an imperfect market, characterised by economies of scale and economies of agglomeration, history matters and there is no unique economic outcome that is predestined by exogenous economic forces. There is an economic case to be made for regional policy, even though in the less determinate environment of imperfect markets, there are no guarantees that regional policy as implemented, will be successful.

Economic rents may be earned when markets are imperfectly competitive. The existence of such rents makes the relationship between employer and employee more conflictual, as both sides wish to maximise their share of the rents. The division of rents depends on the bargaining power of both sides. Legal protection of workers rights improves the bargaining power of workers and the quality of work. Higher wages, and other rights that the Social Charter seeks to protect, may reduce profits, but that does inevitably mean a fall in the level of economic activity and an increase in redundancies. If there is an economic rent component to profit, then a reduction in that rent does not require that the optimal level of investment or economic activity be lower as a consequence.[9]

Of course, there is always the danger of firms leaving to locate in countries where the labour market is more deregulated, thus guaranteeing higher profits. This danger is most acute where multinationals are concerned, especially if the investment is of a footloose character. This would have given the UK a competitive advantage over other member states in the attraction of mobile investment if it had persisted in its decision not to join the Social Protocol. As it is, it serves to highlight the importance of a widespread adoption of the Social Charter if workers rights in the EU are to be protected.

It is only if the Social Charter causes capital and firms to leave the EU altogether, in order to find more favourable conditions elsewhere, that unemployment might increase. The importance of the EU market globally makes it unlikely that such a phenomenon will be widespread. Furthermore, a single market with low paid labour working in insecure jobs may not be what the electorates of the EU member states desire. Apprehension already exists among sizeable minorities in EU that the European experiment is tailored to meet the needs of business and not of workers (who also happen to be the majority of citizens). The provisions relating to in-

---

[9] In Britain, the share of profits in national output went up since 1979, yet investment remained static (Hutton, 1996).

creased worker participation and control in enterprises are a recognition that labour is more than a commodity and that the welfare of workers is determined, not just by the purchasing capacity of their earnings, but also by conditions of work and the opportunities that work affords for self-expression and self-development.

## Reservations

Despite the increased recognition that cohesion has received in the Maastricht Treaty, the reality of the Structural Funds and Social Charter is that they represent no more than minor constraints on the hegemony of the market as the dominant form of social organisation. Regional funding, for example, is discretionary and finite and designed to help regions overcome the obstacles that are inhibiting their effective economic performance. Most actual funding goes to improving the infrastructure of peripheral areas. The assumption is that markets will achieve the rest. However, if markets have agglomerative tendencies, then economic efficiency is not compatible with spatial justice. The effective use of regional aid may require focused spending and lead to increased spatial inequality within a country or region. In addition, if regional aid does not achieve its objective of enabling regions (and countries) to compete in the more competitive environment of a single currency market, there exists no safety net against the economic free fall of that region/country. Currency devaluation is no longer an option, national initiatives must not undermine free market competition, and national fiscal policy is constrained by budgetary considerations and the conditions laid down for entry into the currency union. Renewed assistance in the form of the Structural Funds will depend on the degree of solidarity that exists among the richer and poorer EU member states and the level of competition that exists among disadvantaged regions for such assistance.

Social equity will be enhanced by economic integration only if the gap between rich and poor is narrowed. If we broadly classify the poor as lower paid workers, the unemployed and those dependent on transfers from the state, then a reduction in social inequality depends on the effect that the EU has on wages in general, and on the functioning of the welfare state. Theory does not help us to predict whether social inequality will increase or decrease. Some theorists argue that growth will promote the cause of equality. This is not obvious. Growth in the US economy over the last 15 years, and more recent growth in the UK economy, has been accompanied by growing inequality. High levels of growth in Ireland in the last few years have still failed to touch the most disadvantaged in our society. Countries with high public expenditure output ratios tend to have less social and economic inequality in comparison with countries where public expenditure is a small percentage of national output. High levels of public expenditure are normally financed by progressive taxation which reduces income inequality. The nature of public goods is that they tend to be democratic, in that consumption cannot be confined to the few. The cap on public expenditure which is a precondition to membership of the single currency must inevitably lead to increased inequality.

Markets reinforce individualistic behaviour. If markets are imperfect, then they can prove wasteful as a form of social organisation designed to provide for human welfare. Getting the balance right between a) considerations of efficiency and equity and b) the market provision of private goods and the provision of public goods, requires institutional structures that reinforce the human capacity for solidarity and that provide a mechanism for citizens to express their demand for public goods. Despite institutional reforms introduced at Maastricht, such as the increased power of the European Parliament and the creation of the Committee of the Regions, there still remains a serious democratic deficit in the operations of the EU. The democratic deficit makes it harder for competing individuals and groups (social, ethnic and national) to recognise the legitimacy of the other position. Such recognition is a precursor to the solidarity required if cohesion is to remain a viable objective.

## 8. CONCLUSION

Vaclav Havel, in his address to the European Parliament in 1994, asserted the common destiny of Europe, despite the differences that exist between nations that make up the European mosaic. Countries can choose to fight for their places on a common boat, or they can choose to agree peacefully (Havel, 1994). The European Union that he envisages is one based on close co-operation between European nations and citizens, which would limit, if not exclude, the possibility of new conflicts. Such beneficial co-operation would be based on principles of democracy, respect for human rights, civil society and an open market economy.

The current structures facilitate the achievement of open market economies but more needs to be done to redress the democratic deficit and to strengthen civil society. The institutional expressions of solidarity within the EU (the Structural Funds and Social Charter) are limited in their scope and intent. Both initiatives are ancillary to the main project of creating a single economic space that facilitates business. The increased centralisation of decision making in the EU, which is a consequence of economic integration, is creating a very serious democratic deficit.

A current malaise which is evident in most advanced industrial countries is the extent to which individuals have disengaged from civil society. This phenomenon has been very pronounced in the last quarter century, in particular in countries where social organisation is dominated by market capitalism. The market reinforces individualism, but this is not sufficient to explain the quite dramatic fall in civic and political participation. The role of technology in privatising leisure is one possible explanation. The power of the media in promoting private consumption is another candidate. The general conception of the good life has shifted in an increasingly consumerist direction. Many citizens are critical of current democratic structures and feel powerless to influence the political agenda. It is, therefore, not surprising that individual identity has become increasingly personalised and that individual activities are becoming increasingly self-oriented. If one accepts that individualism and competitive behaviour are a product of, *inter alia*, technology and political disempowerment, then prospects for increased solidarity among countries and citizens of the EU are not promising. The direction of technological change is accelerating the process of social atomism, while the current institutional structure of the EU is not conducive to democratic participation, despite the rhetoric on subsidiarity.

The human capacity for solidarity needs to be encouraged. This capacity is strengthened by a recognition of our common humanity and destiny. Social contact and social exchange, especially when it is related to issues that concern all members of the community, should also increase feelings of fraternity. More devolved government, which would give local communities a greater say in the political decisions that affect their area, would be one example of a facilitating mechanism designed to boost social solidarity at a local level. Increased worker participation in the control of enterprises should aid co-operation among workers and between workers and management. Opportunities for increased contact among workers of different countries should enhance international worker solidarity. Improved fora to address common threats (such as the environmental problem) should encourage countries to search for solutions in a co-operative manner. Governments of EU member states need to be constantly aware of the potentially destructive consequences that can emanate from excessive inter-country rivalries.

If material prosperity is the necessary and sufficient condition for individual welfare and social stability, and if the EU experiment can deliver on its economic promise, then its chances of political and social success are good. However, the complexity of human nature suggests that, while material prosperity may be an important input into human welfare, it is by no means sufficient. Moreover, there are no guarantees that the EU will make all countries, regions and social groups economically better off. Market forces could lead to increased economic disparities between rich and poor countries and between rich and poor individuals within countries. Increased inequalities could give rise to greater levels of social disaffection and reduced levels of public security.

Market forces might give rise to environmentally damaging levels of private production and consumption. Market forces might displace socially beneficial production of public goods.

This scenario is admittedly hypothetical. We do not know *ex ante* what the consequences of European Union will be in terms of the creation and distribution of private and public goods in the future. The important point is that the operation of the market in an EU context could produce unexpected social bads, which can only be rectified by political co-operation among countries and among citizens. Unless federally-based automatic structures are created to promote solidarity among citizens, the political will to address and redress problems that might arise as a consequence of competitive market activity, will not exist. The market ideology does not take account of the fact that individuals are social animals, and certainly does not cater for their spiritual or non-materialistic needs. As Havel said, entities will only work if they offer some key to emotional identification and incorporate values for which people are willing to make sacrifices. He suggested a charter for the EU which would explicitly define the ideals on which it is founded and the values that it wishes to incorporate. The Charter would be a moral code for EU citizens.

If solidarity cannot be nurtured among governments and citizens of the various EU member states, then the new Europe will rest on very unstable foundations.

## References

Bentham, J., Burns, J. and Hart, H. (1990): *A Fragment on Government,* Burns, J. and Hart, H. (eds.) Cambridge: Cambridge University Press.

Cohen, G.A., (1993): "Equality of What? On Welfare Goods and Capabilities", in Nussbaum, M. and Sen, A. (eds.), *The Quality of Life*, Oxford: Clarendon Press.

Dahrendorf, R. (1972): "On the Origin of Social Inequality", in Laslett, P. and Runciman, W.C. (eds.), *Philosophy, Politics and Society*, second series, Oxford: Blackwell.

Davis, K., and Moore, W.E. (1945): "Some Principles of Stratification", *American Sociological Review*, Vol. 10, No. 2.

Driffil, J., Mizon, G. and Alph, A. (1990): "Costs of Inflation", in Friedman, B. and Hahn, F. (eds.), *Handbook of Monetary Economics*, Amsterdam: North Holland.

Dworkin, R. (1977): *Taking Rights Seriously*, London: Duckworth.

Dworkin, R. (1981): "What is Equality? Part I: Equality of Welfare; Part II: Equality of Resources", *Philosophy and Public Affairs*, Vol. 10, No. 3-4.

Etzioni, A. (1988) *The Moral Dimension: Towards a New Economics*, New York: Free Press.

Etzioni, A. (1993): *The Spirit of Community: The Reinvention of American Society*, New York: Touchstone.

Graham, F. (1923): "Some Aspects of Protection further Considered", *Quarterly Journal of Economics*, Vol. 37.

Hausman. D. and McPherson, M. (1994): "Economics, Rationality and Ethics", in Hausman, D. (ed.) The *Philosophy of Economics: An Anthology*, Cambridge: Cambridge University Press.

Havel, V. (1994): Speech to the European Parliament.

Hegel, G., Knox, T. and Pelczynski, Z. (1964): *Political Writings*, (translated by Knox, T. and introductory essay by Pelczynski, Z.), Oxford: Clarendon Press.

Hutton, W. (1996): *The State We're In*, London: Vintage.

Kemp, M. (1962): "The Gains from International Trade", *Economic Journal*, Vol. 72.

Kenen, P. (1969): "The Theory of Optimum Currency Areas: An Eclectic View", in Mundell R. and Swoboda, A.K. (eds.) *Monetary Problems of the International Economy*, Chicago: University of Chicago Press.

Kymlicka, W. (1990): *Contemporary Political Philosophy: An Introduction*, Oxford: Clarendon Press.

Le Grand, J. (1991): *Equity and Choice*, London: Harper-Collins.

Locke, J. and Wooten, D. (1993): *Political Writings*, (edited and with an introduction by Wooten, D.), London: Penguin Books.

Mankiw, G. (1990): "A Quick Refresher Course in Macroeconomics", *Journal of Economic Literature*, Vol. XXVIII, No. 4. pp 1645-60

McKinnon, R.I. (1963): "Optimum Currency Areas", *American Economic Review*, Vol. 53.

Meade, J. (1953): *Problems of Economic Union*, London: Allen & Unwin.

Mill, J.S. (1969): *On Liberty and Utilitarianism*, Oxford: Oxford University Press.

Mundell, R. (1961): "A Theory of Optimum Currency Areas", *American Economic Review*, Vol. 51.

Myrdal, G. (1957): *Economic Theory and Underdeveloped Regions*, London: Duckworth.

Nozick, R. (1974): *Anarchy, State and Utopia*, New York: Basic Books.

O'Donnell, R. (1992): "Economic and Monetary Union", in Keatinge, P. (ed.), *Maastricht and Ireland: What the Treaty means*, Dublin: Institute of European Affairs.

Ohlin, B. (1933): *Interregional and International Trade*, Cambridge: Harvard University Press.

Poole, R. (1991): *Morality and Modernity*, London and New York: Routledge.

Pope John Paul II, (1991): *Centesimus Annus (One Hundred Years)*, London: Catholic Truth Society.

Putnam, R. (1995): "Bowling Alone: America's Declining Social Capital", *Journal of Democracy*, Vol.6, No. 1.

Rawls, J. (1973): *A Theory of Justice*, London: Oxford University Press

Ricardo, D. (1963): *The Principles of Political Economy and Taxation*, Homewood, IL: Irwin (first published 1817).

Rousseau, J-J., Ritter, A. and Conway Bondanella, J. (1988): *Rousseau's Political Writings: new translations, interpretative notes, background commentary*, Ritter, A. and Conway Bondanella, J.(eds.), New York: Norton.

Sabine, G.H. and Thorson, T.L. (1973): *A History of Political Theory*, London: The Dryden Press.

Samuelson, P. (1939): "The Gains from International Trade", *Canadian Journal of Economics*, Vol. 5.

Samuelson, P. (1957): "Wage and Interest: A Modern Dissection of Marxian Economic Models", *American Economic Review*, Vol. 47.

Samuelson, P. (1962): "The Gains from International Trade Once Again", *Economic Journal*, Vol. 72.

Sandel, M. (1982): *Liberalism and the Limits of Justice*, Cambridge: Cambridge University Press.

Scaperlanda, A. (1993): "Christian Values and Economic Ethics", *International Journal of Social Economics*, Vol. 20, No. 10.

Scitovsky, T. (1958): *Economic Theory and Western European Integration*, London: Allen & Unwin.

Sen, A. (1973): "Behaviour and the Concept of Preference", *Economica*, Vol. 40.

_____ , (1992): *Inequality Re-examined*, Oxford: Clarendon Press.

Smith, A. and Skinner, A. (1986): *The Wealth of Nations*, (Introduction by Skinner, A.), London: Penguin.

Taylor, C. (1979): *Hegel and Modern Society*, Cambridge: Cambridge University Press.

_____ , (1985): *Philosophy and the Human Sciences: Philosophical Papers II*, Cambridge: Cambridge University Press.

Thomson, D. (1974): *Europe since Napoleon*, Harmondsworth, Middlesex: Penguin Books.

de Tocqueville, A. and Reeve, H. (1961): *Democracy in America*, (translated by Reeve, H.), New York: Schocken Books.

# 2

# INTERNATIONAL TRADE AND EUROPEAN INTEGRATION[1]

*David Jacobson* and *Terrence McDonough*

## 1. INTRODUCTION

The Irish economy is one in which, as in Europe in general, industrial activity is unevenly distributed. Some sectors perform — and have developed — better than others. Some have become spatially concentrated to a greater extent than others. Yet this uneven development has been the basis for Ireland's recent economic growth. The causes include a complex interplay of historical, cultural and institutional factors in addition to traditional comparative advantage. All of these forces operate in the context of an increasingly integrated Europe.

Ireland's economy can be characterised as one that is small and open. As such it provides an interesting example of the dynamics of development which have occurred in such economies. Ireland's history provides instances both of sustained underdevelopment and, since the appearance of the "Celtic Tiger", rapid growth. A large percentage of Ireland's economic activity takes place in the international sector, through exports and imports. The Irish Economy is an appropriate context in which to examine the applicability of both traditional trade theory and its more recent innova-

[1] The authors wish to thank Dr Siobhán McGovern and Dr Eamon O'Shea for comments on an earlier draft of this paper.

tions. In this paper, we examine the different schools of trade theory and their respective explanations of differential industrial development between countries and regions. We examine to what extent these theories can describe Irish experience to date. We conclude by drawing out the implications for Irish trade and industrial policy in the future. Critically evaluated, these conclusions may provide insight into the challenges facing policymakers in countries in similar situations. In general, what we show is that "lumpiness" in the spatial concentration of industry is consistent both with theories of international trade and theories of industrial development.

The context for recent developments in the Irish economy has increasingly become one of free flows of both goods and services, and factors of production. This is in large part due to Ireland's participation in the Single European Market; fundamentally this has been a programme for the removal of non-tariff barriers (tariff barriers were removed through the integration process over the 25 years following the Treaty of Rome in 1957).

The removal of barriers satisfies some of the assumptions of orthodox theories, and should lead, in accordance with those theories, to increasing evenness in the distribution of economic activity across the EU. However, economic activity seems to continue to concentrate in cores, both within the EU as a whole and within the different regions and countries that make up the EU. The main concern of this chapter is this apparent tendency for economic activity to concentrate spatially.

In the next section we examine the theory of comparative advantage; this leads to a discussion in section 3 of revisions to this theory, as expressed particularly in the work of Paul Krugman. In section 4 we turn to the question of industrial agglomeration and clustering — processes which are consistent with Krugman's conception of the international economy. The best known framework for analysing clusters, introduced in this section, is that of Michael Porter. This leads to a brief examination in section 5 of uneven development and cumulative causation. Section 6 summarises all the foregoing, with a categorisation of ways in which firms interrelate to form industrial or inter-firm structures. We consider applications to Ireland in section 7. Section 8 offers some conclusions, including consideration of implications for policy.

## 2. COMPARATIVE ADVANTAGE

According to the traditional Ricardian comparative advantage theory of international trade, countries will specialise in the production and export of those goods in which they have a comparative advantage. Even if Country A can produce, say, both cars and refrigerators better than Country B, as long as A is relatively better (cheaper, more efficient) at producing cars, then A will produce cars and export them to B, and B will produce refrigerators and export them to A. What follows from this is an expectation that when barriers to trade are removed, there will be inter-industry specialisation; the countries involved will begin to specialise in different industries, some countries producing and exporting more cars, and others producing and exporting more refrigerators. Moreover, those that increase their production of cars will, it would be expected, transfer resources out of the refrigerator industry and, therefore, produce fewer refrigerators. All countries theoretically benefit from the increased productivity brought about by this process of specialisation.

Comparative advantage has been at the base of all neo-classical international trade theory (i.e. since the late 19th century). The major innovation in neo-classical theory this century came with the development of the Heckscher-Ohlin-Samuelson (HOS) model. This model was at the core of neo-classical international trade theory at least up to the end of the 1980s, and is still the central model in many textbooks. The HOS model rests heavily on comparative advantage. It states that, with free trade, a country will export the good that uses most intensively the factor of production with which that country is most richly endowed. The rich endowment of the factor makes it relatively cheaper and, therefore, the production of that good relatively less expensive. With lower relative production costs, this good is the one that is

exported. It is in the latter sense that HOS is based on comparative advantage.[2] The conclusion from HOS is little different from
that of simple comparative advantage, namely that, in a free trade
context, there will be inter-industry specialisation among countries. What HOS adds is that the reason for this inter-industry
specialisation is the difference between countries in endowments
of the different factors of production.

The policy implication of these theories is that all countries
would be better off if there were no intervention by states in international trade, allowing each country to specialise in its most
efficient, least cost industry. However, both the comparative advantage theory and this policy conclusion have come under critical scrutiny. Development economists (Donaldson, 1984; pp. 260-
81), for example, have for long held that:

- The assumptions upon which comparative advantage theory
  is based, such as perfect competition and perfect mobility of
  resources, do not hold, and therefore the theory itself does not
  hold;

- Comparative advantage theory is static, and does not allow
  for dynamic effects, as in the case of planned, created, comparative advantage and the important role of leading industries;[3]

- The theory does not take into consideration distribution effects, such as the extent to which inter-industry specialisation
  within an economy may reduce the welfare of those whose

---

[2] For an excellent treatment of international trade theory that includes both the
standard neo-classical approaches and some of the oligopoly-based models of
international trade, see Södersten and Reed (1994).

[3] From a dynamic perspective it is possible to plan comparative advantage. Thus,
a state institution can intervene to create an industry in which that country does
not yet have, but can develop, a comparative advantage. Specialisation in a
leading industry, through its associated infrastructure and expertise, has implications for future innovations in other industries. It does matter whether a
country specialises in potato chips or computer chips.

livelihood depended on the good whose production is cut back; and

- Among relatively less developed countries (LDCs), a dualism can emerge as a result of trade with more developed countries (MDCs), in which there is an advanced, wealthy, high employment sector and a technologically backward, poor, high unemployment sector, with little relationship between them.[4]

Donaldson (1984: p. 267), having considered such issues, concludes that "free trade (that is, trade that is carried on without LDC government intervention of any kind) for a developing LDC in the real world situation is only rarely the optimal policy".

Other criticisms of comparative advantage and/or HOS have followed from the Leontief Paradox. In the 1950s and 1960s, Leontief undertook research on US trade patterns. His results unexpectedly showed that the US seemed to export labour intensive products. HOS would have predicted that, as the US is a capital-rich country, it should export capital rather than labour intensive goods. Alternative theories were therefore required.

To account for Leontief's Paradox a number of theories provided alternative explanations for the flows of goods and services between countries. Of the economists whose work has influenced post-Leontief international trade theory, the most important is probably Paul Krugman.

### 3. ECONOMIES OF SCALE AND TRANSPORTATION

Krugman (1987a, 1987b, 1993) has been prominent in international trade theory, strategic trade policy, and the geography of trade, though the originality of his contributions has sometimes been questioned (McGovern, 1994; Kindleberger, 1993; p. 56). He has argued that, in addition to comparative advantage as a determinant of the nature and direction of flows of goods and serv-

---

[4] This argument, though not exclusive to, is most developed by, various schools of dependency theory.

ices between countries, product differentiation, economies of scale and imperfect competition must be added.[5]

The need for alternative explanations for the nature and direction of trade flows followed not just from Leontief, but also from other empirical work (NESC, 1989). At its simplest, what this work showed was that when barriers to trade were removed in Europe, the expected inter-industry specialisation did not emerge. When the common market was formed, the economies that had been involved in car production, for example, continued to manufacture cars. Those involved in the production of other consumer durables, such as refrigerators and washing machines, continued to manufacture these too. It was expected that some would move out of cars and specialise in other products. What did change was that a greater proportion of output was exported, and a greater proportion of local purchases was imported. The choice facing consumers broadened.

There was more product differentiation, expressing itself as intra-industry trade. Intra-industry specialisation took place, by which firms in one country produced certain types or makes of cars, while those in other countries produced other models. There was specialisation within industries and not, as was expected, across industries.

A related factor is one of economies of scale. Once it is shown that the market structure is not perfectly competitive — which necessarily follows from the fact that the product is differentiated — then the neo-classical, perfectly competitive, long run equilibrium in which firms are producing at the bottom of their long run average cost curves no longer holds. It becomes reasonable to assume that expanding firms could benefit from increasing returns to scale. A firm (let us call it Firm A, in the market for a good X)

---

[5] This awareness of the role of factors such as product differentiation and increasing returns to scale was not incorporated into international trade theory until the 1980s. For discussions on product differentiation and international trade, see Krugman (1983), and McGovern (1994). McGovern points out that Lovasy (1941) had already, decades before the "new international trade theorists", used product differentiation to explain aspects of international trade.

may now have an advantage in competition with other firms, domestic and foreign, simply because Firm A is producing on a larger scale and is, therefore, further down its average cost curve, that is, because it has higher volumes, it has lower unit costs. There are a number of possible reasons why Firm A may have higher volumes than its competitors, even assuming that the two firms have identical production functions: perhaps Firm A began producing earlier (first mover advantage); that Firm A's local market is bigger; or Firm A began exporting earlier.

Imperfect competition and economies of scale contribute to an understanding of uneven development. They are elements of a process whereby, even in the absence of state intervention of any kind, production of a good can become concentrated in a particular place. Firm A defeats all other firms in the market for X because it has lower costs. Due to transportation costs, all upstream and downstream production, distribution, and other services associated with the production of X are now more likely to be located near Firm A. Other products using similar inputs — or downstream services — to those of X may now also have an incentive to locate near to Firm A. The result is a concentration of economic activity in that place.

It is important to emphasise that this result could be a consequence of factors other than comparative advantage. Firm A may experience lower costs arising from economies of scale, for example, which more than offset relatively higher costs of factors of production in that place. Krugman (1993: p. 98) sums up the impact of economies of scale by concluding that "producers have an incentive to concentrate production of each good or service in a limited number of locations". He factors in "the costs of transactions across distance" and makes the following point:

> the preferred locations for each individual producer are those where demand is large or supply of inputs is particularly convenient — which in general are the locations chosen by other producers. Thus concentrations of industry, once established, tend to be self-sustaining; this applies both to the localisation

of individual industries and to such grand agglomerations as
the Boston-Washington corridor.

This kind of analysis leads to two somewhat contradictory results.
It explains why, in the period following the removal of barriers to
trade, various goods continued to be produced in more than one
of the member countries of the European Economic Community.
But it can also be used to explain why industry and multi-
industry agglomerations developed in specific locations. The reason concerns the relative weights of the different factors: the more
important product differentiation — or intra-industry specialisation — the more likely it was that production in this industry
continued to take place in a number of locations. The more important the economies of scale, and the more advantageous the
local conditions in one particular place, the more likely it was that
production would become concentrated in that place. Local conditions, high transaction costs across distance and economies of
scale in a number of industries together explain "grand agglomerations" emerging at different levels of industrial disaggregation.[6]

It might appear from these conclusions that there is a justification in Krugman's work for strategic trade policy. This is policy
that is aimed, for example, at developing a comparative advantage in a particular industry. Strategic trade policy is often applied as industrial policy, focusing on positive encouragement of
development, for example through subsidies, rather than through
negative prevention of competition through tariffs. However,
Krugman has consistently argued that free trade (and the absence
of strategic trade policy) continues to be best from an international welfare perspective. "The problem is", he writes, "that
while strategic trade policies may be in any one country's interest,
if all countries pursue them the result may be to block mutually
beneficial integration" (1987b: p. 121). It is therefore best, in his

---

[6] The fact that firms and industries will tend to agglomerate was well docu-
mented by early economists, and, in particular, Marshall. Krugman's work in
this area explicitly builds on that of Marshall.

view, if no country pursues such policies. While perhaps theoretically defensible, this vision of universal international forbearance appears utopian.

Analogously, it could be argued that a particular state's industrial policy encouraging inward foreign direct investment (FDI) could be beneficial to that economy, but, if other states introduced similar policies, this could cease to be the case. The "price" to be paid for the FDI would be bid up. The end result would be a redistribution of wealth from the relatively poorer taxpayers in each state to the relatively wealthy owners of the multinational corporations (MNCs). It follows though that a country's strategic trade policies can succeed if other countries either are not aware of them or are tardy in implementing their own. A second possibility is that richer states are willing to tolerate these policies in the poorer state for developmental or other political reasons.

Ireland has been relatively successful in encouraging FDI because it was among the first European countries to have a well-organised strategy of this kind, and because, although the policy contravenes the spirit of the Treaty of Rome, it has been allowed as a means of bringing Ireland's level of economic development up to the European average. The gap between levels of economic activity in Ireland and the European core was, in fact, reduced by the industrial strategy of encouraging FDI. In the future, however, Ireland must beware of bidding away any potential benefits in competition with other states.

## 4. AGGLOMERATION AND CLUSTERS[7]

What follows from the work of Marshall, as updated by Krugman (1993), is that, under certain circumstances, firms within an industry or in related industries will agglomerate, that is, they will locate in the same place, close to one another. The agglomeration economies will be greater than the benefits that firms could de-

---

[7] Some of the discussion on Porter in this section draws on Jacobson and Andréosso-O'Callaghan (1996: pp. 119–21).

rive from a more diffuse locational distribution. A locality or region may become the site for an expansion of common pools of labour, capital and infrastructure. Pecuniary externalities may arise when firms in some particular place make new investments. In such a case the reduction in unit costs arising from the externalities are called agglomeration economies (Harrison, 1992).

Agglomerations of various kinds are probably the norm. It is likely that a higher proportion of the industrial output of the economies of the world is accounted for by production in agglomerations than by production in stand-alone firms, evenly distributed around geographic space. This is consistent with Porter's (1990, p. 18) argument that "firms based in particular nations achieve international success in distinct segments and industries". He rejects the traditional comparative advantage model mainly because its assumptions are unrealistic. The recent revisions in international trade theory around economies of scale and the consequences of other market imperfections, leave unanswered the question that is for Porter (1990: p. 16) the most important: "Which nation's firms will reap them [these economies] and in what industries?" Porter's theoretical and empirical contributions have been in attempting to answer this question.

Porter's primary tool for illustrating "patterns of national advantage" is the cluster chart. This chart includes the successful (competitive) industries of a country, identified as such either by having "a world export share greater than the nation's average share of world exports, or an international position based on foreign investment that was estimated to be as significant" (1990: pp. 287–88). Having identified the patterns of national advantage with the cluster chart, he explains them with four factors he calls the "diamond". These are:

- Factor conditions (including all factors of production, as well as means, such as training and education, for improving those factors of production);

- Demand conditions (for example, the bigger the home demand for an industry's product, the better);

- Related and supporting industries (the presence in a country of internationally competitive supplier industries, for example, will enhance the competitiveness of the buyer industries); and

- Firm strategy, structure and rivalry (including domestic rivalry, and rules and institutions governing that rivalry — the more intense the domestic rivalry, the greater the potential for the firms to be internationally competitive) (1990: p. 71).

Porter's clusters are firms and industries connected through horizontal and vertical relationships. Vertical links are those, such as buyer/supplier, involving firms up or downstream from one anosther in the process of converting raw materials into consumer goods. Horizontal links are those between industries, for example, firms in two industries may have common customers, technologies or distribution channels. Because of agglomeration economies, clustering "works best when the industries involved are geographically concentrated" (Porter, 1990: p. 157). The works of Porter and Krugman on industrial agglomeration reinforce one another. Krugman shows how, from the perspective of international trade, industries can become concentrated in particular places, and Porter shows how, from the perspective of links between firms and industries within a country, agglomeration contributes to international competitiveness.

The work on the potential for industrial agglomerations and their contribution to a country's international trade has not been without critics. Dunning (1992), for example, argues that Porter's focus does not adequately incorporate MNCs. He points out that Nestlé, though a Swiss company, has 95 per cent of sales accounted for by its foreign subsidiaries. The diamonds of competitive advantage of the host countries in which those subsidiaries operate may, therefore, have more to do with Nestlé's contribution to Switzerland's GNP than Switzerland's own diamond of competitive advantage. Dunning suggests the addition of a transnational business variable as a separate factor in the diamond of competitive advantages.

Scasselati (1991) would agree with this,[8] though he goes even further (perhaps too far), in criticising Porter's focus on national entities. He emphasises corporations that in "their inherent drive toward ever expanding accumulation . . . simply cannot afford to tie themselves to any territory". It can be observed, however, that MNCs, though not committed to any one location, are developing long-term relationships in various locations with such collaborative partners as suppliers providing components and services (Sabel, 1996).

Jacobs and de Jong (1991) have two fundamental criticisms of Porter's approach. They argue, firstly, that there is an over-emphasis on end product. In their application of the model to the Netherlands, for example, they find that a cluster may be in an intermediate stage and not at the end-use stage. This makes it difficult to identify accurately the cluster in Porter's chart. Second, the approach is one-sided in that international diversity is stressed. While Jacobs and de Jong accept that both international divergence and convergence are evident, Porter's approach, in their view, does not capture the dynamic relationship between the two tendencies. The first of these observations is most applicable to the Irish case. A full Porterian cluster may be too extensive, spreading beyond the scale and capacity of a small, open economy like Ireland's (O'Donnellan, 1994). In such economies, the domestic market may be too small to generate national clusters. Larger economic spaces may have to be analysed in order to identify the extent to which industries in Ireland may be elements in, for example, a European cluster. Despite these criticisms, Porter is praised for introducing "the idea to an audience of economists that globalisation, somewhat paradoxically, leads to more emphasis on local conditions, and moreover, provides a global

---

[8] Scasselatti also provides a Swiss, though contrasting, example, pointing out that Porter's "applause for the revival of the Swiss watch industry ... neglects the fact that several of the most famous Swiss brands are now owned by a US company, North American Watch".

firm [with] opportunities to take advantage of these" (Jacobs and de Jong, 1991).

The cluster literature contributes to our understanding of why there are differences between the industrial structure in Ireland and that in the European core. If there are advantages to be gained for firms in locating near to other, related, firms, then the relative paucity of industrial development in Ireland, in the first place, was itself a factor in reducing Ireland's attractiveness to industrial enterprises. Relative success in encouraging the establishment of subsidiaries of foreign-owned firms would not, by itself, increase the general attractiveness of Ireland as a location for firms not receiving the artificial attractions of low tax rates, and capital and training grants. Only if linkages develop among firms can the advantages of agglomeration be reaped.

When these linkages do develop, however, they benefit the participating firms, and differentiate the firms in the cluster and their associated location from firms and areas outside it. In this way, while clusters can be the means of reducing the gap between one economy and another, they can also be the means of increasing differences between locations within economies. To the extent that they are spatially concentrated in regions, those regions (or enclaves) will experience increased economic activity, often at the expense of other regions. The growth of cities like Dublin relative to other parts of Ireland, or indeed of counties, like Monaghan, relative to Cavan and Leitrim, may be examples of these tendencies. Markusen (1996) uses the expression "sticky places in slippery space" to denote the ability of such enclaves to attract and keep both capital and labour. We examine various ways in which firms form industrial structures in Section 6.

## 5. UNEVEN DEVELOPMENT AND CUMULATIVE CAUSATION

Basing their arguments on the theory of comparative advantage, many development economists have contended that contact between more and less developed regions will benefit all parties and lead to convergence of living standards. Other development theorists have argued that such contact leads to increasing disparities. While many of their arguments are not meant to apply within the developed world, some can be deployed to understand uneven development within industrialised regions.

The description above of the interactive effects of economies of scale and the benefits of agglomeration can be seen as a specific instance of a broader class of dynamic interactions. The great institutionalist economist, Gunnar Myrdal, described such interactions as cumulative causation, describing virtuous and vicious circles. Prosperous regions attract labour and capital thereby improving conditions, services and infrastructure, which further attract additional labour and capital. Investment increases demand which then draws further investment. This dynamic can be summarised as success breeds success while failure breeds failure (Sawyer 1989: pp. 422–28). The development task in such instances then becomes the breaking of vicious circles of underdevelopment and the institution of virtuous circles of further development.

Mjoset (1992) applied this kind of analysis to Irish development, concluding that among the factors accounting for a vicious circle of relative lack of development in Ireland was a weak national system of innovation. To the extent that the success of the Irish economy in recent years is sustained, this may be evidence of policy — and other factors — having succeeded in breaking the vicious circle and shifting the economy to a virtuous one. We turn to this question in section 7 below.

## 6. INDUSTRIAL STRUCTURES

We are now in a position to categorise the different ways in which firms interrelate to form industrial or inter-firm structures. There are four main ways. First, a firm can stand alone, i.e. it has completely free, open market relationships with suppliers; completely free, open market relationships with customers; and no horizontal strategic alliances with similar firms. A stand-alone firm is a member of no networks, and would generally operate in highly effective markets in which there are, for example, large numbers of buyers and sellers of an undifferentiated product. Such firms are not common anymore, and are more likely in services such as retail shops than in manufacturing.

Second, there are vertical associations of firms, a large number of which can be found in Ireland. Many indigenous firms form close, vertical relationships with subsidiaries of multinationals. Instances include software manual printing firms, producing manuals for particular software firms like Microsoft or Lotus, and Higgins Engineering in Galway producing components for Thermo King, a refrigerated truck company. In vertical associations the buyer firm will trust the supplier to produce to high quality standards, with minimum (or zero) faults, and to a particular time schedule. The buyer firm may have one or two such suppliers of the same component, but it will not call for tenders each time it buys. It will simply select one of its small numbers of preferred suppliers.

Third, there are horizontal associations where groups of firms producing similar products, or different parts of the same product, associate with one another in co-operative relationships. Although there appear to be gains to be derived from this type of inter-firm structure, there are very few identified examples in Ireland. An embryonic association of this type exists in the mid-west region, where a group of small and medium manufacturers of printed circuit boards has discussed the possibility of co-operating so as to obtain better conditions from their buyer companies, usually subsidiaries of multinationals. For similar reasons a group of poultry breeders in Monaghan formed an association which then confronted their monopsonistic buyer, Monaghan Poultry Products. However, there are few examples of firms co-operating horizontally in an integrated production system.

Fourth, there are clusters as described in detail in section 4 above. A cluster is basically a combination of vertical and horizontal associations. Agreements between firms may be formal or informal. Firms may compete against one another in some respects and co-operate in others. Porter (1990) considers a high level of competition to be essential in successful clusters. While there is agreement that competition is important, others consider high levels of both competition and co-operation to be essential for successful industrial structures (de Bandt, 1987). For a group of firms to constitute a cluster, there must be a number of firms producing the same or similar products and a number of other firms that buy from and/or sell to those firms.

There is much evidence that successful firms are those which, particularly through horizontal associations and clusters, have close relationships with other firms. Among the regions where evidence can be found to support this proposition are Emilia Romagna and Abruzzo in Italy, West Jutland in Denmark, and Wales (Cooke, 1996; Dunford and Hudson, 1996). In all these places there are high levels of horizontal association, where groups of small firms co-operate in becoming internationally competitive. They have come to be called "industrial districts", particularly in Emilia Romagna. In Wales, clusters have formed, among them indigenous Welsh firms and subsidiaries of MNCs, including many Japanese MNCs. All these regions have performed extremely well in terms of industrial growth and competitiveness, well above the European average.

There is investment in creating inter-firm structures that improve the competitiveness of the final product. This reduces the "footlooseness" of the MNC participants, and increases their linkages with local industrial structures. However, such inter-firm structures also often increase the dependence of local suppliers on the demand of the multinational (Jacobson and Andréosso-O'Callaghan, 1996: pp. 114–22).

## 7. APPLICATIONS TO IRELAND

We have shown above that one of the factors leading to a change in international trade theory was the observed results of European integration. International trade within Europe increased — as expected — as a result of the creation of the common market. However, the way in which that increase occurred was unexpected.

An important element in the increase was intra-industry trade, in addition to inter-industry trade. Rather than, say, Germany specialising in car production, and importing refrigerators and washing machines from Italy, both countries continued to produce both types of products. Much of the increase in trade following the creation of the common market was accounted for by increases of both exports and imports within industries. Ireland was no exception — accession to membership of the EC in 1973 was followed by an increase in trade with Europe, and a decline in Ireland's dependence on the UK as a trading partner. A significant part of the increase in trade was accounted for primarily by intra-industry trade (McAleese, 1976; Brülhart and McAleese, 1993).

The standard measure of intra-industry trade is the Grubel-Lloyd (GL) index:

$$\frac{\sum_{i=1}^{n} [(Xi + Mi) - |Xi - Mi|]}{\sum_{i=1}^{n} (Xi + Mi)},$$

where Xi and Mi refer respectively to the exports and imports of industry *i*'s goods, and n is the number of industries. The GL index is a measure of the proportion of trade in relation to which goods in a category are both imported and exported. Using five-digit OECD data, weighted by current trade values in each year, Brülhart and McAleese (1993) calculate Grubel-Lloyd indices of intra-industry trade in manufactured goods, as shown in Table 2.1. The table shows that, in 1972, for example, 38 per cent of trade in manufactured goods involved the simultaneous export and import of goods within the same five-digit category.

TABLE 2.1: IRISH INTRA-INDUSTRY TRADE, 1972–1990

| SITC Section | Description | 1972 | 1977 | 1985 | 1990 | Direction of Change | |
|---|---|---|---|---|---|---|---|
| | | | | | | '72–'85 | '85–'90 |
| 5–8 | Manufacturers | 0.38 | 0.49 | 0.47 | 0.44 | + | − |

*Source*: Brülhart and McAleese, 1993.

Brülhart and McAleese actually use a more extensive time series, and show that with the exception of the most recent sub-period, 1985-90, the intra-industry trade trend since 1961 has been upwards. There are questions about how intra-industry trade is calculated. It could be argued, for example, that the more disaggregated the industrial categories, the less intra-industry, and the more inter-industry trade will be found. Brülhart and McAleese (1993) show, however, that "even at a very high level of statistical disaggregation" there are "considerable amounts of intra-industry trade (IIT) in Ireland's external trade, particularly in the manufacturing sectors". Moreover, given that their results are consistent with those of O'Donnell in his work for the NESC study on Ireland and Europe (NESC, 1989), work which used much less disaggregated data, they conclude that this is evidence of "robustness of the trends in Irish IIT (intra-industry trade) detected in this and the previous analyses".

The fact that Ireland's increase in trade with Europe, following its membership of the EC, was accounted for, in significant part, by intra-industry trade does not mean that European integration had no impact on Ireland's industrial structure (NESC, 1993; pp. 250-58). The other 62 per cent of trade in 1972, for example, involved goods exported which were not also being imported, and imported that were not also being exported, that is, inter-industry trade. Using the formula for revealed comparative advantage (RCA),[9] Thornhill (1988) showed that, during the 1970s, Ireland's comparative advantage shifted strongly away from resource-based and low-skill intensive industries, and towards high-skill, capital intensive industries. He identified three main industries accounting for this change: food preparations; organic chemicals; and office machines. The RCA approach clearly shows the increasing importance of several specific industries in Ireland's in-

---

[9] RCA index = $[(x_i/x_{iw})/(x_m/x_{mw})]$ 100, where $x_i$ is the value of exports of product i from Ireland; $x_{iw}$ is the value of "world" exports of product i; $x_m$ is the value of exports of all manufactures from Ireland; and $x_{mw}$ is the value of "world" exports of all manufactures.

dustrial structure and exports. Thornhill's explanations for these results focus primarily on the nature of FDI. MNCs had set up a number of subsidiaries in these industries, and, in particular, in the most important of them, organic chemicals and office machines. Thornhill does not distinguish between Ireland's EC and non-EC trade, nor does he suggest that membership of the EC may have had an impact on the nature of FDI. Rather, he suggests only that Ireland's level of development resulted in the change in the nature of the FDI. We will consider, in later sections, the validity of this omission.

In the mid-1980s Ireland's intra-industry trade stopped growing, and began to decline. Inter-industry specialisation increased, in contrast with the "higher intra-industry specialisation observed at the earlier stages of Irish trade liberalisation" (Brülhart and McAleese, 1993). This inter-industry specialisation, Brülhart and McAleese find, was into "highly trade-oriented and highly productive sectors". (These are the same as the high-skill, highly capital intensive sectors referred to by Thornhill.) Moreover, Ireland's intra-industry trade has, in general, been higher with fellow EC members than with non-members, and the decline in intra-industry trade in the mid-1980s was sharper in relation to intra-EC trade than rest-of-the-world (ROW) trade. This represents an intensification in the 1980s of the trend noted by Thornhill — the increasing sophistication of industry in Ireland. Note, however, that with the exception of food, the industries in which the increasing sophistication is most pronounced are those in which MNCs are most prevalent, namely chemicals and pharmaceuticals, and electronics and engineering (NESC, 1997: Ch. 9). Brülhart and McAleese were the first to note that the increase in trade in the products of the advanced sectors is more pronounced in relation to Ireland's trade with EC partners than with the ROW. This suggests that there is something about Ireland's relationship with the EC that has contributed to these changes in Ireland's industrial structure. It is more than plausible, for example, that Ireland's membership of the EC increased the attractiveness of Ireland as a location for ROW — particularly American —

MNCs, as a satellite platform from which to gain access to the EC markets for their products.

Thornhill (1988) shows three main industries in relation to which Ireland apparently had a RCA in the 1970s: food preparations; office machinery; and organic chemicals. Brülhart and McAleese (1993) show seven industries which had pronounced positive patterns of specialisation in the period 1985 to 1990: office and data processing machines; pharmaceuticals; radio/TV/sound equipment; cocoa, sweets; miscellaneous processed foodstuffs; domestic chemicals and man-made fibres; and spirit distilling and compounding. Given that Brülhart and McAleese used a more disaggregated data set, there is a great deal of similarity between the two sets of industries found to be those in which Ireland has a "revealed" comparative advantage.

All of the main international trade theories discussed above would have predicted specialisation and resultant concentration of resources in one or a few industries. From the work of Porter and others, as discussed above, the question arises as to whether, or to what extent, these concentrations can be explained by traditional comparative advantage, economies of scale and proximity, or the benefits of industrial agglomeration and clustering.

We will consider, in turn, the three industrial groupings discussed above: food, chemicals/pharmaceuticals and computers/electronics. As O'Donnellan (1994) has shown, each of these exhibits some characteristics of a Porterian cluster. In particular, they all have shares of sectoral world exports greater than Ireland's overall share of world exports. Of these, only food has shown evidence of a high level of what he calls "systematic clustering", i.e. highly clustered on the basis of a number of different definitions of clustering. The different definitions of clustering used by O'Donnellan (1994) are:

a.    Trade share;[10]

---

[10] Sector's share of world exports more than four times Irish national average shares. Note that all the definitions are based on data from the mid- and late

b.   Concentration of purchases within own sector;

c.   Domestic share of purchases;

d.   Domestic share of sales;

e.   Concentration of firms within counties;

f.   Concentration of employment within counties;

g.   Association of sectors within regions; and

h.   Share of UK/Irish industrial employment.

Some food-related sub-sectors appear under all these definitions with the exception of d and g. Chemicals/pharmaceutical sub-sectors appear only under a, e, f and g. Computers/electronics sub-sectors appear only under a and e. He goes on to argue that there is little evidence of the productivity and/or innovation enhancing effects with which clustering is supposed to be associated, not even for the food sector.

From the point of view of the revisionists of traditional trade theory, O'Donnellan's results for the food sector send a mixed message. On the one hand, there is evidence of clustering. On the other hand, it would appear that the origin of any specialisation in this sector has more to do with comparative advantage, specifically HOS comparative advantage. The proximity to intensively used raw materials in agriculture must be a large part of any explanation of the success of this sector.

The failure to discover clustering in the chemical/pharmaceutical industry is not surprising. The industry is the result of artificial incentives being offered to MNCs to set up subsidiaries in Ireland (Jacobson, 1991: p. 56). In general, they import bulk chemicals, process them, and re-export them in bulk. Few firms have developed linkages with indigenous firms, or with one another. Their continued presence in Ireland is based on low corporate tax rates, and, at least until recently, relatively lax monitoring

---

1980s; a repeat of O'Donnellan's research based on more recent data could give different results.

of the firms for environmental pollution. As the EU begins to require harmonisation of tax rates and as environmental standards rise, the continuation of a concentration of this industry in Ireland will be called into question.

The failure to find evidence of clustering in the computer/electronics sector is more doubtful. Some of O'Donnellan's criteria, such as domestic purchases and sales cannot be applied to an internationally oriented export industry. The history of the high technology sector contains the paradigmatic examples of clustering in Silicon Valley and the Route 128 area in Massachusetts. It seems unlikely that the continued attractiveness of Ireland for inward high technology investment is unrelated to the presence of existing firms in this sector. There are also concrete examples of high levels of linkage in this sector, among firms, for instance, supplying inputs into Apple's production processes in Cork. The industry began with artificial attractions similar to those which brought the chemical/pharmaceutical MNCs to Ireland. However, it may now have developed into an example of a "created" comparative advantage, with the availability of high levels of relevant skills resulting from a conscious policy of focusing education and training, as well as IDA attention, on this sector.

The indigenous software industry is another example of an industry which may have become a cluster through a conscious policy of education and training. O'Gorman et al (1997: p. 50) conclude that this industry is at least "part of a clustering phenomenon", primarily because of factor conditions, and, in particular, because of the availability of people with software skills, and of an education system capable of generating more people with such skills.

At a more general level, there are a number of reasons why studies such as O'Donnellan's may find it difficult to identify clustering in the Irish case. First, it is possible that the reduction in transport and communication costs has increased the area within which agglomeration must take place for economies to be reaped. This would be consistent with Kennedy's (1991: p. 99) view that:

Ireland, as a member of an increasingly integrated European Community, is becoming more akin to a small region within a large country. In general a region will display a much lower degree of linkage than the country of which it forms part, and the smaller the region the lower the overall degree of intra-regional linkage.

It is likely in relation to information, for example, that the costs of transmission are as similar between Ireland and Bonn, as they are between Munich and Bonn, thus enhancing the possibility of firms in Ireland participating in a European cluster.

Second, evidence of economies of agglomeration may be hidden in the aggregation of the data. Clustering may be taking place on a smaller scale of operations. For example, vertical associations of firms, by definition narrower than clusters, may exist, and may engender economies of agglomeration and/or of association. As O'Donnellan (1994: p. 230) puts it:

> there may well be more subtle and localised clustering happening in some sectors that does make a difference to performance and that should be reinforced by government support for local specialised infrastructure. Possible examples are the dairy industry in Munster, computers and chemicals in Cork, clothing in Donegal, aerospace in Shannon/Limerick, furniture in Navan, and some sectoral pockets of firms in Dublin.

Sub-sectors on which research has been done, and where significant evidence of localised economies of very localised agglomeration and/or association exists, include the software manual printing industry in Dublin (Jacobson and O'Sullivan, 1994), the wooden furniture industry in Co. Monaghan (Mottiar, 1996; Jacobson and Mottiar, 1996), and the indigenous software industry, particularly in Dublin (O'Gorman et al, 1997).

These apparently contradictory explanations for the absence of Porterian clusters are, in fact, reconcilable. On the one hand, as defined by Porter, clusters may require larger economies than Ireland's; O'Donnellan considers the UK and Ireland as an economic area within which clusters might exist, while Kennedy goes even further to consider linkages within the European Community as a whole. On the other hand, small groups of small and medium enterprises (SMEs), as in the software manual printing industry, have sprung up to service subsidiaries of multinationals in Dublin, despite the existence of equivalent firms elsewhere in Europe. The point is that in some cases there are relatively few disadvantages to different parts of a cluster being widely dispersed, for example, where the product has a high value-to-weight ratio. In other cases, there are high costs of transportation and/or high economies of proximity, for example, where just-in-time inventories require close monitoring of the supplier by the buyer.

## 8. CONCLUSIONS

All brands of trade theory suggest that development in the context of an international market is likely to be "lumpy", that is, concentrated in a few sectors and places rather than taking place smoothly across the board. In these circumstances, industrial development must rely on attracting lumps of economic activity within the borders of the state. The debate over industrial policy is about whether a process of specialisation through comparative advantage will arise from purely market driven transactions, or whether there is a role for the state in encouraging the agglomeration of economic activity.

Ireland's experience in the food sector provides some evidence for the comparative advantage perspective, though agriculture can hardly be said to be devoid of government intervention. The success in attracting investment in the electronics/computer sector, a leading industry which may lay the foundations for further development, is a striking instance of the potential relevance of industrial policy. The embeddedness of an industry in the local and regional economy will determine the long-run benefits from inward investment. In this respect, Ireland's flirtation with the chemical industry may prove relatively short-lived as well as ill-advised. Its incompatibility with the "green" image Ireland wishes to project in marketing its food and providing lifestyle amenities for high technology foreign investors militates against further development in this field.

If this analysis is correct, then Ireland's recent success as the "Celtic Tiger" (Sweeney, 1998), to the extent that it is dependent on sectors like chemicals/pharmaceuticals, is likely to be fragile. To the extent that it is dependent on the processes by which Ireland has specialised into the food and electronics/computers sector, it is likely to be more lasting. Even in these sectors there are significant challenges, such as the decline in funds available to agriculture through the Common Agricultural Policy, and the competition to electronics/computers from low cost third world producers. This last includes some countries like India where there are increasingly high levels of such skills as software design and development and an English-speaking workforce.

The policy conclusions that may be drawn from Irish experience include the identification of those sub-sectors in which there are no incentives for agglomeration or, in contrast, incentives for dispersal. Relatively costly attempts to encourage linkages in these sub-sectors must be avoided. More positively, it will be important to identify localised clusters and sub-clusters — industrial districts, networks and *filières* (Jacobson and Andréosso-O'Callaghan, 1996: Ch.3) — and encourage them through appropriate physical and financial infrastructures. It is particularly important to provide general incentives for higher levels of co-operation among Irish firms.[11] In our view, without such development, Irish economic success is unlikely to be sustained in the long run.

If one problem for policy is encouraging or attracting "lumps" (centres of development) within the economy, a complementary problem is the encouragement of development in the economic spaces between the lumps. Traditional perspectives have as-

---

[11] "There has historically been hardly any long-term cooperation between Irish small firms in the provision of purchasing, marketing, financial services or through supply linkages" (O'Sullivan, 1995: p. 386).

sumed that development would spread organically through the expansion of the market which would result from increased economic activity and rising incomes. This kind of process was behind the balanced development of the pioneering capitalist economies of Europe and America. A different prospect faces late industrialisers in the context of a global economy. Even heavily clustered industries will link backwards to intermediate good suppliers and forwards to industrial customers across borders. While prosperity is partially based on international exporting, it is also true that a significant portion of the resulting increase in incomes will, in turn, be spent abroad. It follows that, even in the face of substantial success, economic prosperity will be unevenly spread. Continuing high levels of unemployment in Ireland following several years of more than healthy growth can be partially attributed to this factor. Public intervention designed to spread the benefits of growth will be necessary. Local development policies, increased public employment, and more generous social welfare provision must play a part in this effort.

## References

de Bandt, J. (1987): "French Industrial Policies: Successes and Failures" in Beije, P.R. et al. (eds.) *A Competitive Future for Europe? Towards a New European Industrial Policy*, New York: Croom Helm.

Brülhart, M. and McAleese, D. (1993): "Intra-industry Trade, Adjustment and the EC Single Market: The Irish Experience", Typescript, Dublin: Trinity College Dublin.

Cooke, P. (1996): "Enterprise Support Policies in Dynamic European Regions" in *Networking for Competitive Advantage*, Dublin: NESC.

Donaldson, L. (1984): *Economic Development: Analysis and Policy*, St. Paul, MN: West Publishing.

Dunford, M. and Hudson, R. (1996): *Successful European Regions: Northern Ireland Learning From Others*, Belfast: Northern Ireland Economic Council.

Dunning, J.H. (1992); "The Global Economy, Domestic Governance Strategies and Transnational Corporations: Interactions and Policy Implications", *Transnational Corporations*, 1(3): pp. 7-45.

Harrison, B. (1992): "Industrial Districts: Old Wine in New Bottles?" *Regional Studies*, 26(5): pp. 469-83.

Jacobs, D. and de Jong, M.W. (1991): "Industrial Clusters and the Competitiveness of the Netherlands", TNO Policy Research Paper, 90/NR/064, May.

Jacobson, D. (1991): "Europe's Pharmaceutical Industry: Tackling the Single Market", Special Report No. 2085, London: Economist Intelligence Unit.

Jacobson, D. and Andréosso-O'Callaghan, B. (1996): *Industrial Economics and Organization*, London: McGraw-Hill.

Jacobson, D. and Mottiar, Z. (1996): "Globalisation and Modes of Interaction among Small Firms in Ireland", Paper to the 23rd International Small Business Congress, November, Athens.

Jacobson, D. and O'Sullivan, D. (1994): "Analysing an Industry in Change: The Irish Software Manual Printing Industry", New Technology, Work and Employment, 9(2): pp. 103-14.

Kennedy, K.A. (1991): "Linkages and Overseas Industry" in Foley, A. and McAleese, D. (eds.), *Overseas Industry in Ireland*, Dublin: Gill and Macmillan.

Kindleberger, C.P. (1993): "How Ideas Spread among Economists: Examples from International Economics" in Colander, D. and Coats, A.W. (eds.) *The Spread of Economic Ideas*, Cambridge: Cambridge University Press.

Krugman, P.R. (1993): *Geography and Trade*, Cambridge, MA: Leuven University Press/MIT Press.

Krugman, P.R. (1983): "New Theories of Trade Among Industrial Countries", *American Economic Review*, 73(2): pp. 3430-47.

Krugman, P.R. (1987a): "Is Free Trade Passé?" *Journal of Economic Perspectives*, 1(2): pp. 131-44.

Krugman, P.R. (1987b): "Economic Integration in Europe: Some Conceptual Issues" in Padoa-Schioppa, T. (ed.) *Efficiency, Stability and Equity: A Strategy for the Evolution of the Economic System of the European Community*, Oxford: Oxford University Press.

Lovasy, G. (1941): "International Trade under Imperfect Competition", *Quarterly Journal of Economics*, August, 55: pp. 567-83.

McAleese, Dermot (1976): "Industrial Specialisation and Trade: Northern Ireland and the Republic", *Economic and Social Review*, 7(2): pp. 143-60.

McGovern, S. (1994): "A Lakatosian Approach to Changes in International Trade Theory", *History of Political Economy*, 26(3): pp. 351-68.

Markusen, A. (1996): "Sticky Places in Slippery Space: A Typology of Industrial Districts", *Economic Geography*, 72(3): 293-313.

Mjoset, L. (1992): *The Irish Economy in a Comparative Institutional Perspective*, Dublin: NESC.

Mottiar, Z. (1996): "The Wooden Furniture Industry in Monaghan: An Industrial District?", Unpublished typescript, Dublin: DCU Business School.

National Economic and Social Council (1989): *Ireland in the European Community: Performance, Prospects and Strategy*, Report No. 88, Dublin: NESC.

NESC (1993): *A Strategy for Competitiveness, Growth and Employment*, Report No. 96, Dublin.

NESC (1997): *European Union: Integration and Enlargement*, Report No. 101, Dublin.

O'Donnellan, N. (1994): "The Presence of Porter's Clustering in Irish Manufacturing", *Economic and Social Review*, 25(3): pp. 221-32.

O'Gorman, C., O'Malley, E. and Mooney, J. (1997): *Clusters in Ireland: The Irish Indigenous Software Industry: An Application of Porter's Cluster Analysis*, Research Paper Series, No. 3. Dublin: NESC.

O'Sullivan, M. (1995): "Manufacturing and Global Competition" in O'Hagan, J. (ed.) *Economy of Ireland: Policy and Performance of a Small European Economy*, Dublin: Gill and Macmillan.

Porter, M.E. (1990): *The Competitive Advantage of Nations*, London: Macmillan.

Sabel, C. (1996): *Ireland: Local Partnerships and Social Innovation*, Paris: OECD.

Sawyer, M.C. (1989): *The Challenge of Radical Political Economy*, London: Harvester Wheatsheaf.

Scasselati, A. (1991): "European Integration in the Context of International Capital", *Socialism and Democracy*, May, 13: pp. 1159-65.

Södersten, B. and Reed, G. (1994): *International Economics*, London: Macmillan.

Sweeney, P. (1997): *The Celtic Tiger: Ireland's Economic Miracle Explained*, Dublin: Oak Tree Press.

Thornhill, D.J. (1988): "The Revealed Comparative Advantage of Irish Exports of Manufactures 1969-1982", *Journal of the Social and Statistical Enquiry Society of Ireland*, 25(5): pp. 91-146.

# 3

## MACROECONOMIC POLICYMAKING IN THE CONTEXT OF MONETARY UNION

*Stilianos Fountas*

### 1. INTRODUCTION

The creation of economic and monetary union (EMU) in Europe raises a host of issues for macroeconomic policymaking in member countries. The introduction of a single common currency has profound implications for national monetary and exchange rate policy. In addition, a monetary union (MU) and the associated loss of monetary policy independence will necessarily affect fiscal discipline and raise questions concerning the degree of independence awarded to national fiscal policies.

The first issue addressed in this chapter is whether joining a monetary union represents a welfare improving policy for the countries contemplating participation. Which countries should maintain their policy autonomy and opt out of a single currency and which countries should relinquish their autonomy and agree to have their monetary policy decided by a European central bank? The theories of optimum currency areas (OCAs) purport to provide an answer to these questions. An economic analysis of the decision to participate in a monetary union requires a cost-benefit approach where the losses of forsaking the national currency are squared against the associated gains. The literature on OCAs proposes several criteria relevant in deciding whether a country should abandon policy autonomy for a monetary union.

It would be interesting to determine whether these criteria are empirically valid for Europe. As monetary union in Europe has not yet reached its final stage, the experience of other monetary unions can be useful in predicting whether a European MU has a chance of success.

Assuming that a MU is considered a desirable outcome, the optimal path or transition towards the union deserves careful consideration. Should a gradual approach towards the issue of a single currency be preferred to a shock-therapy approach? The advantages and disadvantages of each proposal need to be analysed before a decision is reached.

Finally, the case of Ireland's participation in an EMU deserves special treatment, given its traditional links with the UK, a non-participant in the single European currency to be launched on 1 January 1999. As the UK still represents Ireland's most important trading partner, the (sterling/punt) exchange rate represents a sensitive variable. The experience of the exchange rate mechanism (ERM) period has shown that periods of weak sterling against the punt are associated with increases in Irish interest rates. In other words, the commitment of Ireland's exchange rate policy in the ERM comes under severe pressure during periods of weak sterling and raises questions about the appropriateness of Ireland's decision to join the MU (Baker, FitzGerald and Honohan, 1996). More recently, a strong sterling and inflationary pressures in Ireland, due to domestic and external factors, have cast doubt over the much celebrated benefit of the single currency — a low inflation rate — and caused concern over the loss of an independent national monetary policy.

The chapter is organised as follows: section 2 analyses traditional and modern theories of OCAs and the costs of a single currency, while section 3 provides a short overview of the benefits of a single currency. Section 4 combines the costs and benefits in a simple analytical framework. Section 5 looks at the feasibility of a MU in Europe in the light of the experience of already established monetary unions. Section 6 discusses the implications of a MU for national fiscal policies. Section 7 compares alternative scenaria on the issue of transition towards the MU. Finally, section 8 presents the case of Ireland's participation in the MU in light of its strong economic ties with the UK.

## 2. OPTIMUM CURRENCY AREAS AND
## THE COSTS OF A SINGLE CURRENCY

A monetary union is a set of countries which join a system of irrevocably fixed exchange rates or decide to use a common currency. Mundell (1961), in his seminal contribution to the theory of OCAs,[1] looked at two determinants of a country's decision on whether to give up policy autonomy and join a MU: the type of disturbances likely to face the country in question; and the existence of adjustment mechanisms to facilitate the response to these disturbances. Let us look first at the type of disturbances. Consider two regions (countries) contemplating the formation of a MU. If these regions face symmetric shocks, i.e. the same disturbances, then, provided they have the same preferences, they will favour the same policy response, which will be accommodated by a European central bank. Therefore, the loss of exchange rate policy autonomy will not represent a major cost for the two regions. If, however, the shocks facing the two countries are negatively correlated across the two regions[2] (i.e. asymmetric or country specific shocks), then the loss of policy autonomy can have a profound impact on the countries involved, depending on a) the size of the shocks and b) the response mechanisms available to

---

[1] For a survey of the theory of OCAs, see Ishiyama (1975), Tower and Willett (1976), and Tavlas (1993a).

[2] Symmetric shocks can also have asymmetric effects across member countries. De Grauwe (1994: pp. 18–24) shows how differences in labour market institutions across countries can account for asymmetric effects of a symmetric supply shock.

the two countries in dealing with such shocks. Asymmetric shocks will not represent a constraint in forming a monetary union provided they can either be of negligible size or can be effectively dealt with through an appropriate response mechanism. In dealing with the shocks affecting a MU it is important to look at the similarity of the industrial structures across member countries and the degree of commodity diversification. According to Mundell (1961), economies that share similar industrial structures are expected to face similar aggregate disturbances (i.e. symmetric shocks), as these disturbances are the sum of industry-specific shocks. Also, economies with high industrial diversification are less likely to be affected by aggregate disturbances as the effect of a shock on aggregate output will be smaller than the effect on an individual industry's output. In a highly diversified region, workers in an industry laid off because of an industry-specific shock could move to other industries within the same region, thus making the movement to other regions unnecessary (Kenen, 1969). Hence, this literature predicts that countries which share the same industries or are highly diversified would be good candidates for a MU since for these countries asymmetric shocks would be of negligible size.

Let us focus now on the available adjustment mechanisms. Consider two countries, X and Y, faced with the following sizeable asymmetric demand shock: consumers in both countries increase their demand for goods produced in X and reduce their demand for goods produced in Y. Hence, an asymmetric demand shock effects the two countries in exactly the opposite way. Using a standard aggregate demand/aggregate supply framework (Figure 3.1), the shift in demand leads to higher prices and lower unemployment (higher output) in Country X and lower prices and higher unemployment (lower output) in Country Y. Basic economic theory suggests that, to restore the equilibrium in the two countries, there is a need for price and/or quantity adjustment. Under the classical assumption of full price adjustment, growing

unemployment in Country Y will push nominal wages downward and, provided nominal wages fall as much as prices, real
wages and unemployment will return to their original levels. In
terms of Figure 3.1, the aggregate supply schedule will shift to the
right as the cost of production becomes lower. Hence, under this
scenario, all real variables (real wages, output and unemployment) will remain unchanged. Exactly the opposite type of adjustment will take place in Country X. More specifically, de-
creasing unemployment will lead to higher nominal wages, thus
shifting the supply schedule to the left. As prices and nominal
wages increase by the same proportion, all real variables obtain
their original values.

FIGURE 3.1: ASYMMETRIC DEMAND SHOCKS

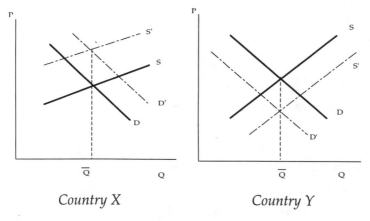

Country X                         Country Y

Under the Keynesian assumption, also made by Mundell (1961),
that nominal wages are sticky downwards, the only available
type of automatic adjustment is through labour mobility across
regions. Unemployed workers will flow from Country Y to
Country X thus restoring equilibrium in the labour and product
markets in the two countries. However, as suggested by Bean
(1992), one should be looking at real wage stickiness as opposed
to nominal wage stickiness since exchange rate policy stabilises
the real economy through its effect on real wages. Given the evi-

dence of sticky real wages in Europe, Bean (1992) argues that exchange rate changes do not represent a good stabilisation device.

An alternative adjustment mechanism ignored by Mundell
(1961) is a regional fiscal redistribution scheme that automatically
transfers income from one member country to another (Kenen,
1969). In our example above, Country X's fiscal authorities would
increase taxes (and hence reduce aggregate demand) and redistribute the proceeds to Country Y which would, as a consequence, face an increase in its aggregate demand. Such a scheme
is available in federal states like the US and works through the
centralisation of the government budget but does not seem a
likely possibility for sovereign countries and, in any case, at the
moment, there is no EU budget for stabilisation purposes.

In the presence of wage rigidities and inter-regional labour
immobility, and the absence of a fiscal redistribution scheme, exchange rate flexibility represents the only channel for adjustment.[3]
More specifically, in our example, a devaluation of Country Y's
currency relative to X's would reduce its real wage (provided real
wages are not rigid) and depreciate its currency in real terms,
thus increasing the demand for its products, reducing the demand for Country X's products and, therefore, offsetting the impact of the asymmetric shock on the aggregate demand in the two
countries. Of course, the exchange rate instrument, which represents a very effective policy in dealing with asymmetric shocks, is
not part of a country's stabilisation policy arsenal once the country has joined a monetary union. In this sense, the important policy implication of this analysis is that participation in a MU leads
to a loss of policy autonomy associated with the exchange rate
instrument.

The above policy implication is based on the presumption that
the loss of independent exchange rate/monetary policy is welfare

---

[3] Bayoumi (1994) presents a theoretical model that combines several criteria relevant to the choice of participation in an OCA.

reducing. However, this presumption is subject to certain qualifications. First, it is possible that monetary policy independence cannot deal effectively with asymmetric shocks because changes in money supply have no real effects on the economy. However, several macroeconomic theories predict that money can have short-run real effects due to the existence of nominal contracts, menu costs and other sources of price/wage inertia (McCallum, 1989; Hillier, 1986).

Second, even if monetary policy autonomy is forgone, there may not be a big loss for the country, provided there is another stabilisation policy instrument, i.e. fiscal policy, to take up the slack. There are several reasons, however, why fiscal policy is an imperfect substitute for the loss of the monetary policy instrument.

- The capacity to raise tax revenues is diminished in a MU with unrestricted labour and capital mobility, as factors of production flow into the jurisdiction of the least tax burden. In anticipation of this loss in the capacity to raise tax revenues, capital markets impose a constraint on the borrowing capacity of national governments to finance their deficits;

- Member countries in a MU can face statutory restrictions on their fiscal autonomy as exemplified, for example, by the fiscal criteria of the Maastricht Treaty. The rationale for such fiscal limits on the government finances of member countries is to prevent the free riding problem where some countries issue excessive amounts of debt in the hope of being bailed-out by other members; and

- Compared to monetary policy fiscal policy is a rather inflexible tool, as in most industrialised countries it is influenced by the political process.

Third, the loss of monetary policy independence can actually increase welfare if the monetary policy instrument is misused by the monetary authorities and is the actual source of the demand shocks. For countries with a tendency to succumb to the temptation to exploit the short-run inflation/unemployment trade off implied by the Phillips curve, giving up monetary policy flexibility can be a welfare-enhancing option. This approach has been taken by the so-called "new theory of optimum currency areas" based on two developments in macroeconomic theory over the last three decades: first, the formation of inflationary expectations and its association with the existence of a short-run and long-run trade off between inflation and unemployment and, second, the subject of time inconsistency which has implications for the credibility of policy announcements to reduce inflation (Tavlas, 1993a, 1993b).

A future policy action is credible if the public believes that the government will follow its policy plans. In other words, a policy is credible when the monetary authorities have no incentive to fool the public and not carry out their announced plans. Equivalently, when the announced policy intentions are executed in the future, the policy is named time consistent. Time consistency can be achieved through pre-commitment to a rule (e.g., money supply growth of x per cent annually). Such a pre-commitment is undesirable in the case of a fixed rule as the presence of shocks deems necessary changes in the rule. In addition, in the case of feedback rules,[4] a policy rule may not be sustainable as the monetary authorities are tempted to exploit the short-run trade off between inflation and unemployment and insert an inflationary bias into policy. Private economic agents tend to expect inflation and, accordingly, build their expectations into their wage and price-setting behaviour.

---

[4] In a feedback rule, the policy instrument depends on the current state of the economy.

The new theory of OCAs predicts that countries whose monetary authorities cannot credibly commit to low-inflation policies, can gain credibility by "tying the hands" of the policymaker through, for example, the participation in a MU with a low-inflation country (Giavazzi and Pagano, 1988). In the case of the European MU, high-inflation countries can choose to peg their currency to the DM (the currency issued by the country with the most credible counter-inflationary monetary policy in Europe), thus borrowing the anti-inflation reputation of the German Bundesbank.

According to the fourth and final qualification, the exchange rate will not be an effective policy instrument for very open economies because, in these economies, a depreciation of the nominal exchange rate will more than likely not be accompanied by a significant depreciation of the currency in real terms (i.e. a gain in real competitiveness) and hence it will not have any real effects on the economy. In very open economies, the domestic price level largely depends on the prices of imported goods. Assuming a high import pass through coefficient (i.e. a large effect of a currency depreciation on import-good prices), the increase in the domestic price level will nearly offset the exchange rate effect, thus leading to a small improvement in competitiveness (McKinnon, 1963). Therefore, according to this argument, the more open an economy is, the more likely that it will face a lower cost from relinquishing its autonomy on exchange rate policy.

### 3. THE BENEFITS OF MU

In contrast with the costs of MU, which basically fall in the field of macroeconomic policy, the benefits of MU are primarily microeconomic in nature. These benefits are:

- Reduced transaction costs;
- Reduced economic uncertainty; and
- Enhanced policy discipline.

## Transaction Costs

A single currency will lead to the elimination of all transaction costs involved in converting one national currency into another. The elimination of these costs represents a net gain to society provided the resources (e.g., bank employees) previously employed by this activity are employed in another profitable activity. In this sense, the net gain to society is the deadweight loss from currency exchange (analogous to the deadweight loss due to a monopoly). These direct savings in transactions costs are estimated by the European Commission (1990) to reach a maximum of 0.5 per cent of the EU GDP. Most of these savings relate to the corporate sector (i.e. intra-EU trade) as retail transactions account for only a small share of the EU GDP. To derive an estimate of these savings one has to sum all transactions costs (i.e. bid-ask spreads plus other commissions) involved in intra-EU transactions. It is important to note that transaction costs will only be eliminated if a common currency is introduced. A system of irrevocably fixed exchange rates where national currencies remain in circulation will still be associated with currency exchange as such a system will not be perfectly credible. Moreover, bid-ask spreads will continue to exist since evidence (de Grauwe, 1994: p. 62) has shown that these spreads are largely independent of the degree of exchange rate variability. The savings in transaction costs are the direct, static benefits of MU. Indirect dynamic benefits[5] would also arise as the disappearance of intra-EU exchange rates would increase trade and capital flows. An additional dynamic benefit arises from the increased efficiency associated with a common currency which leads to an increase in the marginal productivity of capital. This would raise investment and output, hence multiplying the static output effects.

---

[5] Static benefits arise at the start of the MU or with a lag. Dynamic benefits develop gradually over time as capital accumulation or other stock adjustments take time to materialise.

## Economic Uncertainty

A single currency eliminates real exchange rate uncertainty and improves the quality of the information provided by the price mechanism. Nominal exchange rate uncertainty implies uncertainty about future prices of goods and services and the real exchange rate. Real exchange rate uncertainty introduces errors into the production and investment decisions of companies and leads to misallocation of resources. These single currency efficiency gains are microeconomic in nature but have macroeconomic effects as the improved resource allocation leads to higher output.

Exchange rate uncertainty also leads to higher real interest rates and lower economic activity. This is because price uncertainty makes the expected rate of return on investment more uncertain, thus imposing a higher risk premium to compensate risk-averse investors. The existing information asymmetry between borrowers and lenders implies that the increase in real interest rates will be accompanied by the selection of riskier investment projects due to the creation of moral hazard and adverse selection problems. Moral hazard applies when one side of the market cannot observe the actions of the other side. Hence, once a transaction (e.g., a loan) occurs, the incentives of the borrower change at the expense of the lender. Under adverse selection, one side of the market cannot observe the "type" or quality of the other side of the market.[6]

In the present case, the moral hazard problem implies that an interest rate increase provides a stronger incentive to the borrower to undertake riskier investments as all proceeds over the cost of the loan will be reaped by the borrower. Lenders might decide to protect themselves by not charging a higher interest rate

---

[6] The problems of moral hazard and adverse selection are particularly relevant in the market for insurance where under moral hazard people's behaviour becomes riskier after they obtain insurance, whereas under adverse selection customers who are "bad" risks are more likely to buy insurance than those who are "good" risks.

(which would accentuate the moral hazard problem) but instead by restricting the supply of credit (a form of credit rationing), thus further slowing down the economy.

The adverse-selection problem implies that, as interest rates increase, low-risk borrowers reduce their demand for credit (since this group invests in low risk/low expected return projects and cannot afford paying a high interest rate) and therefore, the pool of prospective loan applicants includes mostly high-risk entrepreneurs who are likely to cause an adverse outcome for the lender (i.e. default on their debt). The introduction of a single currency would reduce price uncertainty and improve the quality of information supplied by the price mechanism, thus reducing interest rates and the moral hazard and adverse-selection problems. As a result, economic efficiency would improve and output gains would result.

### Policy Discipline and Credibility

Section 2 identified a case where the loss of a country's monetary policy independence as it joins a MU represents not a cost but rather a benefit if monetary authorities in the specific country cannot credibly pre-commit to a lower inflation rate. Hence, according to this argument, by joining a MU, a high-inflation country benefits from the improved policy discipline and anti-inflation credibility which result in a lower inflation rate (de Grauwe, 1994; Tavlas, 1993a).[7] Moreover, there will be long-run gains due to increasing production efficiency in the high-inflation country. This improvement in efficiency will result from the reduction in inflation as inflation tends to disguise absolute price changes for relative price changes and hence leads agents to the wrong produc-

---

[7] As Germany is historically the country with the strongest anti-inflation reputation, there must be a guarantee that the future MU is capable of producing low inflation for the country to be willing to join the union. One such guarantee is the fact that the future European central bank would be a close copy of the Bundesbank as the only objective of monetary policy would be price stability.

tion, investment and consumption decisions. The decision to give up the national currency and join a MU in anticipation of this benefit seems a rather drastic step according to Melitz (1995) who argues that policy credibility could improve by pursuing, instead, the independence of the national central bank.

It is interesting to note here that the above analysis to the costs and benefits of a single currency implies a rather eclectic approach since one has to use different paradigms to analyse the different issues. For example, the microeconomic paradigm of competitive markets and flexible prices is used to analyse the efficiency gains of a single currency. In contrast, the cost of losing policy autonomy is justified within a Keynesian framework of imperfect integration and sticky prices. Moreover, the analysis of credibility in the MU is done under a third paradigm with emphasis on theories of expectations and modelling of strategic behaviour.

## 4. THE BENEFITS AND COSTS OF MU

A common approach[8] to the cost-benefit analysis of MU focuses on the relationship between trade integration in the EU and the benefits and costs of a single currency for each prospective member of a MU (Krugman, 1990; de Grauwe, 1994). Trade integration in the EU is measured by the degree of openness of a country relative to other prospective member countries of the MU. The latter is proxied by the share of the country's intra-EU trade (exports plus imports) in the national GDP. Following the analysis of sections 2 and 3, we can determine the relation between the benefits and costs of MU and the openness of a country. As McKinnon (1963) argued, a large degree of openness implies that the ex-

---

[8] This analytical approach ignores the examination of the type of shocks affecting prospective participants of a MU because the effect is ambiguous from a theoretical point of view. This issue is examined from an empirical point of view in section 5.

change rate is not an effective policy instrument as, e.g., a depreciation of the domestic currency will not succeed in reducing relative domestic wages and prices (in other words, depreciate the domestic currency in real terms) but will simply increase domestic inflation. Hence, the more open a country is, the lower the cost of foregoing the national currency and joining a MU. In Figure 3.2, we plot the benefits and costs of MU as a percentage of national GDP against the trade share in GDP. In agreement with the above analysis, the Costs line in Figure 3.2 has a downward slope. In words, the greater the share of intra-EU trade in national GDP (degree of openness), the higher the level of trade integration in the EU and, following McKinnon (1963), the less useful the exchange rate as a policy instrument. Therefore, the cost of a MU associated with the loss of the national currency becomes smaller with a larger degree of integration, thus explaining the downward slope of the Costs line.

The benefits of MU are also directly related to the openness of a country. Small and open economies where transactions with foreign member countries represent a large percentage of the total volume of transactions (e.g., Belgium, Ireland and Netherlands) will enjoy the most benefits from a single currency associated with the elimination of transactions costs and exchange rate uncertainty. Therefore, the Benefits line in Figure 3.2 is upward sloping. According to Figure 3.2, countries with degree of integration over T* would receive a net benefit from becoming full members of a MU.

FIGURE 3.2: THE BENEFITS AND COSTS OF MONETARY UNION

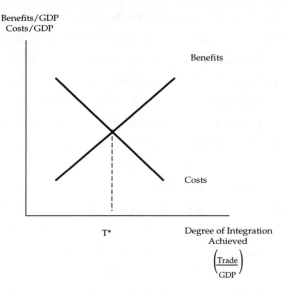

## 5. IS EUROPE AN OCA?

To answer this question most studies consider the size and type of shocks affecting member states and the available adjustment mechanisms in dealing with these shocks.[9] As there is no absolute yardstick to judge the optimality of a given currency area, a common is to compare results derived for European countries with those for already established MUs (e.g., US, Canada). However, comparisons between the US (or Canada) and the EU are subject to the caveat that the former has operated with a common currency for over 200 years, and the occurrence of shocks and labour mobility may change as the process of economic integration deepens in Europe. Let us look at the various criteria for an OCA presented in section 2 and the evidence for Europe in each case.

Mundell's assumption that labour mobility is the principal mechanism facilitating the adjustment to the original equilibrium position has been given empirical support in the US. Blanchard

---

[9] The rationale for the focus on the costs of MU is that one component of the benefits of MU (i.e. the dynamic indirect benefits) is very elusive (Melitz, 1995).

and Katz (1992) look at the relative contribution of alternative adjustment mechanisms in response to negatively correlated disturbances across US regions. Their major findings are, firstly, that among the different adjustment mechanisms considered, i.e. inter-regional migration, changes in relative wages, changes in labour-force participation rates or capital mobility, inter-regional migration is relatively the most important mechanism. Secondly, the importance of adjustment mechanisms tends to differ across regions. For example, very little adjustment in relative wages takes place in the US manufacturing belt. Similar support for highly mobile labour has not been provided for a number of prospective MU countries. Applying the same approach to European regions, Decressin and Fatas (1995) find that the main equilibrating mechanism appears to be an increase in regional unemployment. More recently, Bayoumi and Prasad (1997) compared the US and EU labour market adjustment mechanisms and concluded that inter-regional labour flows are a more important adjustment mechanism in the US than labour flows across European countries, an expected result given the cultural and linguistic differences that apply across the EU-member countries. Using an alternative framework, Eichengreen (1993) found that the elasticity of inter-regional labour flows with respect to internal wages and unemployment differentials is smaller in the UK and Italy than in the US. Evidence compiled by the OECD (1987) shows that labour is not as mobile in Germany and France as it is in the US. There are also differences in intra-regional labour mobility across EU countries with countries in the south (e.g., Spain and Italy) enjoying less mobility than countries in the north of Europe (UK, France and Germany) (de Grauwe and Vanhaverbeke, 1993).

Gros (1996a) argues that the emphasis in the majority of empirical works on the degree of international labour mobility as a requirement for MU has been exaggerated. What is more relevant, as Mundell (1961) himself stressed, is the difference between inter-regional migration (within member states) and international migration. If the evidence implies, as Gros (1996a) finds, that in-ter-regional and international migration are of similar order, then, for given asymmetric shocks, an EMU should not be expected to lead to more problems than the existing monetary unions that coincide with national states. Hence, according to Gros (1996a), the existing empirical evidence on the low level of international migration in the EU, as compared to the US, does not imply that the potential costs of EMU are high.

Some economists have taken a more optimistic view than the studies finding weak evidence for labour mobility in Europe, ar-guing that high capital mobility in Europe can substitute for low labour mobility (Froot and Rogoff, 1991). Hence, even if unem-ployed workers cannot move to other countries, capital equip-ment can move to the depressed region and generate new em-ployment opportunities. However, such a scenario might sound over-optimistic given that, even within countries, movements of capital towards depressed areas have not led to significant nar-rowing of regional disparities (e.g., the south of Italy, north of England).

As mentioned in section 2, the use of the exchange rate as a stabilisation instrument depends on the degree of real-wage flexi-bility. In the case of full real-wage rigidity due, for example, to full wage indexation nominal exchange rate changes cannot have any real effects. In the other extreme case of perfect real wage flexibility, nominal exchange rate changes are very useful in the presence of sticky prices/nominal wages[10] as the change in the nominal exchange rate is the only mechanism to support a change in the real exchange rate. Evidence by Bruno and Sachs (1985) shows that Europe is closer to the case of perfect real-wage rigid-

---

[10] In the presence of flexible prices/nominal wages, the real exchange rate can change due to price level changes and, therefore, nominal exchange rate changes are not necessary, as they are under nominal stickiness, to induce real adjust-ment.

ity than the US, suggesting that the exchange rate is a more effective policy instrument to offset asymmetric real shocks for the US.

Another criterion considered in section 2 is the similarity of industrial structures and the degree of industrial diversification in the member states. Presently, a very large percentage of intra-EU trade is of the intra-industry variety, where member states trade the same categories of products with each other. This phenomenon reflects, to a large extent, the high degree of industrial diversification in member states and the similarity of industrial structures. The question then arises, how will the increasing degree of trade integration in the EU affect the present situation? Will there be more or less similarity in the member states' industrial structures? There are two opposite effects at work. First, more integration will lead to more growth in intra-industry trade thus leading to further convergence in the industrial structures across countries. This effect will make it more likely that the member states will be subject to more symmetric shocks.[11] Second, increasing trade integration[12] can lead to higher regional concentration of the production activity in order to take advantage of economies of scale (Krugman, 1991). This effect makes it more likely that member states will be hit by asymmetric shocks since sector-specific shocks may become country-specific.[13] Therefore, theoretically speaking, the effect of additional trade integration on the type of shocks facing the member countries is ambiguous.

Given this theoretical ambiguity, several recent empirical studies examine the issue of the desirability of a European MU and can be separated into two main groups, those measuring the

---

[11] For evidence that increasing integration tends to make shocks more symmetric, see Emerson et al (1992: p. 143).

[12] Intra-industry trade represents between 57 per cent and 83 per cent of intra-EU trade, excluding Portugal and Greece (EC Commission, 1990: p. 142).

[13] Frankel and Rose (1996) provide empirical evidence that integration leads to more diversification, thus rejecting Krugman's claim.

variability of shocks affecting member states and those identify-
ing whether aggregate demand and supply disturbances are
positively or negatively correlated across countries. Studies in the
first group include Poloz (1990) and Eichengreen (1992). Poloz
looked at the variability of real exchange rates (i.e. exchange rates
adjusted for price level changes) and concluded that regional real
exchange rates within Canada (the standard of comparison) were
more variable than national real exchange rates in Europe. Assuming that real exchange rate variability captures the variability
of economic shocks, and given that Canada has a single currency,
Poloz concluded that Europe could form a MU. Eichengreen
(1992) using the US as the standard of comparison concluded that
real exchange rate variability among European countries exceeds
variability among large US regions implying that Europe is a
poorer candidate for MU than the US regions.

The approach of focusing on the variability of relative prices is
subject to the criticism that it cannot separate the effects of shocks
and policy responses. Hence, a number of studies (Bayoumi and
Eichengreen, 1993, 1994; Chamie, DeSerres and Lalonde, 1994)
have used modern econometric techniques to identify aggregate
demand and supply shocks and distinguish them from subsequent policy responses. Bayoumi and Eichengreen (1993, 1994)
find substantial positive correlation between demand and supply
shocks in Germany and several northern European countries
(Austria, Belgium, Denmark, France, and Netherlands). Hence,
they conclude that only these countries should form a MU at first,
thus providing support for a two-speed Europe. Chamie, DeSerres and Lalonde (1994) look at both the degree of shock asymmetry and the degree of nominal rigidities for a number of European
countries and the US. The consideration of nominal rigidities (in
contrast to other studies) is justified because both shock asymmetry and nominal rigidities are necessary for the loss of mone-

tary policy independence to be costly.[14] The authors conclude that the current core EU countries are not subject to highly positively correlated shocks and hence would face significant costs in joining the MU. Another conclusion is that, even though peripheral EU countries are characterised by a large degree of shock asymmetry, they also show a large degree of price flexibility. This would imply that peripheral EU countries can cope effectively with asymmetric shocks through price level adjustment.

An issue overlooked by the empirical literature on the variability and type of shocks affecting member states is the empirical relevance of external shocks (i.e. shocks to exports and/or the exchange rate) for unemployment in member states. This point is made by Gros (1996a) who provides evidence that changes in export demand cannot account significantly for changes in employment in all member states included in the study. This indicates that external shocks are not very important and, therefore, the loss of the exchange rate stabilisation instrument would not be such a big cost as other studies have concluded.

## 6. FISCAL POLICY, THE CONVERGENCE CRITERIA AND THE INS AND OUTS OF MU

The subject of fiscal policymaking within a MU deserves significant attention as it represents one of the most controversial issues in the economic analysis of integration. Two questions arise. First, is a central fiscal authority necessary for the functioning of the MU? Second, do independent national fiscal authorities threaten the successful functioning of a European central bank (ECB)?

In the presence of factor immobility and price rigidities that inhibit the free working of the market mechanism, a centralised

---

[14] As mentioned in section 2, real exchange rate adjustment will be useful only if member countries face asymmetric shocks. In addition, prices and wages must be sticky due to nominal rigidities so that monetary policy can stabilise the economy through its effect on the real exchange rate (Eichengreen, 1993).

fiscal authority can redistribute income towards regions adversely affected by region-specific shocks. However, such a mechanism is not necessary if member states maintain the option of discretionary national fiscal policy that can respond to offset region-specific shocks. In addition, as Giovannini (1993) argues, a centralised and permanent system of income transfers may be an inefficient one which acts as a disincentive to the implementation of necessary structural adjustments in the national economies.

The second question concerns the impact of the creation of the EMU on the size of fiscal deficits and the incentives of member states to run lax fiscal policies, and the spill-over effects of these policies on the union as well as the implications for the ECB. It is widely believed that the EMU will lead to stronger incentives to undertake unsustainable fiscal policies. The lax budget discipline resulting from the EMU can be explained along the following lines:

- First, the cost of expansionary fiscal policy, which takes the form of a higher interest rate paid by the domestic country on its debt, would be smaller under a MU as a given expansionary fiscal policy would lead to a smaller increase in interest rates. This is the case for several reasons:

  ◊ The creation of a common market for financial capital will make financial assets issued by different member countries closer substitutes for each other, thus making the demand for these assets more interest elastic. Hence, a given increase in the supply of government debt will put a smaller upward pressure on interest rates;

  ◊ As, under the EMU, countries can no longer inflate their economies to reduce the real value of their debt, there would be no country-specific inflation risk premium, thus leading to lower interest rates; and

◊ The default risk premium imposed on each country's debt would be lower since to minimise systemic risk in the monetary union's financial system, a bail-out would be necessary by the union in the event of default of a member country.

- Second, the increasing integration among the union's member countries will reduce each country's ability to raise revenues from taxing mobile factors of production. Furthermore, the lack of coordination among tax policies in member states will lead to tax competition and the undertaxation of mobile factors. If member states cannot either cut government spending or impose higher taxes on the immobile factors, tax competition will lead to an increase in the size of debt issued by national governments.

- Third, the creation of the single currency will remove the use of seignorage (issue of money) from the list of the government's revenue sources. It is likely that a country will substitute debt finance for money finance[15] (seignorage) with the danger of running unsustainable debts[16] (Dornbusch, 1988, 1989; Masson and Taylor, 1993).

- Fourth, as mentioned above, lax fiscal policies will lead to overborrowing of national governments (in particular in cases of tax competition and loss of seignorage) and hence possible bail-out by the union, thus undermining the stability of the

[15] De Grauwe (1994) argues that because of the "harder" budget constraint facing the member states of the MU following the loss of seignorage, there will be less incentive to expand spending and increase budget deficits.

[16] The national debt/GDP ratio becomes unsustainable (i.e. under current policies, it tends to grow without limits) when the interest rate on debt exceeds the growth rate of the economy, unless either the primary budget enjoys a large surplus or money creation is sufficiently large (de Grauwe, 1994: pp. 194-99).

common currency.[17] The bail-out might take two forms: An *ex ante* bail-out where the union implements policies to keep interest rates on government debt at artificially low levels to prevent the unsustainability of government debt; and an *ex post* bail-out through the monetisation of government debt. Both policies would cause inflation across the union, thus threatening the stability of the single currency. A possible scenario leading to a bail-out is as follows: Suppose the government of a MU participating country runs into fiscal difficulty leading to an excessive supply of its debt. Investors fearing debt repudiation might impose market discipline by liquidating the government's bonds, thus leading to a sharp decline in bond prices and capital losses to major bondholders like banks. The end result is bank runs and adverse repercussions in the bond markets and banking systems of other member countries. In a bail-out attempt, the ECB buys the bonds issued by the government in distress in order to prevent a crisis in the local banking and financial system and contagion effects as the crisis spreads to other national markets in the union.[18] This is an example of an international negative externality where a country running excessive fiscal deficits and over-borrowing does not bear the full costs of its actions but imposes negative external effects on the other members of the union which face a higher bail-out risk. This moral hazard problem implies that as a country does not internalise the bail-out costs, its incentives for lax fiscal policies become stronger; hence an argument for multilateral intervention by the ECB.

---

[17] It is not clear whether the bail-out risk will be at the maximum or minimum level at the start of MU. For two contrasting arguments see McKinnon (1997) and von Hagen and Eichengreen (1996).

[18] Such a scenario is more than a theoretical curio as the Mexico crisis of 1994-95 and, more recently, the debt problems of Thailand and South Korea have shown.

The major argument in favour of fiscal restraints is that excessive budget deficits may lead to monetisation of the debt for the government to satisfy its inter-temporal budget constraint and hence undermine monetary stability (Sargent and Wallace, 1981). Along these lines, the Delors report recommended binding fiscal policy rules on the member states. Such binding rules have been criticised on several grounds:[19] First, ceilings on budget deficits severely restrict the much-needed flexibility of macroeconomic policy given the loss of monetary autonomy implied by the MU[20] (Buiter and Kletzer, 1991). Of course, this argument is based on the assumption that fiscal policy plays an important role as a macroeconomic stabilisation tool. Second, under the assumption of efficient capital markets, the negative externality mentioned earlier will not apply as expansionary fiscal policy in, for example, Italy, will increase only the Italian interest rates and will leave unaffected interest rates in all other member states. In other words, different interest rates will apply in different member states and hence it is inappropriate to consider *the* interest rate of the MU (Dornbusch, 1997). Such an argument is only valid if member states agree not to bail-out another member state facing a debt crisis. A "no bail-out" clause, introduced in the Maastricht Treaty, is necessary for the capital markets to work efficiently, i.e. to attach a higher risk premium to member states with a high default risk. However, such a "no bail-out" clause is not fully credible because a debt crisis affecting the Italian government will spill over to countries with financial institutions holding Italian government debt. To prevent the crisis from spreading to their countries in case of an Italian default, these other member states will

---

[19] See also, Buiter and Kletzer (1991), van der Ploeg (1991) and Wyplosz (1991).

[20] Fountas and Papagapitos (1997) provide econometric evidence that following the creation of the ERM and the partial loss of monetary autonomy, several ERM-member countries have substituted fiscal policy for monetary policy for stabilisation purposes.

most likely be willing to buy Italian debt, thus lowering the market-determined risk premium on this debt. Third, binding fiscal rules are difficult to enforce as shown, for example, by the Gramm-Rudman-Hollings legislation setting explicit targets on the US federal budget deficit which was circumvented through the use of off-budget items. Moreover, a sanction mechanism for countries not abiding by the rules might not be credible as it would carry a high political cost. Finally, the proposed rules do not address the issue of debt crises. This would require the use of entry requirements on the debt/GDP ratio, as adopted by the Maastricht Treaty on European Union.

The Maastricht Treaty sets five nominal convergence criteria for countries contemplating full membership in the EMU. These criteria refer to inflation, long-term interest rates, exchange rate realignments and the fiscal finances of national governments.[21] These Maastricht convergence requirements have a poor theoretical basis according to both the traditional and "new" theories of OCAs (de Grauwe, 1996). For example, convergence of inflation rates, interest rates and budgetary policies is neither necessary nor sufficient, according to the traditional OCA theory, to create a successful MU. It is not necessary because two countries with different inflation rates prior to the union may still have very similar economic structures such that they do not face large asymmetric shocks. The difference in inflation rates may simply reflect different institutional features in monetary policy, for instance, different degrees of central bank independence. It is not sufficient because two countries can have the same inflation rate, but very different structures so that a MU between them is sub-optimal. If, for example, Belgium satisfies the inflation convergence criterion, the existence of full wage indexation along with the absence of the scheme in Germany, would mean that an oil price shock during the course of MU would cause problems in the competitiveness of

---

[21] See de Grauwe (1994: p. 147) for a detailed description.

the Belgian industry. De Grauwe (1996: pp. 5-20) shows why the Maastricht convergence criteria have a poor theoretical basis under the "new" theory of OCAs too.

One of the prominent features of the Maastricht Treaty is the excessive deficit procedure (EDP) which restricts the conduct of fiscal policy in the member states. Under the provisions of the EDP, member states should avoid "excessive deficits" during the transition to MU. Moreover, following the launch of the MU, temporary deficits in excess of, but close to, the reference value will be allowed only in exceptional circumstances. The rationale is to prevent overborrowing of member states which would put pressure on the ECB to act as a lender of last resort and bail-out national governments. As part of the EDP, the Maastricht Treaty introduced two fiscal norms as a prerequisite to entry to EMU: first, the general government budget deficit cannot exceed 3 per cent of GDP and, second, gross government debt cannot exceed 60 per cent of GDP unless it is approaching its reference value at a satisfactory pace.[22] These fiscal norms have led to severe fiscal tightening in most prospective EMU countries and have been deemed excessive and lacking any economic justification as the rest of the Maastricht criteria (de Grauwe, 1996).

The Pact for Stability and Growth agreed in the Dublin summit in December 1996 and finalised at the Amsterdam summit in June 1997 defines the conditions that must be satisfied for the participants of the EMU to be allowed to run deficits in excess of the 3 per cent ceiling which are deemed not to be excessive.[23] To avail

---

[22] The two fiscal criteria are linked. Gros and Thygesen (1998: p. 340) show that a country that meets the 3 per cent deficit threshold, under ordinary circumstances, should observe an automatic decline in its debt/GDP ratio towards the 60 per cent upper bound. This indicates that the deficit is the crucial variable and explains the focus of the Maastricht Treaty only on an excessive *deficit* procedure.

[23] For a comprehensive analysis of the costs and benefits of the stability pact, see Eichengreen and Wyplosz (1998).

of this exemption, a country must experience at least a 2 per cent decline in GDP and the excessive deficit must be small and temporary. Countries facing a GDP decline in the range 0.75 per cent to 2 per cent might also be exempt from the 3 per cent deficit ceiling at the approval of the Council of Ministers. Finally, MU members facing milder recessions and deficits over the 3 per cent ceiling will be subject to sanctions if the excessive deficit runs for more than two successive years. These sanctions will be non-remunerated deposits starting at 0.2 per cent of GDP and rising by one-tenth of the value of the excess deficit up to a maximum of 0.5 per cent of GDP. The required amount deposited will keep rising unless the excess deficit is eliminated. If the excess deficit persists for more than two years, the deposit will become a fine; alternatively, it will be returned. In times of positive output growth, the stability pact calls for a balanced budget or a surplus so that the operation of automatic fiscal stabilisers is not hampered.

The above provide a clear indication that the stability pact's provisions are more restrictive than those of the Maastricht Treaty as they introduce limits on the size of output decline leading to the excessive deficit and on the period over which this deficit is permitted. Nevertheless, some flexibility still remains as the imposition of fines is conditional upon the severity of the recession faced by the country and some time is allowed for the elimination of excessive deficits.

Proponents of the stability pact emphasise the benefit of creating a commitment to a credible anti-inflation, tight fiscal policy stance (a monetarist approach). Critics of the pact argue that the loss of monetary policy as a stabilisation tool necessitates the increasing use of countercyclical national fiscal policies which seems to be in conflict with the stability pact (a Keynesian approach). As activist fiscal policy is subject to long implementation lags and hence, practically, not very useful,[24] fiscal restrictions would affect primarily the working of automatic fiscal stabilisers. During a recession, for example, as economic activity slows down, tax revenues fall while, at the same time as unemployment increases, unemployment benefits and government expenditure rise. These adjustments are automatic, i.e. do not require any action by the government and represent the non-discretionary component of fiscal policy. However, evidence shows that automatic stabilisers are not necessarily incompatible with the stability pact because their effect on fiscal deficits is small and, even if their effect becomes large in the future, they will not be in conflict with the fiscal criteria provided the fiscal positions are balanced or in surplus during good times (Gros and Thygesen, 1998). Moreover, Melitz (1997) finds that in the EU, current public expenditure has been procyclical in recent decades (i.e. it increased at times of above average income growth) thus implying that the importance of automatic stabilisers has been exaggerated.[25] This line of research concludes that fiscal policy is not a useful stabilisation tool. In summary, the preceeding discussion seems to indicate that there is not necessarily a need for the EU budget to take a stabilisation role, even in the presence of fiscal restrictions on national fiscal policies.

Restrictive fiscal policy in many countries seeking future participation in the single currency in the 1990s resulted in eleven countries satisfying the convergence criteria, including the deficit criterion, by the end of 1997. Table 3.1 shows the major economic indicators included in the Maastricht Treaty (except for the exchange rate criterion) in 1997 and their forecast levels for 1998. In

---

[24] For evidence on this for the five largest EU countries, see Gros and Thygesen (1998: p. 358).

[25] Lane (1998) provides evidence that Irish fiscal policy proxied by government expenditure has been procyclical, thus making the stability pact less of a constraint for Irish fiscal policy.

some of these countries creative accounting and once-off fiscal measures were required to abide by the 3 per cent deficit ceiling. Following the recommendation of the European Monetary Institute (the forerunner of the ECB), in early May 1998, eleven countries were admitted to Stage Three of EMU which coincides with the launch of the single European currency, the euro, on 1 January 1999. These countries are Austria, Belgium, Finland, France, Germany, Ireland, Italy, Luxembourg, Netherlands, Portugal and Spain. Denmark and the UK opted out, Sweden does not satisfy the ERM membership criterion, and Greece does not satisfy any of the convergence criteria. An interesting issue arising is the future relationship between the countries that join EMU from its start (the "ins") and those that stay out but are likely to join in the future (the "outs"). It is envisaged that the outs will have to gear their domestic policies towards meeting the convergence criteria, hence ensuring a stable monetary relationship between the ins and the outs. Under the ERM II agreed upon in the Dublin summit in December 1996, the outs may enter a "new ERM" with the euro. Participation in the "new ERM" is voluntary but may become a precondition for entry to the EMU. ERM II will differ from the present ERM as it will be based on central rates against the euro, not a grid of bilateral parities. The bands of fluctuation around the central euro rates will be relatively wide so that it becomes less likely they will be challenged by speculators, but the option for narrower bands will also be available.

TABLE 3.1: ECONOMIC INDICATORS IN THE EUROPEAN UNION

| | Inflation | | Long-term Interest Rate | | General Government Surplus (+) or Deficit (–) to GDP Ratio | | General Government Gross Debt to GDP Ratio | |
| | 1995 | 1996 | 1995 | 1996 | 1995 | 1996 | 1995 | 1996 |
|---|---|---|---|---|---|---|---|---|
| Belgium | 1.4 | 1.8 | 7.5 | 6.5 | -4.1 | -3.3 | 133.7 | 130.6 |
| Denmark | 2.3 | 1.9 | 8.3 | 7.2 | -1.6 | -1.4 | 71.9 | 70.2 |
| Germany | 1.5 | 1.2 | 6.9 | 6.2 | -3.5 | -4.0 | 58.1 | 60.8 |
| Greece | 9.0 | 7.9 | 17.3 | 14.8 | -9.1 | -7.9 | 111.8 | 110.6 |
| Spain | 4.7 | 3.6 | 11.3 | 8.7 | -6.6 | -4.4 | 65.7 | 67.8 |
| France | 1.7 | 2.1 | 7.5 | 6.3 | -4.8 | -4.0 | 52.8 | 56.4 |
| Ireland | 2.4 | - | 8.3 | 7.3 | -2.0 | -1.6 | 81.6 | 74.7 |
| Italy | 5.4 | 4.0 | 12.2 | 9.4 | -7.1 | -6.6 | 124.9 | 123.4 |
| Luxembourg | 1.9 | 1.2 | 7.2 | 6.3 | +1.5 | +0.9 | 6.0 | 7.8 |
| Netherlands | 1.1 | 1.5 | 6.9 | 6.2 | -4.0 | -2.6 | 79.7 | 78.7 |
| Austria | 2.0 | 1.8 | 7.1 | 6.3 | -5.9 | -4.3 | 69.0 | 71.7 |
| Portugal | 3.8 | 2.9 | 11.5 | 8.6 | -5.1 | -4.0 | 71.7 | 71.1 |
| Finland | 1.0 | 1.5 | 8.8 | 7.1 | -5.2 | -3.3 | 59.2 | 61.3 |
| Sweden | 2.9 | 0.8 | 10.2 | 8.0 | -8.1 | -3.9 | 78.7 | 78.1 |
| UK | 3.1 | - | 8.3 | 7.9 | -5.8 | -4.6 | 54.1 | 56.2 |
| EU-15 | 3.0 | 2.4 | 8.9 | 7.5 | -5.0 | -4.4 | 71.3 | 73.5 |

*Source:* European Monetary Institute, *Annual Report* (1996).

*Notes:* 1) The inflation rates for 1995 and 1996 were constructed using the interim indices of consumer prices (IICPs) and harmonised indices of consumer prices (HICPs), respectively, published by Eurostat; 2) The 1996 data on general government deficit and gross debt are provisional and based on EC's autumn 1996 forecasts; 3) 1996 HICPs inflation data for Ireland and UK were not available.

## 7. THE TRANSITION TO MU

Once the decision to join a MU has been made on economic or political grounds, the issue of the optimal transition to the final stage of the MU (i.e. the issue of the single currency) comes to the forefront. There are two approaches to this transition: a gradualist approach and a shock-therapy approach.

The rationale for a gradualist approach is to provide time for nominal and real convergence before the introduction of the common currency. The lengthy transition period involved, and the absence of capital controls, carries a danger from instability due to currency substitution and speculative attacks (Masson and Taylor, 1993). Currency substitution takes place when individuals or large firms substitute one or more international currencies for the national currency even for domestic transactions. Currency substitution can apply even if exchange rates are not expected to change. The motivation might be that the relative attractiveness of certain currencies (e.g., the DM) increases because these currencies are widely used in intra-EU transactions. Currency substitution can be destabilising as it leads to large short-term shifts in money demand in member countries which make the interpretation of national monetary aggregates more difficult.

Speculative attacks on the currency issued by a member country in a system of quasi-fixed exchange rates would arise if the market doubts the commitment of the authorities to support a certain parity. As the ERM crisis of 1992-93 showed, speculative attacks can be self-fulfilling and hence lead to a currency realignment. Two common examples of speculative attacks are the case of a hard-currency policy and the case of a country that has issued a large stock of debt with a large proportion about to be refinanced. A hard-currency policy applied for a long period of time by a high-inflation country would lead to a sharp loss in competitiveness and raise expectations for a possible devaluation. This would generate a speculative attack which would be more likely to be self-fulfilling (i.e. lead to a devaluation) with a dwindling stock of foreign exchange reserves. A country with a large stock of public debt outstanding, which is about to refinance a significant proportion of this debt, would face difficulty in defending its currency through short-term interest rate increases because of the increasing cost of debt service. On the contrary, the country would prefer to reduce its debt through a devaluation, thus prompting an intense speculative attack on the currency.

A rapid transition to MU or a shock-therapy approach is, historically, the most common approach to the transition to a MU. An example of this strategy is the recent monetary unification of East and West Germany. The major advantage of a rapid transition is that exchange rate stability is fully credible as intra-EU exchange rates are abolished. Therefore, nominal interest rate convergence is facilitated in the absence of expected exchange rate changes.

The Delors report and the Maastricht Treaty supported the strategy of gradualism where monetary unification is a three-stage process and MU is accomplished in the last stage. The Delors report provided only the blueprint and the Maastricht Treaty formalised this strategy. The first stage started on 1 July 1990 and led to the abolition of all capital controls by the EMS countries with some exceptions. The second stage commenced on 1 January 1994 and its objective is to enhance the co-ordination of monetary policies among national central banks. For this purpose, the European Monetary Institute was founded as a precursor to the ECB or Eurofed. The third and last stage on 1 January 1999, at first, irrevocably fixed exchange rates in the union and then, on 1 January 2002, the newly created ECB will issue the euro.

## 8. IRELAND AND THE MU

Ireland represents a unique case in the ERM due to its close economic ties with the UK, a non-participant in the ERM and the EMU at its inception, which remains Ireland's most important trading partner, even though its importance has fallen over time. Following the break-up of the punt's parity link with sterling, the participation of the Irish currency in the ERM presented Irish policymakers with a serious dilemma at times of weak sterling. The dilemma was that at periods of sterling depreciation against the DM, policymakers had to balance the commitment to keeping their currency inside the ±2.25 per cent fluctuation band against the loss in competitiveness with respect to sterling. On two occasions, August 1986 and January 1993, weak sterling led policymakers to reveal a preference towards maintaining Irish competitiveness and, consequently, to devalue the punt against the rest of the ERM currencies. The trade-off between maintaining competitiveness and commitment to the DM peg becomes less of a dilemma with the widening of the permitted exchange rate fluctuation band as, in this case, the Irish monetary authorities may more easily achieve both objectives. The width of the exchange rate band increased significantly in August 1993, from ±2.25 per cent to ±15 per cent thus changing the nature of the EMS from a system of fixed but adjustable rates to one of nearly flexible rates and providing more flexibility to the policymakers.

Econometric evidence provided by Thom (1995) shows that the rigid peg to the DM followed by the Irish monetary authorities in the years preceding the currency crisis of September 1992 has been succeeded by a more flexible strategy where deviations in competitiveness from some target level are marginally more important than the ERM commitment. This result implies that Ireland may encounter difficulties in its participation in a MU that does not include the UK. In particular, assuming that exchange rate policy can have real effects in the short to medium term, as is the case under slow price/wage adjustment, Mundell's theory of OCAs analysed in section 2 can be used to explain why the exclusion of the UK from a MU can raise difficulties for Ireland. Consider, for example, a sharp nominal depreciation of sterling (Neary and Thom, 1996). This would have real effects (i.e. affect the real exchange rate, competitiveness and employment) provided the purchasing power parity (PPP) does not hold. Such a scenario is more likely in the short run when domestic prices and wages are relatively rigid. In the long run, with full adjustment in domestic prices/wages, the real exchange rate remains fixed and therefore, monetary/exchange rate policy does not have any real effects on the economy. Evidence reported in Baker, FitzGerald and Honohan (1996) shows that the response period to exchange rate shocks is three to four years for prices and four years for nominal wages. This evidence points towards severe adjustment problems as the loss in Ireland's competitiveness implies lower exports and an increase in unemployment. This analysis highlights the fact that giving up exchange rate policy autonomy would represent a significant cost for Ireland. Hence, under these circumstances, the creation of a MU and the associated loss in flexibility in monetary and fiscal policy necessitates a reform of labour market institutions to facilitate the adjustment in response to asymmetric shocks. Of course, this analysis would only be relevant if the occurrence of asymmetric shocks is a likely scenario for Ireland. In agreement with earlier analysis, this would be mostly the case when trade is not of the intra-industry variety. Such seems to be the case according to Gros (1996b) who presents evidence that Ireland is ranked eleventh on intra-industry trade among the EU member countries.

The pessimistic view of Neary and Thom (1996), which is based primarily on the cost side of the MU, contrasts sharply with that of Baker, FitzGerald and Honohan (1996) who conclude that the benefits from a single currency (lower interest rates and savings in transactions costs) outweigh the losses in competitiveness.

The net gains according to these authors have been estimated to be 1.4 per cent of annual GNP, assuming the UK joins the single currency, and 0.4 per cent of GNP in the case where the UK opts out of the common currency.

Barry (1997) claims that the employment losses have been underestimated by Baker, FitzGerald and Honohan (1996) for two reasons: First, the response of nominal wages to upward and downward price movements is asymmetric as nominal wages are relatively rigid downwards. Therefore, periods of weak sterling against the Irish pound would result in higher real wages and unemployment but periods of strong sterling would not lead to employment gains. Second, hysteresis effects in unemployment are more likely to happen in the traditional industry, due to the concentration of less skilled workers, which is more sensitive to sterling fluctuations. Taking these criticisms into account, Barry (1997) finds that the net gains for Ireland of joining the single currency if the UK stays out have been overestimated.

It is worth noting that while most attention by Irish academic economists and politicians over the past few years has focused on the deflationary impact of a weak sterling on the Irish economy, recently a strong sterling performance and strong domestic output growth have switched the focus to higher domestic inflationary pressures. Table 3.2 reports the most recent inflation rates in the EU countries. The Irish annual inflation rate in May 1998 was second only to the inflation rate in Greece. The much-celebrated benefit of joining the EMU — low inflation due to a credible anti-inflation policy at the EU level — does not seem to be present. Moreover, ceding interest rate policy to the ECB means that Irish monetary authorities will not have any control over future inflation rates. To avoid this constraint, Lane (1997) argues in favour of a policy of inflation-targeting outside the EMU.

TABLE 3.2: ANNUAL INFLATION RATES IN THE EUROPEAN UNION (MAY 1998)

| Country | Inflation Rate (%) |
|---|---|
| Belgium | 1.3 |
| Denmark | 1.4 |
| Germany | 1.1 |
| Greece | 5.0 |
| Spain | 2.0 |
| France | 1.0 |
| Ireland | 2.4 |
| Italy | 2.0 |
| Luxembourg | 1.3 |
| Netherlands | 2.1 |
| Austria | 1.0 |
| Portugal | 2.2 |
| Finland | 1.6 |
| Sweden | 1.6 |
| UK | 2.0 |

*Source*: Eurostat.
*Note*: The inflation rates are annual percentage changes constructed using the Harmonised Indices of Consumer Prices (HICPs).

## 9. CONCLUDING REMARKS

This chapter has examined a number of theoretical and policy issues surrounding the creation of the EMU in Europe. It first analysed various OCA theories which place emphasis on the disadvantages created by the issue of a single currency. The main disadvantage is the loss of discretionary monetary policy in dealing with asymmetric demand and supply shocks. The benefits of a monetary union take the form of savings in transactions costs, elimination of exchange rate uncertainty and credibility gains. The theoretical model which we presented concentrated on both the benefit and cost sides of the MU and showed that small open economies would gain most from a single currency. However, the empirical evidence to date, given the difficulty in measuring the dynamic indirect benefits of a single currency, concentrated on the cost side of the MU and, more specifically, the size and type of shocks affecting the member states. This body of research concluded that Germany and some northern European countries would be the most likely candidates for participation in the EMU.

The Maastricht Treaty supported a gradual approach to EMU where prospective member states should satisfy a number of nominal convergence criteria. These criteria are highly restrictive and lack any theoretical basis. By the end of 1997, the majority of EU countries satisfied the convergence criteria, thus paving the way for the launch of the euro on 1 January 1999. Despite the objections of many economists, which point towards the existence of very little evidence in favour of the criteria making Europe an OCA, it is clear that EMU will soon be underway in order to satisfy the political objective of European unification.

## REFERENCES

Baker, T., FitzGerald, J. and Honohan, P. (eds.) (1996): *Economic Implications for Ireland of EMU*, Dublin: Economic and Social Research Institute.

Barry, F. (1997): "Dangers for Ireland of an EMU without the UK: Some calibration results", *The Economic and Social Review*, 28: pp. 333-50.

Bayoumi, T., (1994): "A Formal Model of Optimum Currency Areas", IMF Staff Papers, 41: pp. 537-55.

Bayoumi, T., and Eichengreen, B. (1993): "Shocking Aspects of European Monetary Integration", in Torres, F. and Giavazzi, F. (eds.) *Adjustment and Growth in the European Monetary Union*, Cambridge: Cambridge University Press.

Bayoumi, T., and Eichengreen, B. (1994): "One Money or Many? Analyzing the Prospects for Monetary Unification in Various Parts of the World", Princeton Studies in International Finance, International Finance Section, No. 76.

Bayoumi, T. and Prasad, E. (1997): "Currency Unions, Economic Fluctuations, and Adjustment: Some New Empirical Evidence", IMF Staff Papers, 44: pp. 36-58.

Bean, C. (1992): "Economic and Monetary Union in Europe", *Journal of Economic Perspectives*, 6: pp. 31-52.

Blanchard, O., and Katz, L. (1992): "Regional Evolutions", *Brookings Papers on Economic Activity*, 2: pp. 1-61.

Bruno, M. and Sachs, J. (1985): *Economics of World-wide Stagflation*, Oxford: Basil Blackwell.

Buiter, W. and Kletzer, K. (1991): "Reflections on the Fiscal Implications of a Common Currency", in Giovannini, A. and Mayer, C. (eds.) *European Financial Integration*, Cambridge: Cambridge University Press.

Buiter, W., Corsetti, G. and Roubini, N. (1993): "Excessive Deficits: Sense and Nonsense in the Treaty of Maastricht", *Economic Policy*, 16: pp. 57-100.

Chamie, N., DeSerres, A. and Lalonde, R. (1994): "Optimum Currency Areas and Shock Asymmetry: A Comparison of Europe and the United States", Working Paper 94-1, Bank of Canada.

Decressin, J. and Fatas, A. (1995): "Regional Labour Market Dynamics in Europe and Implications for EMU", *European Economic Review*, 39: pp. 1627-55.

Dornbusch, R. (1988): "The European Monetary System, the Dollar and the Yen", in Giavazzi, F., Micossi, S. and Miller, M. (eds.) *The European Monetary System*, Cambridge: Cambridge University Press.

Dornbusch, R. (1989): "Credibility, Debt and Unemployment: Ireland's Failed Stabilisation", *Economic Policy*, 8: pp. 174-209.

Dornbusch, R. (1997): "Fiscal Aspects of Monetary Integration", *American Economic Review, Papers and Proceedings*, 87: pp. 221-23.

EC Commission (1990): "One Market, One Money: An Evaluation of the Potential Benefits and Costs of Forming an Economic and Monetary Union", *European Economy*, 44, Brussels: Commission of the European Communities.

Eichengreen, B. (1992): "Is Europe an Optimum Currency Area?" in Borner, S. and Grubel, H. (eds.) *The European Community after 1992: Perspectives from the Outside*, Basingstoke: Macmillan.

Eichengreen, B. (1993): "Labour Markets and European Monetary Unification", in Masson, P. and Taylor, M. (eds.) *Policy Issues in the Operation of Currency Unions*, Cambridge: Cambridge University Press.

Eichengreen, B. and Wyplosz, C. (1998): "The Stability Pact: More than a Minor Nuisance?" in Begg, D., von Hagen, J., Wyplosz, C. and Zimmerman, K. (eds.) *EMU: Prospects and Challenges for the Euro*, Oxford: Blackwell.

Emerson, M., Gros, D., Italianer, A., Pisani-Ferry, J. and Reichenbach, H. (1992): *One Market, One Money*, Oxford: Oxford University Press.

Fountas, S. and Papagapitos, A. (1997): "Policy Effectiveness in the Post-ERM Era: Evidence from Six Countries", *Open Economies Review*, 8: pp. 189-201.

Frankel, J. and Rose, A. (1998): "The Endogeneity of Optimum Currency Area Criteria", *Economic Journal*.

Froot K. and Rogoff, K. (1991): "The EMS, the EMU, and the Transition to a Common Currency", National Bureau of Economic Research Working Paper No. 3684.

Giavazzi, F. and Pagano, M. (1988): "The Advantage of Tying One's Hands: EMS Discipline and Central Bank Credibility", *European Economic Review*, 32: pp. 1055-82.

Giovannini, A. (1993): "European Monetary Reform: Progress and Prospects", in Das, D. (ed.) *International Finance: Contemporary Issues*, London: Routledge.

de Grauwe, P. (1994): *The Economics of Monetary Integration*, Oxford: Oxford University Press.

de Grauwe, P. (1996): "The Economics of Convergence: Towards Monetary Union in Europe", *Weltwirtschaftliches Archiv*, 132: pp. 1-27.

de Grauwe, P. and Vanhaverbeke, W. (1993): "Is Europe an Optimal Currency Area? Evidence from Regional Data", in Masson, P. and Taylor, M. (eds.) *Policy Issues in the Operation of Currency Unions*, Cambridge: Cambridge University Press.

Gros, D. (1996a): "A Reconsideration of the Optimum Currency Area Approach: the Role of External Shocks and Labour Mobility", National Institute Economic Review, 158: pp. 108-17.

Gros, D. (1996b): "Towards Economic and Monetary Union: Problems and Prospects", Brussels: Centre for European Policy Studies, Paper No. 65.

Gros, D. and Thygesen, N. (1998): *European Monetary Integration*, London: Longman.

Hillier, B. (1986): *Macroeconomics: Models, Debates and Developments*, Oxford: Basil Blackwell.

Ishiyama, Y. (1975): "The Theory of Optimum Currency Areas: a Survey", IMF Staff Papers, pp. 344-83.

Kenen, P. (1969): "The Theory of Optimum Currency Areas: an Eclectic View", in Mundell, R. and Swoboda, A. (eds.) *Monetary Problems of the International Economy*, Chicago, IL: University of Chicago Press.

Krugman, P. (1990): "Policy Problems of a Monetary Union", in de Grauwe, P. and Papademos, L. (eds.) *The European Monetary System in the 1990s*, London: Longman.

Krugman, P. (1991): *Geography and Trade*, Cambridge, MA: The MIT Press.

Lane, P. (1997): "EMU: Macroeconomic Risks", *Irish Banking Review*, Spring, pp. 25-33.

Lane, P. (1998): "On the Cyclicality of Irish Fiscal Policy", *The Economic and Social Review*, 29: pp. 1-16.

Masson P., and Taylor, M. (1993): "Currency Unions: A Survey of the Issues", in Masson, P. and Taylor, M. (eds.) *Policy Issues in the Operation of Currency Unions*, Cambridge: Cambridge University Press.

McCallum, B. (1989): *Monetary Economics: Theory and Policy*, New York: Macmillan.

McKinnon, R. (1963): "Optimum Currency Areas", *American Economic Review*, 53: pp. 717-25.

McKinnon, R. (1997): "EMU as a Device for Collective Fiscal Retrenchment", *American Economic Review*, Papers and Proceedings, 87: pp. 227-9.

Melitz, J. (1995): "The Current Impasse in Research on Optimum Currency Areas", *European Economic Review*, 39: pp. 492-500.

Melitz, J. (1997): "Some Cross-Country Evidence about Debt, Deficits and the Behaviour of Monetary and Fiscal Authorities: A Progress Report", CEPR Discussion Paper No. 1653.

Mundell, R. (1961): "A Theory of Optimum Currency Areas", *American Economic Review*, 51: pp. 657-65.

Neary, P. and Thom, R., (1996): "Punts, Pounds and Euros: In Search of an Optimum Currency Area", WP96/24, Centre for Economic Research, University College Dublin.

Organisation for Economic Co-operation and Development (OECD), (1987): *Flexibility in the Labour Market*, Paris: OECD.

Poloz, S. (1990): "Real Exchange Rate Adjustment between Regions in a Common Currency Area", Mimeo, Bank of Canada.

Sargent, T. and N. Wallace (1981): "Some Unpleasant Monetarist Arithmetic", *Federal Reserve Bank of Minneapolis Quarterly Review*, pp. 1-17.

Tavlas, G., (1993a): "The Theory of Optimum Currency Areas Revisited", *Finance and Development*, pp. 32-5.

Tavlas, G. (1993b): "The 'New' Theory of Optimum Currency Areas", *The World Economy*, pp. 663-85.

Thom, R., (1995): "Irish Exchange Rate Policy under Wide ERM Bands", WP95/15, Centre for Economic Research, University College Dublin.

Tower, E, and Willett, T. (1976): "The Theory of Optimum Currency Areas and Exchange-Rate Flexibility", Princeton Special Papers in International Economics, No. 11.

van der Ploeg, F. (1991): "Macroeconomic Policy Co-ordination during the Various Phases of Economic and Monetary Integration in Europe", EC Commission, European Economy, Special Edition, 1.

von Hagen, J. and Eichengreen, B. (1996): "Federalism, Fiscal Restraints and European Monetary Union", *American Economic Review*, Papers and Proceedings, 86: pp. 134-8.

Wyplosz, C. (1991): "Monetary Union and Fiscal Policy Discipline", EC Commission, European Economy, Special Edition, 1.

# 4

# EUROPEAN REGIONS: PERFORMANCE AND MEASUREMENT

*Michael Keane*

## 1. INTRODUCTION

Perhaps the most paraphrased sentence in the study of the location of economic activity is Perroux's (1955) observation that growth does not appear everywhere and all at once; it reveals itself in certain points or poles, with different degrees of intensity; it spreads through diverse channels. It is this notion of unevenness in the incidence of economic growth that has stimulated interest and concern with regional economic performance and regional development in the European Union. This interest and concern are based not only on the argument that all people in the Community should be given equal opportunities to better themselves and to participate in the gains from closer integration; but also on the realisation that economic growth is interdependent and that the buoyancy of the overall economic system depends to an important extent on how well its parts are doing.

For the EU regional issues have increasingly come to be regarded as an essential part of the integration and cohesion process. Indeed, each step towards integration since 1972 has been accompanied by a strengthening of policy aimed at reducing "spatial disparities" and increasing cohesion (Cheshire *et al*, 1991). The first response of the EU to the disadvantages from which less developed regions suffer was the channelling of European Investment Bank lending to less favoured regions. This was followed by the establishment of the European Regional Development Fund (ERDF) in 1975 and by the development of the Structural Funds — the ERDF, European Social Fund (ESF) and the guidance section of the Agricultural Guarantee and Guidance Fund (EAGGF) — after the incorporation of cohesion objectives in the Single European Act of 1986. The ERDF was required, for example, to "help redress the principal regional imbalances in the Community through participating in the development and structural adjustment of economies lagging behind and in the conversion of declining industrial regions" (Article 130C of the Single European Act) as well as in rural development. The other funds were expected to contribute to these objectives and to combat long-term and youth unemployment and aid agricultural adjustment (Dunford, 1994). These efforts were particularly reinforced in the Maastricht Treaty (Articles 2 and 3) and in the Delors Package with a commitment to increase spending on the Structural Funds by another 67 per cent by 1999.

The focus in this chapter is on how economic unevenness is measured and addressed by policies within the European Union. One of the great paradoxes in regional economic theory is its inability to explain a number of simultaneously occurring convergences and divergences in spatial economic indices (Clark *et al*, 1986). Equally problematic is the nature of the relationship between economic integration and regional convergence or cohesion (Bachtler and Turok, 1997). Both of these uncertainties clearly condition any conclusions reached in this chapter.

## 2. EUROPEAN REGIONAL DISPARITIES, REGIONAL POLICY AND COHESION

The objective of economic and social cohesion, the desire to reduce disparities between the various regions of the Community, was introduced by the Single European Act as an essential complement to the single market. For the formative period of 1994–99 around 170 billion ECU is available from the Community budget for structural and cohesion policies. This represents about a third of total Community spending and around 0.4 per cent of Community GDP. Over the decade 1989-99, spending amounts cumulatively to 6.5 per cent of annual Community GDP. A historical comparison helps to put the significance of this spending in perspective: Marshall Aid from the US to post-war Europe was equivalent to 1 per cent of US GDP per year and amounted cumulatively (1948–51) to 4 per cent of US GDP (European Commission, 1996c).

The concept of cohesion is rather a vague one. It is probably best explained as the degree to which disparities (imbalances) in economic welfare between countries or regions within the Union are socially and politically tolerable. The assumption is that an increase in disparities is detrimental for cohesion and vice versa (Molle and Boeckhout, 1995). Regional economic disparity is about comparing how well people are doing in material terms, e.g. per capita income, in one region of the Union with those living in another. These comparisons are also made over time to see if performances are converging, i.e. becoming more similar, or diverging; i.e. getting more dissimilar. Obviously such comparisons can be made for different kinds of regions and using different measures of well-being. The standard comparison is to define the nation state as the region and examine regional variations in per capita GDP and between member states, see Figure 4.1.

Statistical indices of disparity describe divergence from a norm, measured, for example, as percentage variation from the EU average (as in Figure 4.1), or the difference between units of measurement of the region with the lowest value and the region with the highest value, or in terms of comparing variations in growth rates each in real or nominal terms, and each in per capita,

FIGURE 4.1: REGIONAL VARIATION IN PER CAPITA GDP WITHIN AND
BETWEEN MEMBER STATES (1992)

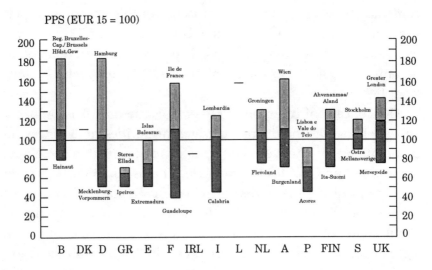

*Source*: European Commission (1996c).

per worker or per household terms — will yield different
results and affect how seriously the gaps in performance between
regions is perceived. Bradfield (1988), for example, illustrates how
the coefficient of variation for market income per capita in Canada
in 1981 was twice as high as that for personal disposable income
per household. Similarly, Davezies (1992) has shown how the
rankings of French regions change substantially when different
measures of per capita income are used (Hansen, 1995). Generally
speaking, one has to be cautious in interpreting summary measures as they can conceal some key issues and consequently contribute little to understanding the true situation (Raynauld, 1988).

There is no particular reason why spatial variation within the
EU should be encapsulated by nation states; supra-national differences and sub-national differences are also significant, perhaps
increasingly so, as the nation state becomes less important in the
European scheme of things, as a unit of economic management,
and maybe also as a unit of political organisation. Clearly, there is

a great deal of flexibility possible in terms of how one might describe economic unevenness, both in terms of the measures used to describe this unevenness and in terms of the units, or regions, used to make the comparisons (Hansen, 1995). For practical reasons which have to do with data availability and the implementation of regional policies the EU has established the nomenclature of territorial units for statistics (NUTS). This geographical classification system provides a single uniform breakdown of territorial units for the production of EU regional statistics. The criteria followed in the definition of the NUTS regions are essentially political. The nomenclature is based primarily on the institutional/administrative divisions currently in favour in the different member states (Eurostat, 1992). The system also forms the basis for the identification of regions which are disadvantaged and for which the European Commission has set development objectives. These are:

- Regions whose development is lagging behind (Objective 1), i.e. regions where per capita GDP is less than 75 per cent of the Community average, or there are special reasons for their inclusion under this objective;

- Areas in industrial decline (Objective 2). These are mainly areas where the rates of unemployment and industrial employment are higher than the Community average and where industrial jobs are in structural decline;

- Vulnerable rural areas with a low level of socio-economic development which also meet two of the following three criteria: a high proportion of employment in agriculture, a low level of agricultural incomes and a low population density or a high degree of out-migration (Objective 5b); and

- Areas with an extremely low population density (Objective 6), i.e. those with fewer than eight people per sq. km.

The resources of the Structural Funds, which amounts to 154.4 ECU (1994 prices) for the period 1994-1999, are available to these regions with the bulk of these resources given to Objective 1 regions.

The NUTS system subdivides each member state into a series of level 1 regions (NUTS 1), each of which is in turn subdivided into a number of level 2 regions, which are themselves subdivided into a number of level 3 regions. The correspondence between NUTS and national administrative units for the EU–15 is shown in Table 4.1. The NUTS 2 level is the one where eligibility for aid from the Structural Funds for Objective 1 and Objective 6 purposes is determined (for other regional Objectives, the level is NUTS 3).

NUTS classifies the territory of the EU-15 into 77 regions at level 1, 206 at level 2 and 1,031 at level 3. The UK, for example, is first divided into eleven standard regions (level 1, or NUTS 1) then thirty-five groupings of counties (level 2 or NUTS 2) and finally sixty-five counties/local authority regions. Ireland is somewhat of a misnomer in this system. The whole country is treated as one region at both NUTS level 1 and level 2. The regional authorities appear as NUTS level 3 in Table 4.1. The new regionalisation proposal submitted by the Irish government to the Commission will change Ireland's entry in the table. It is proposed that there will be two NUTS level 2 regions (one region as Objective 1) but what the number at NUTS 3 will be is, at this stage, unclear.

This NUTS system is used officially to portray and describe the regional dimensions of the EU (Cheshire *et al*, 1995). One of the obvious things which occurs when using the NUTS, or any, system of regions is that the level of detail increases as the degree of spatial or geographical disaggregation itself increases. Consequently, differences between units become more pronounced.

TABLE 4.1: CORRESPONDENCE BETWEEN THE NUTS LEVELS AND
NATIONAL ADMINISTRATIVE UNITS

|  | NUTS 1 |  | NUTS 2 |  | NUTS 3 |  |
|---|---|---|---|---|---|---|
| B | Régions | 3 | Provinces | 11 | Arrondissements | 43 |
| DK | – | 1 | – | 1 | Amter | 15 |
| DE | Länder | 16 | Regierugsbezirke | 38 | Kreise | 445 |
| GR | Groups of development regions* | 4 | Development regions | 13 | Nomoi | 51 |
| ES | Agrupacion de communidades autonomas | 7 | Communidades autonomas + Ceuta y Mellila | 17 / 1 | Provincias + Ceuta y Mellila | 50 / 2 |
| FR | ZEAT + DOM | 8 / 1 | Regions + DOM | 22 / 4 | Départements + DOM | 96 / 4 |
| IE | – | 1 | – | 1 | Regional authority regions | 8 |
| IT | Gruppi di regioni* | 11 | Regioni | 20 | Provincie | 103 |
| LU | – | 1 | – | 1 | – | 1 |
| NL | Landsdelen | 4 | Provincies | 12 | COROP Regio's | 40 |
| AT | Gruppen von Bundesländem | 3 | Bundesländer | 9 | Gruppen von Politischen Bezirken | 35 |
| PT | Continente + Regioes autonomas | 1 / 2 | Comissaoes de coordinacao regional + Regioes autonomas | 5 / 2 | Grupos de Concelhos | 30 |
| FI | Manner-Sucmi /Ahvenanmaa | 2 | Suuralueet | 6 | Maakunnat | 19 |
| SE | – | 1 | Riksomraden | 8 | Län | 24 |
| UK | Standard regions | 11 | Groups of counties* | 35 | Counties/Local authority regions | 65 |
| EU 15 |  | 77 |  | 206 |  | 1,031 |

* Grouping for Community purposes
*Source*: European Commission (1996b).

This can be seen in Figure 4.2 which compares the level and trend
in regional disparities over the period 1983-1993. Disparities between the regions (defined at the NUTS 2 level) are wider than
those between member states. In addition, the trend between the

regions of the Community shows a much varied pattern. The overall tendency seems to have been one of slightly widening disparities during the slow growth years over the first half of the 1980s and a gradual narrowing over the second half of the decade, levelling off in the 1990s. The change in the trend in the mid-1980s could be explained by the improved performance in Ireland and most Spanish and Portuguese regions, which went from marking time, or even retreat, compared to the rest of the Community, to rapid relative advance in the second half of the 1980s.

FIGURE 4.2: DISPARITIES IN GDP PER HEAD, 1983-1993

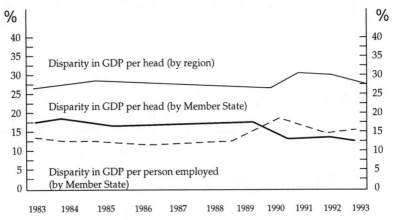

*Source*: European Commission (1996c).

## 3. REGIONAL DEVELOPMENT IN EUROPE

Because of their economic and social differences, the regions of Europe and their inhabitants are not on a level playing field. For a long time, all the member states of the European Union have experienced variations in levels of development and living standards from one region to another (see Figure 4.1) and the gaps become more pronounced when measured across the Union as a whole (Dunford, 1994). However, this kind of historical analysis does not say anything directly about differentials in opportunities between regions to either sustain or promote suitable economic activities. Neither does it provide measures of regional economic potential or regional needs or any meaningful framework for setting realistic regional targets.

Notwithstanding these limitations there is merit in examining economic performance on a regional basis as a means of: establishing the causes of regional growth differentials; gaining some understanding of the interactions between regional economies; understanding the relationship between overall development in the EU (integration, EMU) and development in the regions. With respect to this last relationship two questions (Alonso, 1991) are of particular importance: does increased regional economic disparity adversely affect overall economic growth; and does sustained and rapid economic growth necessarily mean adequate regional economic participation? If, in the context of the EU, the answer to the first question is "Yes" then there can be no successful economic growth policies in the EU without adequate regional economic development policies. If the answer to the second question is "No" then satisfactory EU growth policies by themselves are no guarantee that the gap between the successful and the not-so-successful regions will not widen. These two questions, and their solutions, are critical issues in the debate about the regional dimension of Europe.

The geography of Europe is being dramatically revised by events of recent years. The dynamic created by the Single European Act and the collapse of the East European economic system have created new conditions for development across Europe. The process which is underway is without precedent. While tens of thousands of pages have been written on the formation of the territorially-defined nation state, particularly in the nations of what is today the EU, there is little to go on when trying to foresee the consequences of the impending softening of national boundaries. The world has never seen the peaceful integration of nations on a scale such as this. The consequences will undoubtedly range from the economic and institutional developments which currently hold the spotlight, e.g., the exchange rate mechanism and monetary system, the role of the European Parliament, to future, and perhaps subtler, issues of culture, identity and society. In the territorial dimension, just as the nation states were formed through an amalgamation of regions, one may now expect, what Alonso (1991: p. 8) calls, a certain historic symmetry "as the national units dissolve to one degree or another into the larger community, regional issues and regional initiatives will assume a larger role in the European stage. Indeed, in many of the traditional regions throughout Europe there is already a certain inquietude and even political ferment, as they see in the international integration of the EU an opportunity to reclaim their traditional identities and to downplay their national settings."

Forecasts of what the economic geography of Europe will look like, that is, whether some regions of Europe will gain while other regions lose, are in great demand. It is impossible to identify in clear outline what will happen to the pattern of regional development. There are a number of possible scenarios. Each reflects a particular view of how locational and other economic forces are expected to work to shape future regional patterns. One scenario, for example, is that population and economic activity will concentrate into the largest cities, primarily into those situated in the core of Europe, the "banana"-shaped arc from London over Brussels and Frankfurt to Milan. A second scenario is that instead of being concentrated in the centre, growth will be strongest in peripheral Europe. A third possible scenario is that the demographic and economic development of Europe will not be structured according to any core/periphery pattern, but that it will show a much more complex mosaic in the sense that in all parts of Europe there will be both growing cities and regions and declining cities and regions.

Obviously there is much disagreement on this issue. Prediction is, at the best of times, a difficult task. Each of the suggested scenarios is different because it is based on different views of how key locational processes might actually work. The critical question now is what will happen to the economic prospects of the disadvantaged or peripheral regions as Europe becomes more integrated and various frictions are reduced or eliminated through measures introduced as part of the Single European Act or economic and monetary union. One view, and this is the view favoured by the Commission, is that with improved access of low-wage or low-GDP regions to the centre of Europe, economic activity will want to shift out and relocate to the periphery. This may be how it will work, but Krugman and Venables (1990) have argued, for example, that this presumption is not necessarily right and that, in fact, improved access might actually hurt not help peripheral regions. They offer the following argument: Imagine an industry that can locate in one or both of two places: a "central region" in which the wage rate and hence production costs are high but which has good access to markets; or a "peripheral region" in which labour costs are low but access to markets is less good. One might assume that a reduction in transportation costs, due to the effects of integration, would always tend to shift production away from the centre to the periphery, but Krugman and Venables (1991) suggest otherwise. Their argument is that reducing transportation (or other access costs) has two effects: it facilitates locating production where it is cheapest, but it also facilitates concentration of production in one location so as to realise economies of scale. Krugman (1991) offers a hypothetical example which is fully reproduced here as Table 4.2.

TABLE 4.2: HYPOTHETICAL EFFECTS OF LOWER TRADE BARRIERS

|  | Production Costs | Shipping Costs | | |
|---|---|---|---|---|
|  |  | High | Medium | Low |
| Produce in A | 10 | 3 | 1.5 | 0 |
| Produce in B | 8 | 8 | 4.0 | 0 |
| Produce in both | 12 | 0 | 0 | 0 |

*Source*: Krugman (1991).

Imagine that the good can be produced in either the central region, which we will call region A, or in the peripheral region, which we will call region B. To keep the analysis simple it is assumed that total sales are given so that the problem is one of choosing a location as cheaply as possible, i.e. so as to minimise the sum of production and transportation costs. It is cheaper to produce the good in region B than in A because wages in B are lower: but it is cheaper to produce the good totally in either location than some in both because of economies of scale. On the other hand, producing in both locations minimises transport costs, while producing in region A involves lower transport costs than producing in the periphery. Table 4.2 shows three cases: high, medium and low (in fact zero) transport costs. Not too surprisingly, if transport costs are high, production will take place in both regions, whereas if they are low, it will take place in the low wage region. But a reduction in transport costs, in Table 4.2 (a 50 per cent reduction in costs from the "high" case) actually causes the location of production to shift away from the low-cost periphery to the high-cost centre. The reason is that in the medium transport cost case, costs are low enough to make it worthwhile to concentrate production, but still high enough that access to markets outweighs production cost as a determinant of location. The conclusion of Krugman's model is interesting in what it suggests about the prospects for productive activity, particularly productive activity which experiences increasing returns, in the peripheral regions. The model generates a U-shaped relationship depicting the share of increasing-returns industries which the periphery captures as trade barriers are reduced, and the response of relative wages also follows this pattern.

When barriers are reduced to moderate levels, i.e. from X to C on the horizontal axis of Figure 4.3, the share of production in the peripheral region falls, because the need to produce in each market is reduced. At this point we are towards the bottom of the U-shaped curve, the advantage of proximity to the centre supersedes lower production costs at the periphery and production has moved from the peripheral region to the central region. As barriers are further reduced and, in the limit, become negligible (point D), the cost advantage of the peripheral region begins to dominate. The elimination of trade barriers and the reduction in transport costs largely removes the advantages of locating at the centre.

FIGURE 4.3: ECONOMIC INTEGRATION AND INDUSTRY
AT THE PERIPHERY

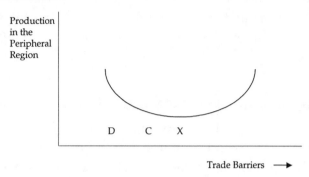

The economic geography models of the type used by Krugman open up the possibility that peripheral regions may lose their increasing return to scale industries as market integration proceeds, in which case, also, real wages will fall relative to the centre. Divergence results in this case. However, if the peripheral region is on the left-hand side of the U-curve, convergence of real wages will result (Barry, 1996).

Models, like that of Krugman and Venables (1990) and Krugman (1991) enable us to develop some basic conclusions about possible patterns in the economic geography of European regions. However, models are, by definition, abstractions or simplifications of reality. This particular model sets out to show in a deductive manner how the interaction of economies of scale, various friction costs due to distance and spatial separation, and local production costs might shape a centre-periphery economic geography. By appealing to the data on location patterns and location shifts one can, perhaps, lend support to the conclusions or predictions of the model. Barry (1996) provides a recent example of this in his examination of how the structure of Irish industry has changed over the course of the economy's adjustment to greater free trade. A difficulty in addressing this question is that of attribution; the necessity of "disentangling the structural transformation of the economy wrought by free trade from the influences exerted by technological and global developments and the major swings in fiscal policy of the last two decades" (Barry, 1996:

p. 354). His conclusion is that Ireland has managed to position itself on the left-hand side of the U-curve but suggests that this result has to be treated with caution because of the many "locational" considerations that relate to the decisions of mobile multinational capital.

## 4. THE INFLUENCE OF REGIONAL AND LOCAL CONDITIONS

An alternative way of trying to construct an explanation of location behaviour is to work from the data at the outset, i.e. attempt
to construct a theory of regional development on the basis of an
analysis of the development in European regions and cities in,
say, the 70s, 80s and early 90s. Illeris (1991) outlines a version of
this inductive approach to theory. His approach has two main
elements. The first stresses the structure of the local economy, its
composition of growing and declining sectors, because this is
what influences the total development of a region. As Illeris (1991:
p. 11) states: "Regions obviously perform well if expanding sectors (e.g. oil production, high tech industries, producer services,
tourism, international organisations) form a large part of the
economy — all other things equal. On the other hand, regions develop negatively if "sunset" sectors dominate, such as agriculture,
coal mines, steel industry, shipyards, or ports."

Economic structure obviously explains a lot of the observed
performance of regions but, equally important, and the second
element in the approach of Illeris, is local conditions. Particular
economic sectors, for example, can perform better in some regions
than in others and consequently "sectors ... influence the total development of different regions differently". Illeris cites the example that while the textile industry generally is a sunset sector in
Western Europe, it is growing, or at least is stable, in Tuscany and
in the Herning-Ikast area of West Jutland in Denmark. Here a
combination of local factors has contributed to a dynamic textile
industry, while it is disappearing elsewhere (Illeris, 1991: p. 12).
The list of local factors identified includes: political conditions,
infrastructure and physical planning, availability of people with

adequate skills, cultural conditions or modes of life, compensating changes in factor prices and advantages of agglomeration. Finally, if it is true that local conditions may sometimes improve in one region and deteriorate in another, it also follows that the possibilities of influencing the development of a region are increasing. The present mosaic-like pattern tells us that the tendencies are quite open. The multiplicity of patterns implies a broad array of opportunities and possibility for regions and local economies to construct their own opportunities.

The reasons why certain regions are disadvantaged appear to go back a very long way and call for structural solutions. Some of these regions are adversely affected by their geographical location but all share certain difficulties, although to different extents: inadequate basic infrastructure (transport, telecommunications, energy, water, environmental protection); a poorly qualified labour force and a low level of research and technological development; local financial markets which do not respond to the needs of small firms for credit. This is a standard list of the kind of structural difficulties faced by some regions. It represents a viewpoint that defines a region's status and prospects as being fairly rigidly prescribed by some kind of Ricardian law of comparative advantage. Describing it through a neo-classical framework one can think of comparing two regions, again region i a central region and region j, a peripheral one. Now we introduce into the model some differences and imperfections in the conditions facing these two, all of which favour region i. Thus, for example, firms in i get higher prices for their goods because of better access to markets, better transport systems, etc., they pay less for capital (real and financial), they benefit from agglomeration economies and they have access to better quality workforces. Each of these advantages may be small but in aggregate terms they can be quite substantial and give a significant overall advantage to the firms located in i. Following Bradfield (1988) it is possible to analyse the significance of these differences using a standard isoquant/isocost diagram, Figure 4.4.

FIGURE 4.4: CUMULATIVE ADVANTAGE ACROSS REGIONS

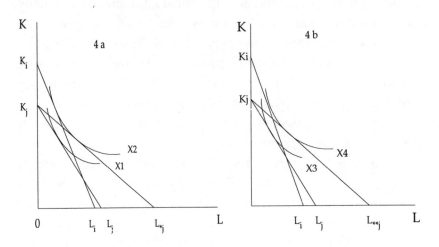

*Source*: Bradfield (1988).

In Figure 4.4a the line $K_jL_j$ is the isocost line for a given level of outlay for a firm located in region j. The line $K_iL_i$ is the isocost line for the same outlay for a firm located in i. The shape and position of $K_iL_i$ relative to $K_jL_j$ reflects the differences already described in the two regions. For the outlay on question a firm in i can reach the output level $X_2$. For long-run equilibrium firms in j must be also able to produce at $X_2$. To achieve this the isocost line must be $K_jL^*_j$ and the wage relative between the regions must be $oL^*_j/oL_i$. What this suggests is that a set of fairly small advantages for firms in region i requires a substantial wage differential to ensure the existence of production in both regions. If region j does not have the kind of advantages found in i, firms will only be attracted to region j, or will only stay in region j, if there is a compensating low wage rate.

The difficulties facing region j are more pronounced if the production technology involved is highly capital-intensive, see Figure 4.4b. A more capital-intensive technology makes it more difficult for the disadvantaged region to compete. It requires a higher wage differential to offset the advantages of the central region. When firms are using a capital-intensive technique, the savings generated by cheaper labour are correspondingly reduced. Therefore, to compensate for the lack of other cost savings, labour must be even cheaper. In Figure 4.4b, a firm in region i can produce $X_4$. With the initial wage differential, a firm in region j can only produce a lower quantity. Only if region j's isocost line were to move to $KL^{**}_j$ could region j compete with i. Bradfield (1988) pushes this analysis further by looking at the prospects for regional growth. If the experience across the EU is one of uneven growth, with some sectors or industries growing more rapidly than others, one could expect different regional effects. If the high growth industries are capital-intensive, growth will be concentrated in the high-wage central region, since this is where the capital-intensive industries will be located. And the capital-intensive industries will expand in the centre region unless and until growth alters some of the underlying conditions. Growth, for example, might cause urban diseconomies at the centre or cause other changes which reduce some of i's advantages. Until the underlying differences are overcome, the analysis suggests that growth will not bring benefit to the disadvantaged j region. The alternative is, of course, that region j, instead of being simply a low-wage location, succeeds in improving its own attractiveness for growth industries.

### 5. STRUCTURAL DISADVANTAGE AND STRUCTURAL FUNDS

An obvious response to the difficulties faced by regions like j is to address the structural deficits. A supply-oriented regional policy can contribute to a solution. This is the thrust of current European regional policy. The Community regional policy tools for achieving economic and social cohesion can be described under two headings: The Structural Funds and other cohesion instruments. The vast bulk of the Community's structural measures are financed out of the following sources: the European Regional Development Fund (ERDF). (Assistance from the ERDF is limited to the most disadvantaged regions (Objective 1) and concentrates primarily on productive investment, infrastructure and the development of small businesses); the European Social Fund (ESF), which concentrates on vocational training and recruitment aid; the Guidance Section of the European Agricultural Guidance and Guarantee Fund (EAGGF), which supports agricultural structures and rural development; and, since 1993, the Financial Instrument for Fisheries Guidance (FIFG), which assists the adjustment of the fisheries sector. Along with the member states, these funds part-finance development measures through non-repayable aid. The amount of these funds has been agreed at 138.2 billion ECU for the period 1994-99. A breakdown of structural assistance, 1994-1999, by Objective (see pp 81-82 for a definition of the different objectives) and by country (in million ECU at 1994 prices) is given in Table 4.3.

The Cohesion Fund was established by the Treaty of Maastricht to work alongside the existing Structural Funds. It was intended to assist preparation for economic and monetary union in the four countries whose per capita GDP was less than 90 per cent of the Community average in 1992 (Greece, Portugal, Ireland and Spain) by supporting projects concerned with the environment and trans-European transport networks anywhere in these countries. The Cohesion Fund has 15.5 billion ECU to cover the period 1993-99. The European Investment Bank (EIB) uses loans to provide support for economic and social cohesion. In 1994 the EIB provided 12 billion ECU for regional development.

Finance for the Structural Funds is not usually used for individual projects proposed or selected by member states or by the Commission but rather is allocated to development programmes, each of which has its own multi-annual budget. The programmes represent the culmination of a process to which all the partners concerned, the member states, the regions, other bodies and the Commission, have contributed. These arrangements are outlined in Figure 4.5. Programmes initiated at national level are drawn up on the basis of regional development plans (in Ireland's case a national development plan) or single programme documents (SPDs), as in Northern Ireland, submitted to the Commission by

TABLE 4.3: STRUCTURAL FUNDS 1994–99, BY OBJECTIVE AND BY COUNTRY (IN ECU MILLION AT 1994 PRICES)

| Country | Objective 1 1994-99 | Objective 2 1994-96 | Objectives 3 and 4 | Objective 5a 1994-99 | Objective. 5b 1994-99 | Community Initiatives | Total |
|---|---|---|---|---|---|---|---|
| Belgium | 730.0 | 160.0 | 465.0 | 194.5 | 77.0 | 233.84 | 1,860.34 |
| Denmark | – | 56.0 | 301.0 | 266.9 | 54.0 | 88.95 | 766.85 |
| Germany | 13,640.0 | 732.9 | 1,942.0 | 1,142.5 | 1,227.0 | 1,901.42 | 20,585.82 |
| Greece | 13,980.0 | – | – | – | – | 1,083.38 | 15,063.38 |
| Spain | 26,300.0 | 1,130.1 | 1,843.0 | 445.6 | 664.1 | 2,315.07 | 32,697.87 |
| France | 2,190.0 | 1,763.3 | 3,203.0 | 1,931.9 | 2,238.0 | 1,421.36 | 12,747.56 |
| Ireland | 5,620.0 | – | – | – | – | 304.02 | 5,924.02 |
| Italy | 14,860.0 | 684.0 | 1,715.0 | 814.4 | 901.0 | 1,703.14 | 20,677.54 |
| Luxembourg | – | 7.0 | 23.0 | 40.1 | 6.0 | 13.12 | 89.22 |
| The Netherlands | 150.0 | 300.0 | 1,079.0 | 164.6 | 150.0 | 231.77 | 2,075.37 |
| Portugal | 13,980.0 | – | – | – | – | 1,410.17 | 15,390.17 |
| United Kingdom | 2,360.0 | 2,142.1 | 3,377.0 | 449.7 | 817.0 | 1,102.26 | 10,248.06 |
| Total | 93,810.0 | 6,975.4 | 13,948.0 | 5,450.2 | 6,134.1 | 11,872.50 | 138,190.20 |

*Source:* European Commission (1996d).

member states. Development plans are then the subject of negotiations with the Commission which lead to Community support
frameworks (CSFs) and then to programmes which again require
adoption by the Commission. Single programme documents
(SPDs), on the other hand, contain proposals for programmes
from the outset and so become operational as soon as they have
been adopted by the Commission, see Figure 4.5. Both the CSFs
and the SPDs specify priority measures and the amount of assistance to be provided.

The work of the Structural Funds is governed by four principles. The first is the principle of programming, which results in
multi-annual development programmes. These are the result of
the process outlined in Figure 4.5. The second is partnership
which implies the closest possible co-operation between the
Commission and the appropriate authorities at national, regional
or local level in each member state from the preparatory stage to
implementation of the measures. The third is the principle of ad-
ditionality which means that Community assistance complements
the contributions of the member states rather than reducing them.
Except for special reasons, the member states must maintain public spending on each objective at no less than the level reached in
the preceding period. The final principle is that of the principle of
subsidiarity. One consequence of the subsidiarity principle in relation to structural measures is that it is up to the appropriate
authorities at national level to select the projects to be financed
and to supervise their implementation.

The rationale behind these principles is to try and extract
greater efficiency, impact and effectiveness from Structural Fund
expenditures. In principle, at least, operational programmes are
now meant to be planned and budgeted on a multi-annual basis
and organised around specific targets and objectives (Dignan,
1995). The framework adopted by Ireland is summarised in Table
4.4. This framework is being implemented through the arrangements described in Figure 4.5.

TABLE 4.4: THE IRISH NATIONAL DEVELOPMENT PLAN
1994–1999, PROPOSED EXPENDITURES

| | Expenditure Shares (%) | | | Sectoral Shares (%) | |
|---|---|---|---|---|---|
| | State and Public Bodies | Private Sector | EU Aid | EU Aid | Total Spend |
| Industry | 16.7 | 62.3 | 21.0 | 11.2 | 21.1 |
| Natural resources | | | | | |
| Agriculture | 14.3 | 23.0 | 62.7 | 12.2 | 7.7 |
| Forestry | 25.5 | 16.7 | 57.8 | 0.9 | 0.6 |
| Fisheries | 9.6 | 46.6 | 43.8 | 0.9 | 0.8 |
| Tourism | 10.5 | 53.3 | 36.2 | 4.5 | 3.3 |
| Local development | 66.3 | 9.5 | 24.2 | 4.4 | 7.2 |
| Human resources | 39.9 | 0.0 | 60.0 | 27.0 | 17.8 |
| Transport | 41.7 | 0.5 | 57.8 | 21.8 | 14.9 |
| Energy | 96.8 | 0.0 | 3.2 | 1.0 | 12.2 |
| Communications | 96.6 | 0.0 | 3.4 | 0.5 | 5.3 |
| Environmental services | 22.4 | 3.4 | 74.2 | 7.0 | 3.7 |
| Hospital infrastructure | 38.1 | 0.0 | 61.9 | 1.0 | 0.6 |
| Community initiatives | 38.2 | 10.9 | 64.5 | 7.5 | 4.6 |
| CSF technical assistance | 25.0 | 0.0 | 75.0 | 0.1 | 0.0 |
| Total | 42.5 | 18.0 | 39.5 | 100.0 | 100.0 |
| Expenditure | 7,428 | 3,621 | 6,907 | | 17,956 |

*Source: Ireland National Development Plan, 1994-1999, Dublin: Government Publications.*

Community initiative programmes, drawn up on the basis of guidelines set out by the Commission itself, complement the CSFs and the SPDs and help provide a solution to problems which have a particular impact on the Community. The Community initiatives in place for the period 1994-1999 have a budget of 13.45 billion ECU in 1994 prices, which is about 9 per cent of total Structural Funds. The initiative will focus on seven broad themes: cross-border and transnational co-operation, rural development,

FIGURE 4.5: PROCESS AND PLANNING IN RELATION TO THE STRUCTURAL FUNDS

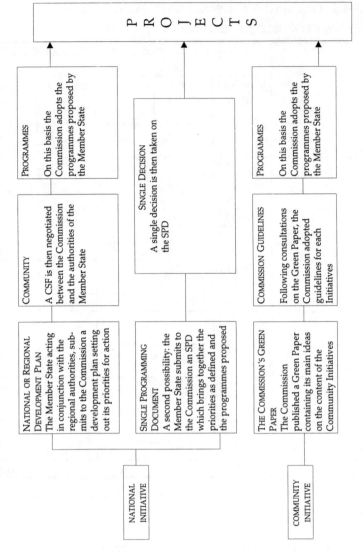

*Source:* European Commission (1996a).

## TABLE 4.5: COMMUNITY INITIATIVES AND IRELAND, 1994-1999

| | |
|---|---|
| **Interreg II** | The main aim of Interreg II is to develop cross-border co-operation and help areas on the Union's internal and external borders to overcome specific problems arising from their comparatively isolated position *vis-à-vis* other national economies and the Union as a whole.<br>Total Budget (million ECU): 2.900.2; Ireland 133.5 |
| **LEADER II** | As part of an overall policy to stimulate rural development, LEADER II is designed to help rural associations and local government in rural areas to exploit their potential better.<br>Total Budget (million ECU): 1.400.0; Ireland 46 |
| **Adapt** | The aims of Adapt are to: adapt workers to changes; improve the competitiveness of firms through training; prevent unemployment by improving qualifications; create new jobs and fresh activity.<br>Total Budget (million ECU): 1.400.0; Ireland 21.20 |
| **SMEs** | The purpose of the SME Initiative is to assist small and medium-sized businesses, whether industrial or in the services sector, particularly in Objective 1 regions, to adjust to the single market and become competitive on international markets.<br>Total Budget (million ECU): 1.000.1; Ireland 28.4 |
| **URBAN** | Urban is intended to help find solutions to the serious social problems caused by the crisis in many depressed urban areas by supporting schemes for economic and social revitalisation, the renovation of infrastructures and environmental improvement.<br>Total Budget (million ECU): 599.9; Ireland 15.5 |
| **PESCA** | The aim of Pesca is to assist the fishing industry in coping with and mastering the social and commercial consequences of the crisis in the fishing sector and to contribute to diversifying the regions affected through the development of job-creating activities.<br>Total Budget (million ECU): 250.0; Ireland 3.7 |

*Source*: *European Commission Guide to the Community Initiatives*, EU Information Sheet, 15 February 1996.

the most peripheral regions, employment and the development of skills, the management of industrial change, urban areas and the fishing sector. The key Community initiatives that Ireland is involved in are summarised in Table 4.5. The total EU allocation for these initiatives amounts to 1,872.5 million ECU (1994 prices) and Ireland's allocation through the different initiatives amounts to 304.02 million ECU.

### 6. THE IMPACT OF COMMUNITY REGIONAL POLICIES

The purpose of the Structural Funds is to assist regions in achieving the living standards and productivity levels of the richer EU regions by bringing about faster economic growth than in the core regions. The general evidence suggests that some regions have made some progress towards convergence in real terms with the rest of the Community. However, the evidence also confirms the view that structural change is a slow process (EU, 1996c). Some summary indicators of developments in the Community's weaker regions 1986-1993 are shown in Table 4.6.

TABLE 4.6: DEMOGRAPHIC AND ECONOMIC INDICATORS IN REGIONS ASSISTED BY THE COMMUNITY, 1986-1993

| REGIONS | Employment (1986=100) | Unemployment Rate | | | GDP per Head (PPS) (EUR12=100)[2] | | | |
|---|---|---|---|---|---|---|---|---|
| | 1993 | 1986 | 1991 | 1993 | 1986 | 1989 | 1990 | 1991 |
| Objective 1 | 109 | 15.4 | 14.3 | 16.7 | 61 | 63 | 63 | 64 |
| Objective 2[1] | 113 | 14.7 | 10.8 | 12.1 | 96[3] | 95 | 95 | 94 |
| Objective 5b[1] | 107 | 8.3 | 6.1 | 7.3 | 84 | 82 | 82 | 83 |
| Other regions | 106 | 8.4 | 6.4 | 8.0 | 117 | 117 | 117 | 116 |
| EUR12 | 107 | 10.7 | 8.5 | 10.4 | 100 | 100 | 100 | 100 |

[1] Figures for Objective 2 and 5b regions cover all NUTS 3 regions where at least 50 per cent of population is eligible for Community assistance.
[2] EUR12 excludes East German *Länder*.
[3] The figure is for 1987.
*Source*: Eurostat, calculations DG XVI.

The data indicate that experience as regards unemployment in the Community's weaker regions has varied significantly in the period since 1986. The latter half of the 1980s was a period of general economic recovery throughout the Community. Unemployment in the Community as a whole fell by 2 percentage points from 10.7 per cent in 1989 to 8.5 per cent in 1991 before increasing to 10.4 per cent in 1993. In respect of unemployment, Objective 2 regions as a whole outperformed other parts of the Community, assisted and unassisted parts alike. Unemployment rates in the Objective 2 regions were 4 percentage points lower in 1991 (10.8 per cent) than in 1986 (14.7 per cent). This fall was partly reversed over the following two years, although the rise in unemployment was not as great as for the Community as a whole. As a result, the difference between the average unemployment rate in Objective 2 regions and that in the Community as a whole narrowed from 4.6 percentage points in 1986 to only 1.7 percentage points in 1993. This can be interpreted as a particularly encouraging outcome given that a reduction in unemployment disparities is the principal aim of Objective 2 assistance.

Part of the explanation for the fall in unemployment in Objective 2 regions is probably related to labour supply developments. Most Objective 2 regions are highly urbanised and, therefore, often among those where demographic changes and population ageing have reduced the number of new entrants to the labour market. At the same time, job losses in traditional industries — coal, steel, engineering — have tended to affect men in middle and older age groups, a significant proportion of whom have presumably withdrawn completely from the labour market. The impact of falling labour supply should not, however, be exaggerated. Tentative estimates of employment change suggest that Objective 2 regions had a faster rate of net job creation than the rest of the Community. Over the period 1986-1993 the average rate of increase was approximately double the Community average, Table 4.6.

The Objective 5b regions (vulnerable rural areas) generally have relatively lower rates of unemployment, a traditional feature of rural areas outside the Community's least developed regions. From an average rate of 8.3 per cent in 1986, unemployment in the Objective 5b regions fell to only 6.1 per cent in 1991 and increased again to 7.3 per cent in 1993. Although reducing unemployment is not an explicit aim under Objective 5b, the data indicates that there has been a relative improvement in employment. This is underlined by the tentative evidence on employment change — which is likely to be more directly related to the process of structural diversification in rural areas — where the figures suggest gradual net job creation at a rate equivalent to the Community average, Table 4.6.

The data on GDP indicates a slightly downward trend in GDP per capita in the Objective 2 regions over the period. This might be because the economic restructuring taking place in these regions has led to an increase in the share of total employment in sectors with relatively low productivity in Community terms, e.g. certain personal services. In Objective 5b regions there was little change over the period, GDP per head has remained at around 80 per cent of the Community average

In the Objective 1 regions the indicators present a mixed picture. In 1986, the average unemployment rate in these regions was 15.4 per cent, half as high again as the Community average and double the rate in Objective 5b areas. Since then there has been little improvement, the rate declining to 14.3 per cent in 1991, before increasing to 16.7 per cent in 1993. Although the evidence on changes in employment in the Objective 1 regions is more encouraging, rates of increase do not seem to have reached those of the Objective 2 areas. Part of the reason for high and persistent unemployment is labour supply growth in many Objective 1 areas. For the medium term at least, reducing unemployment is likely to represent something of a moving target as new entrants, especially women, come into the labour market in significant numbers. Although the structure of employment in Objective 1 regions is changing, there are still significant numbers employed in agriculture (EC, 1996b) in 1990, the average share of agricultural employment in the Community was 6.6 per cent whereas in the Objective 1 regions it was nearly three times higher at 17.7 per cent. This means that while the Objective 1 regions as a whole accounted in 1990 for one job in six in the Community, in agriculture they accounted for nearly one in two.

It is the change in GDP, measured in per capita terms, and the speed of this change, which is the central indicator of progress in the Community's Objective 1 regions. Disparities in income per head between all member states have narrowed significantly over the period 1983-93. This is due to a catching-up on the part of the cohesion countries — Spain, Portugal, Greece and Ireland — with income per head increasing from 68 per cent to 74 per cent of the Community average. Ireland has recorded the fastest growth of any member state in recent years, maintaining a high rate, even during the recession in the early 1990s. GDP per head, which stood at 64 per cent of the European average in 1983, increased to 80 per cent by 1993, rising further to 90 per cent in 1995.

In terms of the convergence process it is true that the growth of the European Union economy as a whole means that the weaker member states have, in effect, to hit a moving target to achieve convergence. Cohesion requires a better performance by the lower-income countries over a sustained period. Some convergence scenarios are illustrated in Figure 4.6. The evidence illustrated suggests that if the Irish economy continues to grow at a rate of 4.5 per cent a year and the EU growth rate also continues at its 1983-1993 average of 2.5 per cent a year, then Ireland will draw level with the EU level of per capita income before 1999. Spain, growing at 3.0 per cent, will reach the EU average by 2005. Portugal will not achieve convergence until close to 2015 and Greece, growing at 1.8 per cent a year against an EU growth rate of 2.5 per cent, will find itself diverging further from the EU average income level over time. The recent and dramatic growth of the Irish "Tiger" economy indicates that Ireland is more than ahead of schedule in terms of the conclusions in Figure 4.6.

FIGURE 4.6: CONVERGENCE SCENARIOS FOR THE COHESION
COUNTRIES

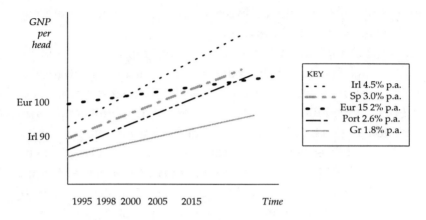

Statistical indicators of regional performance reflect a combination
of cyclical and structural changes affecting the Community's region and not just the impact of Community policies or spending.
Conceptually, the impacts of the Structural Funds occur on two
fronts: there is a macroeconomic impact, or a set of demand-side
effects, and there is their effectiveness in promoting an improved
performance and thus sustained convergence by the beneficiary
regions — supply-side effects. The Structural Funds provide a direct spending stimulus to regional economic activity, construction
projects are commenced, additional jobs are created, trainees receive wages through ESF funding, etc. These demand-side economic impacts can be fairly readily assessed. Thus it is estimated,
for example, that structural funding in the 1989-1993 framework
programme added 3 per cent to GNP in Greece and Portugal, 2
per cent in Ireland and 1 per cent in Spain and Italy (EC, 1996c).
Estimates by the ESRI of the fiscal impact of Structural Funds,
1989-1993 on Ireland's GNP are broadly similar to the Commission figures (Bradley *et al*, 1992). Clearly the funds do have sizeable short-term impacts on spending and growth in the regions.

What the consequences of this "macro" level performance for
regional disparities within Ireland will be is an interesting question. Until recently there was no information available at sub-

national level with which we could look at this issue. Regional accounts for Ireland were first published in 1996; they related to 1991 and a full description of the methodology used can be found in Regional Accounts 1991 (Government of Ireland, 1996). Further sets of accounts are now available for 1993 and 1995. The key variable measured in these accounts is gross value added (GVA) which is closely related to the national accounts concept of GDP. GVA at basic prices is a measure of the value of the goods and services produced in a region priced at the value which the producers received minus any taxes payable and plus any subsidies receivable as a consequence of their production or sale. It is one of the principal concepts used in deciding eligibility for Structural Funds. GVA differs from household income in three main respects. Firstly, GVA includes the total profits of companies (company profits arising in the state, which accrue to non-residents, are considerable). Secondly, the workforce that produces the GVA in a region may not live there and may bring their incomes home to a neighbouring region. Thirdly, personal income includes items such as social welfare benefits and factor incomes from abroad, which are not included in GVA.

The measure for GVA by region for the years 1991, 1993 and 1995 is summarised in Table 4.7. EU comparisons are also provided. The areas for which these accounts have been compiled are the eight regional authority regions. The MidEast region (Kildare, Meath and Wicklow) and the Dublin region are affected by a substantial proportion of their workforce living in one region and commuting to work in another. It is, therefore, considered more meaningful to combine these two regions.

The composition of the regions in Table 4.7 is described as follows:

Dublin:      Dublin County Borough,
             Dun-Laoghaire-Rathdown, Fingal and
             South Dublin
Mid East:    Kildare, Meath and Wicklow
South West:  Cork County, Cork County Borough and Kerry

Mid West:        Limerick County, Limerick County Borough, Clare
                 and Tipperary North Riding
South East:      Waterford County, Waterford County Borough,
                 Carlow, Kilkenny, Wexford and Tipperary South
                 Riding
West:            Galway County, Galway County Borough, Mayo
                 and Roscommon.
Border:          Cavan, Donegal, Leitrim, Louth, Monaghan and
                 Sligo
Midlands:        Laois, Longford, Offaly and Westmeath

The evidence is of considerable unevenness in economic performance across the eight regions. The Dublin region consistently
outperforms the rest while the West is the poorest performer. The
trend in regional differences shows that differences in performance levels across the regions widened over the period 1991-1994
but have narrowed somewhat in 1995. In terms of EU comparisons it is interesting to look at the 1995 data from the perspective
of the eligibility criterion for Objective 1 status (see p. 81), i.e. regions where per capita GDP is less than 75 per cent of the Community average. While the GVA measure is not identical to GDP,
it is, in the Irish context, interpreted as an acceptable proxy. The
1995 comparisons in Table 4.7 show that only three regions —
Border, West and Midlands — meet the 75 per cent criterion for
Objective 1 status. This Irish data again reinforces the point about
the difficult and very long-term task of trying to promote greater
regional evenness in economic performance.

The second, and more important, impact of the Structural
Funds is the supply-side effects. These measure the extent to
which regional policy is successful on the supply side of the economy in raising rates of economic growth in assisted areas and
hence helping to bring about convergence in living standards and
employment levels (Begg *et al.*, 1995). These impacts result from
the creation of new productive capacity, improved workforce
skills, the provision of new infrastructure and the dissemination

TABLE 4.7: REGIONAL ACCOUNTS 1991-1995, INDICES OF GROSS VALUE ADDED (GVA)

| Region | Indices of GVA per capita State = 100 | | | | | Regional GVA as a % of EU Average 1993 EU = 100 | | | |
|---|---|---|---|---|---|---|---|---|---|
| | 1991 | 1993 | 1994 | 1995 | | 1993 | 1994 | 1995 | |
| Dublin and MidEast | 117.6 | 116.3 | 120.0 | 121.0 | | 95.4 | 105.6 | 111.3 | |
| Dublin | 133.2 | 133.4 | 135.5 | 132.1 | | 109.4 | 119.2 | 121.5 | |
| Mid-East | 68.4 | 63.5 | 72.7 | 87.1 | | 52.0 | 63.9 | 80.1 | |
| South-West | 104.9 | 108.2 | 103.3 | 106.2 | | 88.7 | 90.9 | 97.7 | |
| Mid-West | 93.6 | 93.6 | 97.3 | 94.6 | | 76.7 | 85.6 | 87.0 | |
| South-East | 90.0 | 93.1 | 88.8 | 86.4 | | 76.3 | 78.2 | 79.5 | |
| West | 75.2 | 71.8 | 68.9 | 70.0 | | 58.9 | 60.6 | 64.4 | |
| Border | 82.4 | 81.7 | 81.3 | 77.2 | | 67.0 | 71.6 | 71.1 | |
| Midlands | 75.6 | 75.9 | 72.2 | 71.8 | | 62.2 | 63.5 | 66.1 | |
| State | 100 | 100 | 100 | 100 | | 82.0 | 88.0 | 92.0 | |

*Source:* Government of Ireland, (1996)

of new technologies. Such investments, by their very nature, will continue to have an economic impact over a long time period, whereas the demand-side effects have an immediate and fairly short-term impact. The problem is that impact of new investment in infrastructure, in training or new technologies on growth rates is difficult to assess since the policy measures in question are only one of many influences which are taking place simultaneously on economic development. Thus, it is difficult to isolate the impact of policy measures from that of other issues.

The recent ESRI mid-term evaluation of the Community support framework (CSF), 1994-1999, has sought to address the complicated problem. The essential technique used by the ESRI team is that of simulating, with the ESRI medium-term model of the economy, the "with CSF" scenario and various "without CSF" scenarios and then comparing the outcomes of the usual macroeconomic variables of interest such as GNP, employment, etc., (Honohan, 1997; Barrett, 1998). What these simulation exercises show is that the initial impact of spending under the CSF, 1994-1999, is much greater than the more permanent effects shown for the period after 1999. This is because the demand-side impact is, of course, purely transitory and it fades away when the current round expenditure is assumed to end in the year 1999. The supply-side impact takes some time to build up but persists long after the funds are spent. The cumulative effect, according to the ESRI evaluation, is to raise GNP by about 3 percent by 1998-1999. When the demand-side effects have disappeared in the year 2000, and the supply-side effects have built up, the permanent effects of the 1994-1999 round is to raise the level of GNP by around 1 per cent compared with the level it would have been.

The really fundamental question in all exercises like this is how much the policymaker knows about the supply side of the economy, about the nature of development processes and about the efficacy of particular types of policy interventions on performance and growth. Is it sufficient, for example, to argue that by overcoming deficiencies in a region's infrastructure one removes the critical barrier to better performance and higher growth? It has long been argued that deficiencies in Ireland's transport infra-structure were a critical obstacle to development. Clearly a trans-portation improvement, or indeed any other piece of investment, is only one of many factors which can contribute to change in a regional economy. The complexity of most regional economic systems makes it difficult to isolate the influence of any single measure, be it a new transportation investment or a new training programme or whatever. It is increasingly recognised that most measures are a necessary, but not a sufficient, condition for eco-nomic development to occur. Thus, in the context of decision-making and policy, it seems more appropriate to shift the focus in impact assessment from trying to demonstrate some causal rela-tionships between different investment and economic develop-ment, which one can never prove anyway, and concentrate in-stead on trying to operationalise the "necessary condition" crite-rion (Huddleston *et al*, 1990). This makes it difficult for those de-signing the various programmes to make the right choices and to project the development impact flowing from the choice of one set of measures rather than any other.

The situation can be made even more difficult if there is no process of strategy formulation to guide such choices. The danger must be that, in order to avail of EU funding, a peripheral region will adopt sub-optimal investment programmes, or ones that simply fit EU requirements. This could potentially distort public policy choices in the peripheral regions, a development which it-self could potentially promote ongoing dependence on transfers from Brussels (Dignan, 1995). A second element in the ESRI's mid-term evaluation of the Structural Funds was to look at such issues within the context of the individual measures of the different op-erational programmes. In doing so it identified some measures that it considered inefficient or ineffective — poorly designed ru-ral relief, under-priced business services and expansion grants for immobile firms — and others that warranted more attention and greater allocations of resources — upgrading of rural networks, broad-band telecommunications and better-managed urban transport (Barrett, 1998).

It is important that structural or any other EU funds should be used efficiently and effectively. To ensure this, it is important that there are mechanisms for the evaluation and monitoring of the various measures and programmes and that there is an opportunity for open debate on the issues (Matthews, 1993). The overriding concern for the regions, however, must be with trying to identify the factors that really matter if less developed regions are to achieve successful regional development. The experiences of individual member states with years of regional policies confirm the fact that it is not simply a question of increasing the resources of the Structural Funds. Current thinking points to a number of diverse factors which matter if the less-developed areas are to achieve successful regional development (Begg *et al*, 1995). The future of regions in Europe depends more on economic changes than on any regional or national policies, even though these have an important role to play in the realisation of regional infrastructures, transregional networks and images (Lever and Bailly, 1995). In this context Jacobs (1984) has pointed to the importance of creating conditions conducive to improvisation and flexibility as the key to regions developing. The contribution of Porter (1990) is also important in this respect. His analysis emphasises balanced development within a nexus of sophisticated markets, suppliers and support services, which have evolved over long periods in successful regions. The challenge is to develop the means of replicating these conditions in less successful regions. This challenge is also identified by O'Sullivan (1996: p. 391) in her analysis of industrial policy in Ireland. She describes government policy in the countries that have had successful industrial development, e.g. Japan and the East Asian Tigers, as being "less concerned with the degree of government intervention that is appropriate than about the most efficacious means to develop the organisational basis for a sustained process of development. In Ireland, in contrast, capabilities were not created within the government or the private sector. At the heart of Irish industrial policy was the hope that given the right financial incentives, such capabilities would simply emerge, a hope that reflects a lack of understanding of the complexity of the social process underlying the process of development. "Similar resonances can be found in the recent investigation into local partnerships and social innovation in Ireland" (Sabel, 1996). These different contributions point to how uncertain our understanding is of these issues and the need for much more intense theoretical and empirical analysis which can guide policy direction and the specifics which will truly matter and properly meet the particular needs and circumstances of Europe's regions.

## 7. CONCLUSION

The logic of markets which function well, which is, after all, what the European Union is about, argues that capital will move to seek its complements, and that the regions on the periphery will benefit from their association with regions of the centre. Equally, the market for labour will become more integrated, and wages will become more equal from one region to another through migration of labour and of capital. Unfortunately, this logic assumes that a number of underlying conditions are being met. If this is not the case, then the prospects for the disadvantaged regions will be poor and there will be a need for some kind of regional insurance mechanism to achieve both stabilisation and a reduction of inequalities throughout the Union. The core principles of fiscal federalism operating in existing federations show how to achieve these goals. However, in the European Union the adoption of these principles appears to be stymied by political resistance and by the size of the EU budget. Consequently, Europe's efforts to achieve overall inter-regional stabilisation is likely to "go no further than co-ordination of national policies and a possibly limited inter-regional insurance instrument" (NESC, 1997) and ongoing questions of regional imbalances will be addressed through the Structural and Cohesion Funds.

Agenda 2000 confirms that the priority policy goal of economic and social cohesion will be adhered to by the Community during the next planning period 2000-06. Within the financial perspectives it is proposed that 275 billion ECU (at 1997 prices) would be set aside for the Structural Funds and the Cohesion Fund compared to 200 billion (at 1997 prices) for the period 1993-99. The debate and the politics will be about proposals to concentrate and simplify the structural measures and to reduce the number of regional objectives from five to two. In the new planning period less developed regions will continue to be eligible for aid under Objective 1. However, the Commission proposes to apply strictly the GDP criterion by which assistance will go only to regions whose per capita GDP is less than 75 per cent of the Union average. For those regions currently eligible under Objective 1, which come out above the 75 per cent threshold, a phasing out mechanism will be defined. The Commission proposes that for regions confronted with major economic and social restructuring needs a "new" Objective 2 will be created. For this critical period in the history of the European integration process, with monetary union, enlargement and future financing high on the agenda, the outcome for the weaker regions is more uncertain and the commitment to cohesion is all the more necessary.

## REFERENCES

Alonso, W. (1991): "Europe's Urban System and its Peripheries", *Journal of the American Planning Association*, Winter: pp. 6-12.

Barrett, A. (1998): "Reporting on the ESRI Mid-Term Evaluation of the CSF, 1994-1999", Paper presented to the NASC West Ireland Europe Liaison Seminar, Westport, March.

Bachtler, J. and Turok, I. (eds.) (1997): *The Coherence of EU Regional Policy*. London: Jessica Kingsley Publishers.

Barry, F. (1996): "Peripherality in Economic Geography and Modern Growth Theory", *The World Economy*, Vol. 19, No. 3: pp. 345-65.

Begg, I., Gudgin, G. and Morris, D. (1995): "The Assessment: Regional Policy in the European Union", *Oxford Review of Economic Policy*, Vol. 11, No. 2: pp. 1-17.

Bradfield, M. (1988): *Regional Economics*, Toronto: McGraw-Hill Ryerson.

Bradley, J., Fitzgerald, J., Kearney, I., Boyle, G., Breen, R., Shortall, S., Durkan, J., Reynolds-Feighan, A. and O'Malley, E. (1992): "The Role of Structural Funds: Analysis of Consequences for Ireland in the Context of 1992." *Policy Research Series Paper No. 13*, Dublin: Economic and Social Research Institute.

Cheshire, P.C., Camagni, R.P., Gaudemar, J-P & Cuadrado, J.R. (1991): "1957 to 1992: Moving towards a Europe of Regions and Regional Policy" in Rodwin, L. & Sazanami, H. (eds.) *Industrial Change and Regional Economic Transformation: The Experience of Western Europe*, London: Harper Collins Academic.

Cheshire, P., Furtado, A. and Magrini, S. (1995): *Analysis of European Cities and Regions: Problems of Quantitative Analysis*, University of Reading Discussion Papers in Urban and Regional Economics, series C, No. 108.

Clark, G.L., Gertler, M.S. and Whiteman, J. (1986): *Regional Dynamics*. Boston: Allen and Unwin

Davezies, L. (1992): "*Reflections sur les Comparisons Internationales de Disparities Interregionales*" (Reflections on international comparisons of interregional disparities), *Revue d'Économie Régionale et Urbaine*, Vol. 2: pp. 241-55.

Dignan, T. (1995): "Regional Disparities and Regional Policy in the European Union", *Oxford Review of Economic Policy*, Vol. 11, No. 2: pp. 64-95.

Dunford, M. (1994): "Winners and Losers: The New Map of Economic Inequality in the European Union", *European Urban and Regional Studies*, Vol. 1, No. 2: pp. 95-114.

European Commission (1996b): *Competitiveness and Cohesion: Trends in the Regions*. Fifth Periodic Report on the Social and Economic Situation and Development of the Regions in the Community. Brussels: EU.

European Commission (1996c): *First Report on Economic and Social Cohesion 1996*. Brussels: European Union.

European Commission (1996d): *Structural Funds 1994: A New Period Makes Fresh Demands*, Inforegio Information Sheet 15, February. Brussels: European Commission.

Eurostat (1992): *Regional Nomenclature of Territorial Units for Statistics*, Brussels: European Commission.

Government of Ireland (1996): *Regional Accounts -Pn 3232*, Dublin: Central Statistics Office.

Hansen, N. (1995): "Addressing Regional Disparity and Equity Objectives through Regional Policies: A Sceptical Perspective", *Papers in Regional Science*, Vol. 74, No. 2: pp. 89-104.

Honohan, P. (ed.) (1997): *EU Structural Funds in Ireland: A Mid-Term Evaluation of the CSF 1994-99*, Economic and Social Research Institute Policy Research Series Paper No. 31, Dublin: Economic and Social Research Institute.

Huddleston, J.R. and Pangotra, P.P. (1990): "Regional and Local Economic Impacts of Transportation Investments", *Transportation Quarterly*, Vol. 44, No. 4: pp. 579-94.

Illeris, S. (1991): "Urban and Regional Development in Western Europe in the 1990s: Will Everything Happen in the London-Brussels-Frankfurt-Milan 'Banana'?", Paper presented to the 32nd European Congress of the Regional Science Association, Lisbon: August.

Jacobs, J. (1984): *Cities and the Wealth of Nations*, New York: Penguin.

Krugman, P. and Venables, A. (1990): "Integration and Competitiveness of Peripheral Industry" in de Macedo & Bliss (eds.). *Unity with Diversity within the European Economy: The Community's Southern Frontier*, Cambridge: Cambridge University Press.

Krugman, P. (1991): *Geography and Trade*, Cambridge: Mass.

Lever, W. and Bailly, A. (1995): *The Spatial Impact of Economic Changes in Europe.* Aldershot: Avebury.

Matthews, A. (1993): *Managing the EU Structural Funds*, Cork: Cork University Press.

Molle, W. and Boeckhout, S. (1995): "Economic Disparity under Conditions of Integration: A Long-Term View of the European Case", *Papers in Regional Science*, Vol. 74, No. 2: pp. 105-23.

National Economic and Social Council (NESC) (1997): *European Union: Integration and Enlargement*, Dublin: National Economic and Social Council.

O'Sullivan, M. (1996): "Manufacturing and Global Competition" in O'Hagan, J. (ed.) *The Economy of Ireland*, Dublin: Gill and Macmillan.

Perroux, F. (1955): *"La Notion de Pôle de Croissance"*,(The notion of the credibility pole) *Économie Appliquée*, pp. 1-2.

Porter, M.E., (1990) *The Competitive Advantage of Nations*, London: Macmillan.

Raynauld, A. (1988): "Regional Development in a Federal State" in Higgins, B. and Savoie, D. (eds.) *Regional Economic Development Essays in Honour of Francois Perroux*, Boston: Unwin Hyman.

Sabel, C. (1996): *Local Partnerships and Social Innovation*, Paris: Organisation for Economic Co-operation and Development.

# 5

# ENLARGEMENT: IMPLICATIONS AND CONSEQUENCES

*Michael Cuddy*

## 1. INTRODUCTION

The peripheral regions of the European Union have been pro-
gressing quite favourably under the various support mechanisms
implemented by the EU Commission and national governments.
However, the catching up process is slow. This is due to a number
of factors that challenge governments, institutions and entrepreneurs. There is continuing rapid technological change in products
and processes requiring radical restructuring of all industry, particularly the primary and secondary sectors. There is significant
absolute and relative increase in the services industry and a
shrinking of the primary and secondary sectors. There is rapid
internationalisation of trade, an increase in competition and a corresponding need to harmonise tax burdens on enterprises and,
therefore, to scale back social support and transfer payments, with
increasing emphasis on self-reliance. Centres of concentrated economic activity are more privileged to take advantage of these
challenges than areas of dispersed economic activity. Consequently, there is a relentless push towards the growth of large and
medium-sized cities and a relative decline of those areas which
lack such centres. The pressure on the less developed areas, peripheral areas and areas of dispersed population, will persist.

Assistance from the centre will continue to be necessary if living standards and life opportunities in these regions are to converge on the EU average. In the meantime, it has been agreed to significantly enlarge the Union by incorporating countries comprising regions which are much less developed than the poorest regions of the Union, thereby lowering the priority demands of the current poor regions.

The proposed eastward enlargement of the EU will stimulate changes in the labour market which will generate labour movement and influence wage rates; it will generate trade effects which will benefit both the existing EU countries and the incoming countries and it will stimulate new investment opportunities. Enlargement will also have direct political implications through the participation of the new members as well as through the very substantial strain on EU finances. The gains and benefits will not fall evenly across the different countries, regions and social sectors of the EU. This is likely to cause certain tensions and undoubtedly opposition to enlargement from those who feel that the balance of gains and losses will fall on the negative side. It is not surprising, then, that proposals to enlarge the Union to the east, incorporating countries from the former Soviet Block in Central and Eastern Europe, whose development lags very significantly behind the EU average, cause concern about the impact that such an enlargement will have, particularly on the existing peripheral regions of the EU.

The strongest pressure for enlargement is coming from the Central and Eastern European countries (CEEC) themselves. This is motivated by a number of considerations. First, there is the argument that association with, or membership of, a democratic Union would help to strengthen democracy in these countries, where democracy is still so fragile. Any economic benefits of this association would make the reform process more acceptable and, thereby, contribute to democratisation. Second, active cooperation with the EU in the fields of foreign, security and legal policy provides a certain guarantee of political protection, particularly in the face of uncertain eastern politics. This would allow the CEEC to get on with the business of internal reform in pursuit of economic development and to devote all their very limited resources to this end.

Third, and, perhaps the most valid reason for joining the EU, is the prospect of raising living standards through access to the large single market, increased direct foreign investment, and transfer payments from EU sectoral, social and regional policies. The present low level of local demand is inadequate to create a buoyant market for domestic production. Easy access to EU markets would boost demand and bring about badly needed increases in local production and income. Low wage costs in the CEEC economies would insure competitiveness. Certain sectors would benefit particularly well, for example, agriculture, food and labour intensive industries. This foreign-led demand expansion could be the motor to prime the whole economy. There are a number of factors which make the CEEC, with access to the large EU markets, extremely attractive to foreign investors: there is a great need for capital investment and technology transfer because of the outdated technology and low level of investment in all aspects of the economy over the past number of years; there is a paucity of local finance because of low local savings and a rudimentary banking system where investment financing is poorly developed; and, at the same time, there is a large pool of relatively highly skilled labour.

Membership of the EU would inevitably mean access to, and transfers from, the various economic development support funds: agriculture, the main sectoral fund, the social fund that supports human resource development, and the regional development fund that finances regional programmes of industrial development and infrastructural support.

The pressure within the EU for an eastward enlargement is motivated, primarily, by political considerations. Political stability on the borders of the EU is desirable in order to ensure external defence and internal security and, thus, internal economic stability and growth. The price to pay in absorbing the CEEC into an economic, political and monetary union is, in political terms, considered more acceptable than the cost of continuing instability on the borders. The humanitarian aspect in contributing to raising living standards in neighbouring countries is, also, not inconsiderable. Trade and, in particular, investment opportunities in the CEEC have also played a role although the expected increase in the overall aggregate demand for EU products coming from the CEEC is likely to be quite small in the short to medium term.

The objective of this chapter is to analyse the principal costs and benefits of an eastward enlargement of the EU, in particular the likely impact on the western periphery of the EU. It uses the relevant theory to predict the impact of enlargement on the labour market, international trade and foreign direct investment, and then draws on the available empirical evidence to support these predictions. Some of the challenges facing the CEEC countries in meeting the membership requirements, which are set down by the EU, are also examined; and, finally, the budgetary implications for the EU in integrating the new members are considered. But, first, some comparisons of key socio-economic variables are made between the EU and the ten CEEC countries that have applied for membership of the EU.[1]

## 2. SOME COMPARATIVE STATISTICS

Membership of the EU for all of the CEEC countries will not be achieved at the same time, given the different levels of economic development in the various countries and their progress in transition to a political democracy and a market-oriented economy.

---

[1] Hungary and Poland applied for membership in 1994; Romania, Slovakia, Latvia, Lithuania, Estonia and Bulgaria in 1995; and the Czech Republic and Slovenia in 1996.

Various agreements have already been concluded between the EU and the 10 countries that have so far requested membership. Interim Agreements were concluded with them, which allowed the integration process to commence even before Europe Agreements[2] were concluded. In December 1997 the first wave of entrants was agreed, Hungary, Poland, Slovenia, Estonia and the Czech Republic, and membership negotiations will now commence. The new enlargement, when finally accomplished, will be the most significant since the founding of the EC and will radically alter the political, economic and geographic nature of the Union.

With the eastern enlargement, there will be a 50 per cent increase in geographical territory, 30 per cent increase in population, 30 per cent increase in cities of over one million and 25 per cent increase in cities with over 500,000 of a population (Table 5.1). There will be a very significant shifting eastwards of the EU centre of gravity.

The gross domestic product (GDP) per capita in the EU is eight times that in the CEEC. Recognising the deficiencies in this parameter as an index of economic development and living standards, it is, nevertheless, clear that the level of economic development in the CEEC countries lags considerably behind that of the EU. This has very important implications for the level of funding in the economic sectors, social policy and infrastructure, which must be injected into these countries and the period of time it will take in order to bring living standards into line with the EU average. It also has important implications for the CEEC countries in their capacity to meet membership obligations, particularly in regard to the application of common legislation, institutions, policies and practices.

---

[2] The Europe Agreement is the basis of relationships between individual CEEC and the EU. It confers certain privileges: CEEC member in trade and access to EU funds to assist in the transition to political democracy and a market-oriented economy and thus easing the future integration process.

The principal sectoral differences between the EU and CEEC economies relate to the significantly greater importance of agriculture and the significantly lesser importance of services in the latter. Although the share of the labour force engaged in industry is comparable in the EU and the CEEC, there is, however, a very significant qualitative difference. The latter concentrates in traditional and heavy industry and has only a limited modern component. Also, technology and production processes in the CEEC are considerably lagging behind the EU and indeed very often are quite obsolete (Hitchens *et al*, 1996).

Unemployment is similar in both the EU and the CEEC. However, whereas the unemployment rate in the EU fairly accurately reflects the real labour market situation, this is not the case in the CEEC, where there is considerable disguised, or hidden unemployment. The inevitable radical structural adjustments, which must take place, will considerably increase this component of overall unemployment. The extent of the structural adjustment (or the lack of it) which has taken place varies between the different countries and is partly reflected in the very wide variation in inflation rates, between 10 and 131 per cent a year.[3]

The greater openness of the CEEC economy, as indicated by the export-to-GDP ratio, is more a reflection of its smaller size of GDP than of greater internationalisation of trade. The significantly large negative trade balance, like the high inflation rates, is linked to public debt and loose credit policy.

---

[3] Transfers to enterprises which have not implemented or have not successfully implemented the necessary restructuring contribute to the government budgetary deficits which expands the money stock and gives rise to inflation.

TABLE 5.1: KEY SOCIO-ECONOMIC VARIABLES IN EU AND CEEC, 1993

|  | EU (15) | CEEC (10) | EU (25) % Increase |
|---|---|---|---|
| Population (m) | 369 | 108 | 29 |
| Area (1,000K2) | 2,239 | 1,104 | 49 |
| Cities > 1m | 19 | 6 | 32 |
| Cities > 500K | 52 | 13 | 25 |
| GDP/capita (ECU) | 15,944 | 1,799 | – |
| Labour Market (%) | – | – | – |
| Agriculture | 5.8 | 22.3 | – |
| Industry | 33 | 29 | – |
| Services | 61 | 49 | – |
| Unemployment | 11 | 12 | – |
| Inflation (%) | 3.1 | 10-131 | – |
| Exports (% GDP) | 8.2 | 27 | – |
| Trade Balance (% of exports) | 0.4(+) | 22(-) | – |
| Higher Education (% of population) | 0.4 | 5.4 | – |
| Life Expectancy (males) | 73 | 67 | – |

*Source*: Eurostat (1995a), Eurostat (1994), *Encyclopaedia of the Nations of Europe* (1995).

One of the important aspects of the centrally planned economy in the CEEC has been the high level of social services relative to GDP, including education and health. The human-capital stock is high as reflected in the much larger percentage of the population with a higher education, 5.4 per cent of the population versus 0.4 per cent for the EU (although, again, there are shortcomings in the comparability of statistics). The lower life expectancy in the CEEC is a reflection of the deterioration in the health support system, due to the rapid decline in GDP, the decoupling of social services from the commercial activities of enterprises, and deteriorating health of the population due to the physical and psychological pressure imposed on the society through the break-up of the socialist system.

### 3. THE LABOUR MARKET AND MIGRATION

Labour mobility reflects a lack of acceptable employment opportunity in one location and its availability in another. Such mobility may be viewed as an investment in which costs are borne in an early period in order to obtain returns over a longer period of time. If the present value of the expected benefits associated with mobility exceeds the costs, then people will decide to change jobs or move. The present value of the net benefits of mobility will be larger, the greater the expected benefits to be derived from the new job, the smaller the benefits of the existing job, the smaller the immediate costs associated with the change and the longer one expects to be in the new job or live in the new area. This can be stated formally as follows:

$$\text{PV of net benefits} = \sum \frac{(B_{jt} - B_{0t})}{(1+R)^t} - C$$

$B_{jt}$ = the benefit derived from the new job (j) in year t;

$B_{0t}$ = the benefit derived from the old job (0) in year t;

$t$ = the length of time one expects to work at job j;

$R$ = discount rate;

$C$ = costs associated with the move itself.

Addressing the aggregate labour market and assuming that the wage rate alone, which is equal to the marginal value of labour, is the only factor which determines the amount of labour supplied, the linking of labour markets in the EU and CEEC, through enlargement, with full freedom of mobility, will bring about labour flows and will equate wage rates in both markets (Figure 5.1). Before the linking of markets, there are OL′ workers employed in the EU, with an average wage rate of W₁EU; there are OL′

employed in the CEEC with wage rate $W_1CEEC$. It can be stated in general terms that a unifying of the labour markets will bring about migration, L'L from the CEEC to the EU, a lowering the average wages in the EU and a raising of them in the CEEC to $W_2EU(=W_2CEEC)$.

FIGURE 5.1: LABOUR MARKET IN EU AND CEEC AND THE JOINT MARKET AFTER INTEGRATION[4]

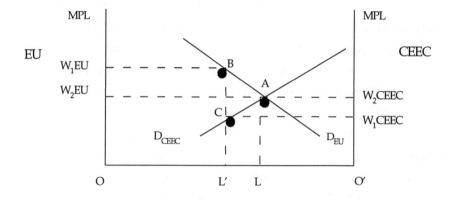

The labour market is not, however, homogeneous, either from the demand or supply side; the market is also spatially distributed, on both the demand and supply sides; and there are various other factors which cause friction and inertia. So, whereas migration of labour from east to west may be predicted, it must also be qualified to allow for these factors.

Recent studies (Sahling and Smith, 1993; Ulman *et al*, 1993) suggest that while people are more attracted to places where earnings are expected to be better, they do not necessarily come

---

[4] The vertical axis on the left-hand side of Figure 5.I measures the marginal product of labour and the wage rate in the EU; the demand for labour in the EU slopes downward, from left to right; the vertical axis on the right-hand side measures the marginal product of labour and the wage rate in the CEEC; the demand for labour in the CEEC slopes downward, from right to left. The quantity of labour supplied is measured on the horizontal axis, in the EU from left to right, and in the CEEC from right to left.

from areas where opportunities are poorest, nor do they go to the most attractive labour market location as measured by the unemployment rate. However, the number of people moving with a job already in hand is three times as large as the number moving to look for work. Migration is closely correlated with youth: the younger one is, the greater the potential returns from any human capital investment; also, unmarried people are more likely to migrate between states than married ones. Within age groups, education is the single best indicator of who will move: the more educated workers are then the more likely they are to move. Distance is, also, a factor, with the propensity to move far away being smaller than the propensity to move shorter distances. Education, however, appears to be a bigger deterrent to long-distance migration than does age.

However, the overwhelming experience in the EU is, that despite the absence of legal barriers and, at the same time, with significant wage differences between countries, labour mobility has been very restricted (European Commission, 1994). This suggests that the economic incentives are unable to overcome the non-legal barriers, like language and social relationships. In 1994, less than 2 per cent of EU nationals were in another member state. The majority of these moved between 1950 and 1970 and were mainly unskilled workers. The 1980s and early 1990s has seen a slowing down of large scale movement of labour from the periphery and an increasing number of migrants returning to their native countries (Italian, Greeks and Portuguese, in particular). At the same time there has been an increase in movement between countries with similar living standards (Germany, France, Benelux countries). Also, recent indications suggest that movement of the higher skilled workers is between two and four times more likely than for manual and clerical workers.

The EU experience then suggests that if wage and living condition differences are really high and opportunities exist, then movement will take place. This may be reversed later as the differences are reduced and opportunities in the countries of origin open up, which encourage reverse migration flows. The experience with CEEC countries, to date, does seem to suggest a rerun of the earlier south/north flows. Where opportunities for mobility did exist, for example between the former East and West Germany and for ethnic Germans in other CEEC countries, large flows did take place (European Commission, 1994). The flow increased from 39,000 a year in 1985 to 700,000 before the fall of the Berlin Wall. This led to rapidly declining areas of population in eastern parts of Germany and rapidly growing population in the western part in the late 1980s and early 1990s. Indeed, it is estimated that, between 1994 and the year 2000, the number of immigrants to Germany from the east will increase to 5 million.

On the basis of theory and the existing empirical evidence, significant migration is likely from the CEEC to the EU once the barriers to movement are lifted. It might be expected at least as much from the relatively richer north as from the poorer south of the CEEC; the destinations are likely to be varied, but the neighbouring regions of the EU are likely to be more favoured than distant destinations. Given the relatively high education level in the CEEC, migration to the west is likely to be more intense. This will be further reinforced by the fact that wage differences between skilled and unskilled labour is lower in the east than in the west.

In addition to depressing labour markets in those regions to which there are the largest migration flows, the east/west migration will have a knock-on effect on the labour market in those regions of the EU from which there are currently labour outflows to the more buoyant labour market destinations of the Union. The extent of the east/west labour movement will be tempered by the extent and success of the CEEC reforms which can absorb local labour. Policies which favour labour employment over capital investment (though altering the relative price of these two factors) will have a critical bearing on this outcome, as has already been demonstrated in the former German Democratic Republic (von Furstenberg, 1995).

## 4. INTERNATIONAL TRADE

International trade is determined by international patterns of production and consumption. However, most of the theory concentrates on the production side, using assumptions that neutralise demand as a determinant of trade and its composition. The Heckscher-Ohlin-Samuelson theory, the dominant theory of international trade, suggests that countries tend to export goods that are intensive in the factors of production that are in abundant supply locally and import those goods that are intensive in the factors of production that are in scarce supply locally. The current assumption is that the CEEC is labour abundant relative to the EU, and that the EU is capital abundant relative to the CEEC.

The removal of trade barriers between the EU and the CEEC will increase trade flows. The CEEC will expand trade in labour intensive goods, while the EU will expand trade in capital intensive goods. With trade expansion, the demand for the abundant factor will increase and the demand for the scarce factor will decline in both trading areas. This will have important income distribution effects, where the owners of the abundant factors gain while the owners of scarce factors lose. Thus labour will gain in the CEEC and lose in the EU, while capital will gain in the EU and lose in the CEEC. The theory assumes that factor prices are equal to the value of their marginal products and product prices are equal to their marginal costs. It assumes that production functions are linear and homogenous and that there are no transport costs, only two factors of production, two products and two countries.

However, the failure of the Heckscher-Ohlin-Samuelson theory to explain the bulk of international trade, the large intra-industry and intra-firm trade, the large trade between countries with seemingly similar factor proportions, the relatively high level of trade between neighbouring countries and the increasing role of monopolistic firms in international trade has led to new explanatory perspectives (Krugman 1991, Krugman and Obstfeld, 1994). The weakening of the link between the share of intra-industry trade and differences in factor composition (Helpman, 1981) is undoubtedly related to the expansion of multinational corporations. Also, intra-industry trade between similar high-income countries comes from the fact that they are neighbours and/or are members of free trade associations.

In view of the importance of trade for economic transition, the EU decided not to wait for the ratification of the Europe Agreements but adopted Interim Agreements, covering the trade provisions of the Europe Agreements, which opened up the EU's market to the partner countries' exports. The initial timetable, under which the EU abolishes tariffs and quantitative restrictions for most industrial products over five years, was later shortened, giving free access by 1 January 1995, instead of 1 January 1997, for the Visegrad countries (Hungary, Poland, Czech Republic, Slovakia and Slovenia) and by 1 January 1996 instead of 1 January 1998 for Bulgaria and Romania. The schedules for Romania and Bulgaria were again shortened by a year, following the Essen European Council meeting in December 1994. This ensured that they would be aligned with those of the Visegrad countries. As a result, industrial products from the associated countries have had virtually free access to the EU since the beginning of 1995. Trade in certain sectors, mainly textiles, agricultural products and fisheries, is regulated and thereby restricted by specific rules.

Already prior to complete trade liberalisation, there has been a very significant increase in trade between the EU and the CEEC, although still relatively small in global terms. However, the trade pattern now established is indicative of the impact that further liberalisation and eventual integration is likely to have on the EU. Two clear patterns emerge. First, the trade with the CEEC is effectively a re-establishing of traditional trade links, and, second, high technology, capital intensive products are emphasised in EU exports to the CEEC, while low technology, labour intensive products are emphasised in the imports from the CEEC. The data on the importance of the CEEC as a trading partner[5] indicates that Greece, Germany and Italy are the most important beneficiaries of developing eastern trade links, while Ireland, Portugal and Spain are the least important beneficiaries. The CEEC destination is the most important for Greece, Germany and Italy and least important for Ireland, Portugal and Spain (Table 5.2). The CEEC origin of imports is most important to Germany, Greece and Italy and least important to Portugal, Ireland and the UK. Clearly, proximity to the CEEC is a very important factor in determining the destination of their exports and the origin of their imports. The greatest sectoral concentration in imports from the CEEC is in the low-technology sectors, like textiles, footwear, wood, stone, etc. (Table 5.3). On the other hand, the greatest sectoral concentration on the export side is in the high-technology machinery and electrical equipment sectors.

TABLE 5.2: SHARE OF CEEC TRADE IN THE TOTAL EXTRA-EU TRADE BY COUNTRY, 1993

| Country | Exports % | Imports % | Country | Exports % | Imports % |
|---------|-----------|-----------|---------|-----------|-----------|
| Belgium | 7.1 | 4.7 | Ireland | 3.5 | 1.5 |
| Denmark | 9.0 | 9.7 | Italy | 12.0 | 10.4 |
| Germany | 14.8 | 16.1 | Netherlands | 9.6 | 4.7 |
| Greece | 25.3 | 13.1 | Portugal | 2.3 | 2.0 |
| Spain | 4.2 | 3.6 | UK | 3.7 | 4.1 |
| France | 4.8 | 4.4 | EU 12 | 9.6 | 8.7 |

*Source*: Derived from Eurostat (1996a) and Eurostat (1996b)

---

[5] The measure of importance is trade (exports plus imports) with the CEEC as a percentage of total extra-EU trade.

TABLE 5.3: SECTORAL SHARE OF EU TRADE WITH CEEC, 1994

|  | Imports<br>% Share | Exports<br>% Share |
|---|---|---|
| Agriculture + Food | 7.67 | 9.68 |
| Mineral products | 6.49 | 1.99 |
| Chemical and Plastics | 8.85 | 14.89 |
| Textiles + Footwear, etc. | 28.91 | 17.87 |
| Wood, Stone, Base metals | 25.07 | 11.66 |
| Machinery and Electrical | 14.45 | 29.78 |
| Vehicles and other transport | 7.08 | 11.66 |
| Other | 1.77 | 2.73 |
| Total | 100 | 100 |

*Source*: Derived from Eurostat (1995b)

A comparative static simulation exercise has quantified the impact which changing trade flows, due to the economic reforms in Eastern Europe and its integration into the world economy, will have on EU regional manufacturing. Bröcker and Jäger-Roschko, (1996) show that spatial variation of the effects can be attributed to regional variation in the sectoral mix (structural effect) and variation in the sectoral effect between different regions (locational effect). The overall effect of the reform on the EU is positive, being more than twice as important to the lagging regions as to the non-lagging regions. However, it is six times more important to the lagging regions of the east than to those of the west.[6] The location effects in the lagging regions of the east are four times more important than the structural effects. In the lagging regions of the west, the location effect is negative while the structural effect is positive and a little above the average for all EU regions.

---

[6] The lagging regions of the east include all the lagging regions of Greece and Italy. The lagging regions of the west include all the lagging regions of Ireland, Spain, Portugal and the UK.

The opening-up of trade to the east will lead to a substantial increase in trade, and a very significant reorientation of Eastern European countries towards Western European markets (Fischer and Johannson, 1996). This trade will be extremely important to the development of the Eastern European economies. The impact of trade reform will be twice as high between neighbouring countries as between non-neighbouring countries. The Eastern European countries have a comparative advantage in sectors like textiles and clothing, iron and steel and agricultural products.

It is clear, then, from theory, empirical evidence and results from simulation exercises that the impact of expanded trade with the CEEC will not be evenly distributed throughout the EU, either sectorally or regionally. In the short term there will be more competition from the CEEC for the low-technology sectors and greater trade opportunities in the CEEC for the high-technology sectors, particularly for the neighbouring countries in the EU. In the longer term, the low technology, high labour intensity sectors, located primarily in the less developed and peripheral regions of the Union, will be subject to the greatest competition from the low-technology, low labour cost producers from the CEEC. On the other hand, trade opportunities will be created for the high-technology producers, mainly in the core regions of the EU. However, industrial development in the CEEC, led by foreign direct investment and based on a highly educated and low cost labour force is likely to change the future composition of trade between the EU and the CEEC.

An examination of the latest trade figures between Ireland and the Visegrad countries suggests that any generalisations are difficult to sustain (Table 5.4). While the most important exports from Ireland to the Visegrad countries are in the capital-intensive, mechanical/electrical/electronics industries, the imports from the Visegrad countries are not strongly oriented towards the labour-intensive products, although textiles and primary products like coal do feature. There is, however, very significant intra-industry

trade east/west and west/east even in sectors as narrowly defined as electrical, general machinery or office machines, for example, whereas office machines is the most important Irish export
to the CEEC, it is also the second most important import from the
CEEC. Indeed, the third and fourth most important import categories are generally high-technology, capital-intensive goods.
However, the other more important export categories are quite
mixed in terms of level of incorporated technology and capital
intensity. This suggests that there is already a strong basis for direct competition which, through foreign direct investment, is
likely to intensify in the future.

TABLE 5.4: TRADE BETWEEN IRELAND AND THE VISEGRAD
COUNTRIES, 1995

| SITC No. | Commodity | Rank Order | Exports £,000 | Rank Order | Imports £,000 |
|---|---|---|---|---|---|
| 1 | Meat/Meat Preparation | 6 | 6,732 | | |
| 3 | Fish | 8 | 2,259 | | |
| 6 | Sugars/Sugar Prep. | | | 10 | 3,203 |
| 28 | Metal Ores and Scrap | 2 | 10,174 | | |
| 32 | Coal & Briquettes | | | 1 | 19,567 |
| 55 | Essential Oils/Resinoids | 3 | 9,498 | | |
| 57 | Plastics in Non-Primary Form | 9 | 2,245 | | |
| 65 | Textiles | | | 6 | 3,497 |
| 67 | Iron and Steel | | | 9 | 3,264 |
| 72 | Machinery Specialised | | | 3 | 6,610 |
| 74 | Machinery General | 5 | 8,044 | 4 | 5,223 |
| 75 | Office Machines | 1 | 58,333 | 2 | 8,354 |
| 76 | Telecommunications | | | 7 | 3,388 |
| 77 | Electrical | 4 | 8,783 | 8 | 3,333 |
| 78 | Road Vehicles | | | 5 | 5,153 |
| 87 | Professional, Scientific instruments | 7 | 4,834 | | |
| 88 | Photographic Apparatus | 10 | 2,165 | | |

*Source*: Central Statistics Office (1996).

## 5. FOREIGN INVESTMENT

Investment funds can flow through foreign direct investment, the purchase of equity in existing companies, government or private bonds and through lending to the public or private sectors through banking activities. The main form discussed here is foreign direct investment (FDI).

The distinctive feature of FDI is that it involves not only a transfer of resources but also the acquisition of control. That is, a subsidiary does not simply have a financial obligation to the parent company, it is part of the same organisational structure. Two of the driving forces in foreign investment are access to markets and relative factor costs. A firm's expansion into another country can take any of three forms: horizontal extension (producing the same goods elsewhere), vertical extension (adding a stage in the production process that comes earlier or later in the firm's processing activity), or conglomerate diversification. The overwhelming portion of FDI involves either horizontal or vertical expansion and typically plays a strategic role in oligopolistic competition, in particular, it may serve as an entry deterrent. Domestic factors also remain important in both the magnitude and the composition of inflows. Countries with sound domestic fundamentals have attracted capital on a larger scale and with a higher proportion of long-term investment. Edwards (1991) shows that there appears to be a strong link between economic fundamentals and foreign direct investment. A similar outcome could result from the introduction of institutional reforms, such as the liberalisation of the domestic capital market and policies that result in credible increases in the rate of return on investment. Inflows may also reflect renewed confidence about favourable medium- and long-term investment opportunities in the host country.

The CEEC are desperately behind in technology and even more desperately short on investment funding. The low labour costs due to low wages, and relatively high skills, and the increasing opportunity of exporting to the EU makes the CEEC an attractive place to invest. This should be true for both institutional funds and direct investment. However, given the rather slow evolution in the development of the domestic banking system, the funding of investment through bank loans is, as yet, quite limited. This makes opportunities even more interesting for direct foreign investment. Correspondingly, it makes the regions of the EU relatively less attractive for direct investment. Regions, which previously were marginal in their attractiveness may not now be attractive at all. Therefore, funds, which might normally have been invested in the EU to take advantage of the large EU markets, are now being channelled into the CEEC. The impact on direct investment from sources within the EU is similar to that on direct investment coming from outside the Union.

Foreign direct investment into the CEEC has expanded from a very low base in the 1980s to 5.2 billion ECU in 1995 (EIU, 1995). The EU is the major contributor to this investment, with an EU country being the most important or the second most important investor of all foreign investors in every member of the CEEC, except Estonia (Table 5.5). Indeed, Germany is the first or second most important investor in nine out of 10 CEEC countries. In line with the trade relations, the share of EU members' total direct foreign investment going to the CEEC is highest in those countries which border the CEEC (Table 5.6). Over 35 per cent of Austria's total foreign direct investment and 5.7 per cent of Germany's goes to the CEEC while only 0.7 per cent of the UK's and 0.5 per cent of France's goes to the CEEC.

So, even before any of the CEEC members are admitted into the EU, they are an important destination for EU direct foreign investment. As economic and political stability develops and the relationship with the EU moves from European Agreements to full membership, this investment is likely to increase. The increasing interest from the US and Japan in direct investment in the EU is likely to find the CEEC more attractive than the EU countries as access to the EU markets is eased. Thus, it might be easily construed that this expansion of direct investment eastwards is, at least to some extent, at the expense of the marginal or peripheral regions of the EU.

TABLE 5.5: RELATIVE IMPORTANCE OF EU'S FOREIGN DIRECT INVESTMENT IN THE CEEC, 1992

| CEEC Countries | EU Countries | | | | | | | | |
|---|---|---|---|---|---|---|---|---|---|
| | D | I | F | NL | B | UK | DK | E | GR |
| Bulgaria | 1 | | | 2 | 4 | 6 | | | |
| Czech | 1 | 7 | 3 | 8 | 5 | | | | |
| Hungary | 2 | 9 | 6 | 4 | 10 | 7 | | | |
| Poland | 2 | 3 | 4 | 5 | 10 | 8 | 11 | | |
| Romania | 2 | 5 | 1 | 6 | 9 | 3 | | 10 | 11 |
| Slovenia | 1 | 3 | 4 | | | | | | |
| Slovakia | 2 | 8 | 5 | 7 | | | | | |
| Estonia | 6 | 5 | | | | 7 | | | |
| Latvia | 2 | | | | | 1 | | | |
| Lithuania | 2 | | | | | 1 | | | |

*Source*: Meyer (1995)

TABLE 5.6: SHARE OF EU MEMBER'S TOTAL FOREIGN DIRECT INVESTMENT GOING TO THE CEEC

| EU Countries | % Share |
|---|---|
| Austria | 35.1 |
| Belgium | 0.4 |
| Finland | 2.3 |
| France | 0.5 |
| Germany | 5.7 |
| Italy | 1.8 |
| Netherlands | 3.3 |
| UK | 0.7 |

*Source*: Meyer (1995)

## 6. THE CHALLENGE TO THE CEEC IN MEETING EU ENTRY CONDITIONS[7]

At the Essen Summit in December 1994, the Commission set out a "pre-accession strategy" for the associated countries specifying the following economic and political conditions for membership:

- That the candidate country has achieved stability of institutions guaranteeing democracy, the rule of law, human rights and respect for the protection of minorities;

- The existence of a functioning market economy, as well as the capacity to cope with competitive pressure and market forces within the Union; and

- The ability to take on the obligations of membership, including adherence to the aims of political, economic and monetary union (harmonisation of fiscal and monetary policy with those of the EU countries).

The strategy also indicated ways in which the European Union would assist the associated countries in meeting these conditions.

It is difficult to appreciate fully the degree of restructuring which has to take place if satellite states of the former Soviet Union are to achieve the democratic society and free market economy which is the norm in the EU. The transition from a totalitarian centrally planned to a democratic market economy is an extraordinary process without historical precedent. Moulding the process to ensure representation of the interests of the public and the discharge of the legislative responsibilities by politicians elected on the basis of their political platform who can be democratically removed if they are not fulfilling their obligations, is far from complete. The large number of political parties which result from the failure to gain adherence to a broad base of political

---

[7] This section draws mainly on personal experiences in the CEEC and CIS (Cuddy, 1997).

principles, creates instability. The formation of interest groups, who can articulate and focus issues and have them debated in public fora and who can exert pressure on politicians, has yet to be developed. Despite free elections, and in some cases the capacity to change political direction through the electoral process, many of the key aspects of the democratic process are still missing. The formation of large political groupings with a shared philosophy, but, nevertheless, with a wide spectrum of, very often, competing interests, which is necessary for political stability, must be strengthened. The method by which effective committed candidates, rather than the traditional party elites, can be drafted into the electoral process, must be considerably strengthened. Interest groups, such as trade unions, employers, farmers, consumers, which are the driving forces behind political parties in the EU, must emerge and evolve. The dialogue between elected representatives and the electorate outside of elections must be orchestrated. It will take some considerable time before the democratic process can be realised, when the will of the people is effectively articulated and when responsibility for it is accepted by the political parties, legislated for and implemented.

Going along with the changing political system, the objectives, functions and structures of administrations must be radically reformed to meet the needs of a democratic and market driven economy. The withdrawal of the state from the production process is widespread. The greater emphasis now on social service provision, the creation of an appropriate environment (legislation and policing) for market activity, the promotion of entrepreneurship and planning the broad strategic developments at national and local levels, requires new functions and new competencies. This transition is difficult in terms of degree, pace and precision of implementation.

The process of decentralisation of administration, from national to regional to local, has only commenced. Levels of administration below the central level have no experience and no competence in the assumption and discharge of responsibility for economic development. The EU, through the Phare Programme, is assisting in developing the legislation and structures to accompany the decentralisation of decision-making powers and policy implementation. This process is essential to regional and local development, and will be particularly apt when the CEEC integrates into the EU and shares in its regional development strategies and policies.

Perhaps the most radical changes are taking place at the level of the individual enterprises. A massive privatisation programme has been implemented, although differing in extent and method from country to country. The inter-enterprise linkages, the price fixing of products and factor inputs, product quotas and disposal and capital investment based on political decisions rather than demand, which were all part of the centrally planned system, have been effectively broken up. Privatisation of property has transferred all decision-making with respect to the enterprise onto the management team of the individual enterprise. The most critical functions of market analysis and development, business and financial planning require significant training and retraining of personnel. Many products and technologies, current under the old regime are now obsolete. Substantial capital investment is required if enterprises are to become internationally competitive. Despite its increasing significance, foreign investment can only meet a very limited part of total investment requirements. A drastic restructuring of the banking system is necessary in order to channel savings into domestic investment.

Social services must undergo considerable restructuring as the privatised enterprises disengage from their traditional provision of certain social services. The state, through local or central government, must now assume an enlarged responsibility. The tax base, which was in large part the value added of the state enterprises, has shrunk in accordance with state withdrawal from production, and has only been partially replaced by the value added in fledging, fragile private enterprises and personal incomes and sales. At the same time the liability of the state sector has been increased with the expanded social responsibility and the new phenomena of the unemployed.

The disintegration of the state sector through privatisation and an explosion of new enterprises, particularly in the services area, has given rise to radically new training needs for enterprise management and development. New functions and structures necessitate the training and retraining of public sector personnel at all levels. This in turn places new demands on the training institutions and, therefore, on the trainers of the trainers. The education system, having evolved to meet the needs of an authoritarian political and administrative system and centrally planned economy is itself incapable of responding to these needs and must be radically reformed in order to do so. The sort of time lags necessary to meet these sequential requirements is quite long indeed. All this must take place within national administrative and financial structures which are themselves slowly but surely being radically reformed.

Harmonisation of fiscal and monetary policies is also required in order to be able to integrate fully into the EU. The movement to a market economy and the harmonisation of policies with their EU counterparts will lead to a radical redistribution of income. These conditions will impose tremendous pressure on the associated countries and continuing demands that they undergo radical reforms, which will push society to socio-economic and political difficulties. The needs of national macroeconomic management, with the decline of the public sector and the corresponding expansion of the private sector in the production of goods and services, have radically changed. A groping adjustment to the new requirements continues. The inter-linkage between budgetary deficits, monetary aggregates, exchange rates and trade are moving toward the normal market economy relationships. At the same time, the radical change in the tax base due to privatisation, when combined with the shrinkage in production, less disposable revenue available and increasing social demands due to poor income and employment, is bringing about considerable political tension, and in some cases a slowing down of the restructuring process. Indeed, in many countries there is a cyclical speeding-up and slowing-down of this process with oscillations in elections between progressive governments and conservative governments in many CEEC countries.

The transition to a market economy has led inevitably to increasing disparities in incomes. People who find themselves in the expanding sectors are able to realise higher incomes. Conversely, for those who find themselves in the contracting or disappearing sectors, incomes are rapidly declining. In addition, the freeing-up of markets for agricultural produce and the disappearance of subsidies has redistributed income from the city to the countryside. Convergence with EU farm prices and eventual entry into the EU with its high farm prices will have a very radical redistributive effect from city to country.

As the CEEC countries weave their way toward functioning democracies and advance toward operational market economies, significant successes are already being signalled. Nevertheless, there still remains a plethora of areas where the transformation process has yet to show very tangible results. So, all in all, the restructuring process at all levels will continue over a considerable period of time. It is clear, then, that the conditions laid down for EU membership, including the requirements of fiscal and monetary policy harmonisation, will not be met in the short to medium term (say up to five to ten years) without putting unacceptable pressure on society within the CEEC or without very significant transfers from the EU.[8]

---

[8] The experience of former East Germany with a population of only 18 million, which has absorbed DM879 billion of public transfers over the period 1991-97, representing roughly 4.3 per cent of West German GDP annually (Rummel, 1997), and which is still a long way from matching the conditions and structures

## 7. IMPLICATION FOR THE EU BUDGET AND MEMBER VOTING RIGHTS

The simple fact is that the CEEC are at a very different stage of development from the EU member states. If GDP per capita is even a crude measure of relative standards of living, the EU average is eight times that of the CEEC average. Even the most developed economies of the CEEC, the Visegrad four,[9] with 64 million citizens is now 2.5 times more agricultural and only 30 per cent as rich as the EU average. This makes them more populous, poorer and more agricultural than the four poorest countries in the EU (Ireland, Spain, Greece and Portugal) put together. Even by the year 2000, many of them will not have a GDP per capita much above 40 per cent of the then EU average.

The budgetary implication of the entry of the Visegrad four clearly indicates the impact which enlargement will have, assuming that benefits are extended to the new entrants comparable to those presently being enjoyed by the existing less-developed regions of the EU. Visegrad enlargement would raise the annual cost of CAP expenditures by 47 billion ECU and the Structural Funds by 26 billion ECU (Baldwin, 1995). So, admitting the Visegraders by the year 2000+ would increase EU spending by, approximately, 73 billion ECU or of the order of 75 per cent of the EU's projected budget for the year 2000. It is also reasonable to expect that Visegrad agriculture would grow at the same rate as in Germany over a 20-year period, putting even more considerable pressure on the CAP budget. In effect, this would mean that a drastic cut in transfers to the current net beneficiaries would have to be implemented, or, alternatively, a considerable expan-

---

in West Germany, is a rather significant omen of the implications of EU membership requirements and of the transfers required to realise them.

[9] The Visegrad four are Hungary, Poland, Slovakia and the Czech Republic. Although five countries (the Visegrad four, less Slovakia, plus Slovenia and Estonia) are included in the first wave of enlargement, much of the analysis to date on the impact of enlargement is based on the entry of the Visegrad four.

sion in revenue would take place, which would fall mainly on northern EU taxpayers. The former is more likely. Thus, since EU farmers and poorer regions receive 80 per cent of all EU spending, most of the spending cuts would inevitably fall on these groups. This budgetary problem is likely to remain for decades. Assuming the continuing operation of the "75 per cent of the EU average income" rule for Objective 1 status, if EU income average grew by 2 per cent a year and the Visegraders' average grew by three times that, two decades would pass before the Visegraders reached the 75 per cent mark (Baldwin, 1995).

In the context of enlargement, the CAP is most problematic in its capacity to absorb budgetary funds. Agriculture is important in all the prospective new member states, but particularly in Romania, Bulgaria, Poland and Latvia, in terms of its share in GDP and national employment (Table 5.7). Also, the most important products in all countries are dairy, meat and cereals, which are the principal surplus products in the EU and although small in value terms relative to EU production, the potential is there to add very significantly to the surpluses under the current CAP regime. Lowe and Ward (1998, p. 469) correctly conclude that: "The commitment to enlarging the European Union and the next round of the world trade negotiations mean that the CAP is economically and politically unsustainable in its current form."

The Commission has embarked on a two-pronged initiative to address enlargement and the budgetary implications of CAP, addressing, on the one hand, agricultural development in the CEEC and, on the other hand, the reform of CAP. The Agricultural Strategy Paper (European Commission, 1995) concluded that the CEECs are less in need of high price and income support for their farmers than of targeted assistance for restructuring, modernisation and diversification. It, therefore, recommended pre-accession assistance in the form of modernisation programmes, technical assistance and access to the EU's market. Internally in the EU the main pressure is on continuing the CAP reforms commenced in

1992, reducing agricultural prices to world market levels, emphasising an integrated approach to rural development and providing farmers with direct income support linked to environmental improvements. Agenda 2000 has reinforced this approach resulting in a number of legislative proposals[10] due to come into effect in the year 2000 (European Commission, 1998). This strategy will reduce the budgetary pressure on the EU, raise the international competitiveness of the sector and, at the same time, avoid the prospect of sudden price increases in agricultural products to new members. The latter is critical, given that 30-60 per cent of household income in these countries is spent on food products.

Budgetary reform pressure, resistance to CAP reform and the significance of CEEC agriculture, from the viewpoint both of the producer and the consumer, suggest that the EU will negotiate a long transition period for agriculture for the new member states.

At the Essen European Council in December 1994, the EU decided to establish a comprehensive strategy for preparing the associated countries of Central and Eastern Europe which have Europe Agreements for accession to the EU (European Commission, 1996a). The pre-accession strategy is a comprehensive policy, encompassing all forms of co-operation and focusing them on realising the goal of membership (European Commission, 1996b).

The Europe Agreements, the "structured dialogue" and the Phare Programme are the main tools of this strategy. Europe Agreements provide the means whereby the EU offers associated countries trade concessions and other benefits which are normally

---

[10] The main proposals cover a) revised council regulations for the common market organisations for cereals, arable crops, beef and milk; b) a revised council regulation on olive oil; c) a "horizontal" regulation to introduce some common provisions on cross-compliance with environmental conditions, modulation of payments linked to the labour force and an element of degressivity in large payments; d) a revision to EAGGF Financing Regulation; and e) a new regulation covering rural development measures financed by the EAGGF both from its Guidance Section (in Objective 1 areas) and from the Guarantee Section (elsewhere).

associated with full membership of the EU. The "structured dia-logue" is an innovation in the EU's approach to prospective members, enabling them to become more involved in the EU's activities prior to accession — the associated countries participate regularly in EU ministerial meetings, and join EU leaders at meetings of the European Council (European Commission, 1996c). The "structured dialogue" will familiarise the associated countries with the process of decision-making and the institutional set-up of the EU. The Phare Programme is an EU initiative which provides grant finance to support its partner countries during the process of economic transformation and strengthening of democracy. The programme provides technical know-how, including policy ad-vice and training, for its partner countries. Phare is the main fi-nancial instrument in support of the pre-accession strategy, and in 1995/6 the programme was reoriented towards the objective of integration. For the period 2000–2006 the Phare Programme will focus on accession by setting two priority aims, which were en-dorsed by the European Council at Luxembourg: the reinforce-ment of administrative and judicial capacity (about 30 per cent of the overall amount), and investments related to the adoption and application of the *aquis* (about 70 per cent) (European Commis-sion, 1998). The pre-accession strategy also contains a number of measures which support the process of economic reform and thereby the successful integration of the associated countries into the EU (European Commission, 1996b).

Anxious to bring more drive to the pre-accession period, the Commission has recommended a new framework, an Accession Partnership with each applicant country, and a new system of planning and assessing each country's performance (European Commission, 1997a). This new framework is known as the rein-forced pre-accession strategy, and is part of Agenda 2000. Acces-sion Partnerships will bring together all forms of assistance to the countries of Central and Eastern Europe within a single frame-work.

TABLE 5.7: THE IMPORTANCE OF AGRICULTURE IN THE CEEC, 1995

| Countries | Value of Agricultural Production | | Share of National Employment | Main Products |
|---|---|---|---|---|
| | *Ratio of CEEC to EU (%)* | *Share of National GDP (%)* | | |
| Bulgaria | 1.29 | 12.6 | 22.0 | cereals, dairy, meat |
| Estonia | 0.13 | 7.0 | 7.0 | dairy, meat, cereals |
| Czech Republic | 1.79 | 5.2 | 6.3 | cereals, dairy, meat, oilseeds, vegetables |
| Hungary | 1.97 | 7.2 | 8.0 | cereals, dairy, oilseeds, meat, vegetables, fruit |
| Latvia | 0.11 | 9.9 | 18.0 | dairy, cereals, potatoes, meat |
| Poland | 5.39 | 6.6 | 27.0 | cereals, dairy, meat, fruit, potatoes |
| Lithuania | 0.12 | 9.4 | 24.0 | dairy, meat, vegetables |
| Romania | 4.39 | 20.0 | 34.4 | cereals, meat, dairy, fruit, vegetables |
| Slovakia | 0.68 | 5.8 | 7.5 | cereals, diary, meat, vegetables |
| Slovenia | 0.56 | 4.3 | 7.0 | cereals, dairy, meat, potatoes |

*Source:* European Commission (1997b).

Agenda 2000 also generated a number of legislative proposals in relation to pre-accession aid. The instruments for pre-accession aid proposed in Agenda 2000 comprise:

- A co-ordination Regulation co-ordinating the three pre-accession aid instruments to avoid any overlapping;

- An agricultural pre-accession strategy;

- An instrument for structural policies pre-accession (ISPA); and

- The existing Phare Regulation will continue to provide pre-accession aid (European Commission, 1998).

Actions under the three pre-accession aid instruments will be integrated into the Accession Partnerships with the candidate countries to ensure coherence. The overall amount of pre-accession aid will total 3 billion ECU a year for the period 2000-2006, more than double the amount available in 1999 (European Commission, 1998).

It is clear, however, from the Cardiff Summit that considerable negotiation must ensue before the budgetary position for the next planning period is clarified. In addition to the task of reducing EU policy expenditures in order to accommodate enlargement within a capped budget, there were evident signals that the budgetary funding mechanisms must also be addressed. In particular, the German Chancellor, Mr H. Kohl, demanded a reduction in the net German contribution to the EU budget (Frank Millar, 1998).

Enlargement of the EU will, of course, give voting rights to the new members and, thus, a role in internal decision-making. This will, inevitably, reduce the voting rights of existing members. Decisions are arrived at through a weighted majority. But, of course, not all countries or regions have the same interests, and the strength of alliances along lines of common interest determines the eventual outcomes. Alliances in the past have been formed between countries with peripheral or problem regions, particularly with respect to net transfers to support economic development, through, for example, the Structural Funds. The new countries joining will be well down the scale in terms of development. Clearly these two blocks will be in direct conflict with respect to the sharing out of sectoral, structural and social funds. However, under current rules Visegraders would receive more Council of Minister votes than Ireland, Greece, Spain and Portugal put together. The implications for the latter group of countries of the entry of the most advanced of the CEEC into the EU is clear, first of all, in terms of competing interests and then in terms of the voting power in deciding the outcome.

## 8. CONCLUSIONS

The last enlargement of the EU, with the entry of Austria, Finland and Sweden had no serious distribution effects, since the income level and the overall level of economic development in all these countries was above the EU average. The new enlargement is very different. There are significant labour market, trade, investment and budgetary implications of enlargement. The less developed and peripheral regions of the EU are particularly sensitive to these effects.

Enlargement is also going to pose significant difficulties for the CEEC countries in bringing about reforms whereby their economies are in line with the requirement of members. Radical restructuring of the political, institutional, administrative and industrial systems must take place. Their fiscal, monetary and sectoral policies must also be consistent with the requirement of a market economy and the particularities of the EU. This will inevitably bring hardships, particularly in relation to the social support system, and very significant income redistribution effects are inevitable. The transition period is going to be long and painful.

There are compelling arguments, from both the side of the EU and the CEEC for enlargement. From the EU side, there is the humanitarian aspect of assisting with the economic development of its neighbours; there is the security aspect; and there is the long-term trade, investment and economic development aspect. From the CEEC side, there is the strengthening of the democratic process, the security aspect, the likely budgetary transfers and the labour market, trade and investment advantages. These long-term advantages from both sides, as well as the long historical links between East and West Europe, are likely to override any short term disadvantages.

A clear commitment has now been given to enlargement and it will go ahead. However, given the high level of economic, social and political incompatibility, full membership will only be accorded to the new candidates over a long period. Nevertheless, enlargement will have significant impacts on many aspects of the EU economy, including the budgetary requirements. At the same time, the internal strength and dynamic of the Union can only be guaranteed through maintaining economic, social and political cohesion. Enlargement, therefore, and the new demands which it places on the Union must be balanced with the imperative of continuing internal cohesion.

## REFERENCES

Baldwin, R.E. (1995): "The Eastern enlargement of the European Union", *European Economic Review*, Vol. 39, No. 3/4.

Brocker, J. and Jager-Roschko, O. (1996): "Eastern Reforms, Trade and Spatial Change in the EU", Papers in Regional Science, Vol. 75, No. 1.

Cuddy, M.P. (1997): "Towards Regional development Programmes in Russia" in EC Commission, *European Integration and Economic Transition: Challenges for Regional Policy*, Brussels: Tacis Information Office.

Central Statistics Office (1996): Personal Communication, Dublin: Trade Section.

Edwards, S. (1991): "Capital Flows, FDI and Debt-Equity Swaps in Developing Countries" in Siebert, Horst (eds.) *Capital Flows in the World Economy*, Tübingen: J.C.B. Mohr.

Gale Research Inc. (1995): *Encyclopaedia of the Nations of Europe*, 8th Edition, New York: Worldmark Press Limited.

EIU (1995): "Business Report", 3rd Quarter, 1995, London: Economist Intelligence Unit Limited.

European Commission (1994): *Europe 2000+: Co-operation Territorial Development*, Luxembourg: European Communities.

European Commission (1995): "Study on Alternative Strategies for the Development of Relations in the Field of Agriculture between the EU and the Associated Countries with a View to the Future Accession of these Countries", Agricultural Strategy Paper, Brussels.

European Commission (1996a): "Enlargement: Questions and Answers", Information Memo (96/78), Brussels.

European Commission (1996b): "The European Union's Pre-Accession Strategy for the Associated Countries of Central Europe", Brussels.

European Commission (1996c): "Enlargement of the European Union", (GA/cdv D(96)), Brussels.

European Commission (1997): "The Week in Europe", The European Commission Representation in Ireland, Dublin, 18 July 1997.

European Commission, DGX (1997a): "Agenda 2000: For a Stronger and Wider Union", Information Programme for the European Citizen, Brussels.

European Commission (1997b): "Commission's Opinions concerning the Application for Membership to the European Union (various)", Brussels.

European Commission (1998): "Agenda 2000: The Legislative Proposals", (ip/98/258), Brussels.

Eurostat (1994): *Statistical Yearbook*, Regions, Luxembourg: Office for Official Publications of the European Communities.

Eurostat (1995a): *Europe in Figures*, Fourth Edition, Luxembourg: Office for Official Publications of the European Communities.

Eurostat (1995b): "European Union Trade with Central and Eastern European Countries (CEEC)", *Statistics in Focus* (External Trade), No. 7, Luxembourg: Office for Official Publications of the European Communities.

Eurostat (1996a): "European Union Trade with Central and Eastern European Countries (CEEC)", *Statistics in Focus* (External Trade), No. 7, Luxembourg; Office for Official Publications of the European Communities.

Eurostat (1996b): *Basic Statistics of the European Union*, 33rd Edition, Luxembourg: Office for Official Publications of the European Communities.

Fischer, M. M. and Johannson, M. (1996): "Opening up International Trade in Eastern European Countries: Consequences for Aggregate Trade Flows in the Rhine-Main-Danube Area", Papers in Regional Science, Vol. 75, No. 1.

Helpman, E. (1981): "International Trade in the Presence of Product Differentiation, Economics of Scale and Monopolistic Competition: A Chamberlain-Hecksher-Olin Approach", *Journal of International Economics*, Vol 11, No. 3/4.

Hitchens, D., Wagner, K., Birnie, E., Hamar, J. and Zemplinerova, A. (1996): "Prospects for manufacturing in the Czech Republic, Hungary and East Germany", *Moct-Most, Economic Policy in Transitional Economics* Vol 6, No. 2.

Krugman, P. (1991): "Increasing Returns and Economic Geography", *Journal of Political Economy*, Vol. 99, No. 3.

Krugman, P. and Obstfeld, M. (1994); *International Economics Theory and Policy*, Third Edition, New York: Harper Collins.

Lowe, P, and Ward, N. (1998): "Regional Policy, CAP Reform and Rural Development in Britain: The Challenge for New Labour", *Regional Studies*, Vol. 32, No.5

Meyer, K.E. (1995): "Foreign Direct Investment in the Early Years of Economic Transition: A Survey", *Economics of Transition*, Vol 3, No.3.

Millar, F. (1998): "Expecting Kohl to Swing Thatcher's Handbag", 15 June, *Irish Times*.

Rummel, O. (1997): "Why East Germany Failed to Become an Economic Tiger: Sobering Convergence Lessons from German Unification", *MOCT-MOST*, Vol. 7, No. 3.

Sahling, L.G. and Smith, S.P. (1993): "Regional Wage Differentials", *Review of Economics and Statistics*, Vol. 31, No. 1.

Smith, R.S. and Ehrenberg, R.G. (1994): *Modern Labour Economics: Theory and Policy*, Fifth Edition, New York: Harper Collins.

Ulman, L., Eichengreen, B. and Dickens, W.T. (1993): *Labour and Integrated Europe*, Washington, D.C.:The Brookings Institute.

Von Furstenberg, G.M. (1995): "Overstaffing as an Endgame and Prelude to the Employment Collapse in Eastern Germany", *Communist Economies and Economic Transformation*, Vol. 7, No. 3.

# 6

# SOCIAL POLICY AND THE WELFARE STATE IN EUROPE[1]

*Eamon O'Shea*

## 1. INTRODUCTION

This chapter is concerned with the development, evolution and future prospects of social policy in the European Union. The main focus is on the status of social policy in the Union and the problems associated with the harmonisation and convergence of national systems of welfare provision. While major advances have been made in the areas of the single market, monetary union, economic integration, even political union, the same cannot be said of the social dimension of integration. Whatever progress has been made in the sphere of social policy has, by and large, been confined to the labour market. The task of this chapter is to explain why progress has been so slow in developing a common approach to social policy within the Union.

Addressing this issue requires answers to a range of interconnected questions, including the following: Why has progress been confined to the labour market? Who determines the pace of progress and on what issues? Is it possible to talk about convergence of European welfare states? Is such convergence desirable? What methodologies are available to examine these issues? The exploration of each of these issues requires a good understanding

---

[1] The author wishes to thank Brendan Kennelly for comments on an early draft of this chapter.

of the nature of, and variations in, the welfare state across Europe. For that reason, there will be a major emphasis on models of the welfare state in the early stages of the chapter.

The main argument is that the solution to welfare problems in Europe lies primarily in the creation of a genuinely participative society. Currently, social policy in the EU is focused on a re-stricted range of regulatory measures located mainly within the labour market. The emphasis is on the protection of existing workers rather than the support of people excluded from main-stream economic and social life. This is a very narrow approach to social policymaking, even allowing for the constraints imposed at Community level by the opposition of the majority of the member states to a common social policy in the Union.

A comprehensive social policy would include both welfare and work dimensions. The former is, by and large, ignored in EU social policy, while the latter has been too narrowly confined to paid full-time work. The deepening of European integration will require more federal-type intervention in the area of social policy, which may include direct action on income support at EU level for people currently outside the market system. The prospect may appear somewhat far-fetched at this point in time, given the cur-rent weakness of EU social policy. However, progress on political union may depend ultimately on a wider remit for social policy within the Union.

The chapter begins with a discussion of the typologies which have been used to describe the various patterns of welfare state regimes in the European Union, including a brief discussion of social care models in the Union. The key relationship between the labour market and social protection is explored in section 2. The trade-off between efficiency and equity is fundamental to an un-derstanding of the welfare state and is crucial in the debate about the limits to EU involvement in social protection across the Community. Section 3 deals, in summary fashion, with the evolution of social policymaking in the EU, up to, and including, the Maastricht Treaty. Developments since Maastricht are discussed in section 4. An assessment of EU social policy is contained in section 5. The final section considers possible scenarios for the future development of EU social policy, including a proposal for a Community basic income scheme linked to a participative model of European citizenship.

## 2. WELFARE STATE MODELS

One approach to the basic question of what constitutes a welfare state is to agree a set of criteria for deciding when a country qualifies for the nomenclature "welfare state", given that every country has a more or less, larger or smaller, welfare sector. The criteria-setting approach can lead to problems of classification. The criteria used will quickly limit the domain of enquiry. If, for instance, social citizenship is used as the primary criterion, then comparative analysis of welfare state provision in the EU would be confined to Scandinavian countries, since most other countries would fail the universality test. This would be a very dramatic result, contradicting most of our working hypotheses on the nature of welfare state provision. On the other hand, simplifying matters by using the ratio of social expenditure to GNP as an indicator of welfare state development is equally problematic. The aggregate nature of expenditure is bound to conceal large differences in the mix of provision across countries, and the choice of some arbitrary cut-off ratio to confer welfare state status is also likely to be controversial.

Alber (1988) attempts to side-step some of these issues by examining the historical transformation of state activities. He points out the difficulties of the welfare state as a descriptive concept, given the large cross-sectional and historical variation in its definition and boundaries. He defines two different conceptions of welfare state development: one that supports existing modes of production and distribution, the other that intervenes in these processes. Using this framework, five general phases of welfare state development in Western Europe can be identified, beginning with the minimalist approach to intervention, common in the 19th century, through the various stages of welfare state provision in this century, ending with the current mix of welfare provision between the state, the voluntary sector and private sources. In a similar vein, Ploug and Kvist (1996) define welfare state development as a prolonged historical process that is not yet finished.

While historical schemata of this sort are a useful way of organising our thinking on the evolution of the welfare state, they can never fully account for the reasons behind development in particular countries. Schemes of this type hide differences in the policy process across countries. Neither do we learn much about the relationship between the development of the welfare state and political, cultural and institutional processes within countries. Welfare regimes and associate power structures have led to different forms of development at different times, which are not always captured in aggregate schemes based on the historical transformation of state activities. Not all countries follow the same pattern of development.

Esping-Andersen (1990) argues that social scientists have been too accepting of nations' self-proclaimed welfare status. At the same time, however, it is difficult to blame social scientists for this approach. The alternative is the imposition of a normative construct, based on a subjective view of the optimal coverage a welfare state should provide for its citizens. In that respect, Scandinavia is often used by pro-welfare statists as the model welfare state entity, in spite of the fact that this essentially social-democratic welfare regime only covers at best four countries, and hides divisions between constituent member countries, particularly in recent years.

The basic distinction between residual and institutional welfare regimes provides the framework for more recent attempts to categorise welfare states. In residual models, the state assumes responsibility for welfare only in the event of market, or family failure. The basis for intervention is need; coverage is restricted to marginal groups unable to provide for themselves, and without the support of their families. In contrast, the institutional welfare regime is likely to be more universal in its application, even if sometimes confined to an industrial achievement model which complements the market economy. These basic distinctions are useful because they can be used to classify existing welfare states as either residual or institutional models, as well as mapping the evolution of systems from residual to universal. The problem with the Titmuss dichotomy is the general nature of the classification system, which makes it very difficult to pick-up differences across countries with respect to both evolution and provision. This has led to the development of more finely tuned ideal typologies which seek to locate welfare state provision within three, or four, fields, each one characterised by its own objectives, means, provision, financing and outcomes (Titmuss, 1974; Esping-Andersen, 1990; Leibfried, 1992; Ploug and Kvist, 1996; Ferrera, 1996).

The most influential work on the categorisation of welfare states has been that of Esping-Andersen (1990). He identified three distinct welfare models as follows:

- The Scandinavian, or social democratic, model has a high degree of universality and institutionalisation, and is essentially financed by general taxation. The emphasis is on social rights, with the state the primary agency for ensuring citizenship. The welfare state is inclusive, covering workers in both market and non-market activities. The de-commodification of social goods is, by and large, complete in this model. At the same time, however, the labour market continues to be the primary focus for participation. The state ensures participation through an emphasis on training and education and significant public intervention in the labour market. The state has been the employer of first resort, especially for women;

- The continental, or "state corporate" model is a selective welfare state which is financed mainly by the contributions of employers and employees, through work-based social insurance schemes. The entitlement to social rights is based on an attachment to the paid labour force. People outside the labour market are left to depend on support from families, mutualities, voluntary organisations and the Church (Jarre, 1991). The principle of subsidiarity underpins the selectivity implicit in this system, which has been described by Van Kersbergen (1995) as one of "social capitalism". Because social protection is tied very much to employment status, the redistributive impact of the welfare state is weak. Esping-Andersen (1990) points to the preservation of status differentials as a fundamental aim of the selective welfare state. Germany and Austria are examples of countries with strong conservative and selective traditions in welfare state provision; and

- The liberal Anglo-Saxon model. This is closest to the residual model identified by Titmuss. The system is a combination of modest universality and extensive means-tested assistance. The welfare state is a compensator of last resort. Need is the principle on which the state intervenes on a discretionary basis. Intervention is necessary in order to support people unable to insure themselves, either because they are not attached to the labour market, or because they belong to a high-risk group. Benefits paid by the state are usually flat rate and are financed out of general taxation. This model has been most associated with the United Kingdom.

Leibfried (1992) and Ferrera (1996) have added a fourth category — the "Latin rim" countries, i.e. the southern countries of Western Europe (Greece, Portugal, Spain, Southern Italy) — to Esping-Andersen's three worlds. In these countries, the state does little to regulate employment, or to redistribute income. The solution to traditional welfare state problems has been located primarily in civil society. The emphasis is on family, the Church, and private charity. Leibfried describes the Southern Europe welfare state as rudimentary, but in the process of catching up, in that many of these countries have made promises towards a modern welfare state in their constitutions. In all of these countries, social expenditure has been increasing in recent years. Notwithstanding these changes, social protection in Southern Europe is nowhere near universal, but continues to be mainly categorical and work-focused. For those who are covered, social protection can be generous; for those without protection, coverage is fragmented and weak. For instance, the Greek welfare system lacks any kind of universal minimum income support scheme, except for non-contributory benefits available to old age pensioners (Katrougalos, 1996). Similar fragmentation is evident in other southern countries.

The main criticism of these typological frameworks centres around the difficulty of representing the myriad of social structures, both within and among countries, using only three, or four, distinct classifications. Mishra (1993), for example, points to two different traditions in liberalism. Classical liberalism is associated with a *laissez-faire* philosophy and is best illustrated by reference to the United States. An alternative liberal tradition is firmly rooted in the collectivist philosophies of Keynes and Beveridge. Both of these traditions have influenced the current mix of welfare provision in the United Kingdom. Consequently, that country can be characterised as neo-liberal with respect to social assistance, but social democratic with respect to health care.

The tendency for some countries to fit into more than one regime is not confined to the United Kingdom. The Netherlands, for example, is characterised by a combination of selective and comprehensive provision. Similarly, the welfare system in Ireland has elements of all three regimes, comprehensiveness (general taxation financing), corporatism (social partnerships, associated mainly with labour market participation) and residualism (means-tested, social assistance programmes). Kosonen (1994) also points to differences within regimes. For instance, Sweden is different to the other countries included in the social democratic model. Differences also exist between countries normally included in the continental corporatist model, particularly between Germany, the Netherlands and Switzerland.

Kemeny (1995) has been critical of the absence of theories of power in Esping-Andersen's discussion of welfare state regimes. He claims that some of the ambiguity about the classification of social structures would be removed if more attention was paid to power relationships in different welfare societies. For Kemeny, working class hegemony is the main determinant of the development of national welfare state systems. Other criticisms of Esping-Andersen's work have focused on the male-centred definition of commodification, which tends to lead to a residual treatment of gender issues in welfare state classification (Taylor-Gooby, 1991; O'Connor, 1993). This may explain the absence of any treatment of social care provision, which is mainly the domain of women, in Esping-Andersen's typology.

These problems have led some commentators to reject the typological approach on the basis that it conceals more than it reveals. For example, Cousins (1997) argues that Ireland is not capable of being understood within the core-centric and modernist approach chosen by Esping-Andersen because so much is left out of the explanation, particularly local-specific elements related to history, culture, and religion. In most cases, the circumstances and issues arising from the interaction of these forces are unique to each country. In addition, different European countries are at different stages of economic development, and this is reflected in the shape and form of their welfare provisions.

On the other hand, the recent economic crises of the 1970s and 1980s has brought about some convergence in welfare state coverage and provision, particularly in Northern Europe. The influence of the various economic crises can be seen in the tendency of most systems to reduce both the level and duration of social protection, particularly for unemployed workers. There has been a concern about the creation of a dependency culture with respect to welfare, and criticism of what is perceived as excessive social expenditure in most Northern European countries. While it would be wrong to suggest that recent economic changes have led to the abandonment of welfare ideals, and the subsequent dismantling of the welfare state (Ploug & Kvist, 1996), they have led to a degree of downward convergence in social protection, especially between Scandinavian and Central European countries. When combined with the extension of welfare coverage in southern European countries, it is possible to identify the beginnings of a convergence movement — towards rationalisation and a new welfare mix — but not necessarily involving the complete erosion of national solidarity agreements.

The analysis of welfare state regimes has been mainly confined to social protection and social transfer payments. However, many life-situations, for example the care of children and the care of old people, are mediated outside of, as well as within, the market-state nexus (Alber, 1995). Problems are resolved within families, between families and the voluntary sector, and between the market, state, family and voluntary sectors. There is, therefore, a much richer set of possibilities associated with social care provision than is covered by social protection.

The diversity of social care provision and the complexity of organisation make it difficult, however, to develop typologies of care, as has been done with respect to social security. There are no comprehensive international data sets on social services provision, making it difficult, therefore, to compare the various services across countries. Much of what goes under the general heading of social care, for example, care of the elderly, care of children, and care of physically handicapped people, is, by its very nature, difficult to quantify and, consequently, remains outside scrutiny and measurement (Jones, 1985). In addition, countries tend to be idiosyncratic in the way social care services are described, making it difficult to compare services across countries.

Alber (1995) explores the pattern of social care provision for old people in Europe in terms of regulatory structure, financial structure, the structure of supply, and the degree of consumer power. Based on a detailed examination of social services in three countries, Germany, Denmark and the Netherlands, Alber identifies two crucial sets of relationships in social services provision: one between Church and state, and the other between the centre and periphery. These relationships, rather than a theoretical perspective based on class cleavage, or the power relations between capital and labour, should, according to Alber, form the basis of any future analysis of variations in social care across Europe.

In a recent paper, Anttonen and Sipila (1996) explore potential models for European social care services. Their starting point, once again, is that existing typologies of welfare state provision are too narrow, since too much attention is paid to the relationship between the state and the labour market. In particular, the focus on de-commodification ignores the relationship between the state and the family and, sometimes, the subordination, and dependence, of women within family relationships. Anttonen and Sipila identify four distinct country groupings for two categories of social care consumers — children and older people. Countries with abundant social care services in both of these areas are Denmark, Sweden and Finland. Countries with scarce social care provision in both are Portugal, Greece, Spain, Ireland and Germany. Countries with abundant services for old people, but scarce services for children, are the Netherlands, Norway, and Great Britain. Countries with the alternative mix, abundant services for children, but scarce resources for elderly people, are Belgium, France and Italy. Denmark and Portugal represent the two ends of the social care continuum in Europe — Denmark representing the highest level of provision, Portugal the lowest.

There is some correspondence between the above groupings of social care provision and Leibfried's (1993) classification of income support systems. In particular, it is possible to identify both a Scandinavian universalist model and a Latin rim family care model. Beyond these groupings, classification becomes more problematic. Subsidiarity plays an important role in care of the elderly in Central Europe, particularly in Germany, but it is stretching credibility to talk in terms of a generalised continental model of elderly provision. Differences are even more pronounced in the area of services for children between the countries of continental Europe. Services for children in Belgium and France are, for instance, different from service provision in Germany and the Netherlands. Countries may also fall into more than one regime. It is possible, for instance, to identify both a residualist and family care orientation in the Irish social services mix. The welfare mix of social services provision may also change over time, as witnessed by the movement from a universalist provision to a residual system in the UK in the past two decades.

This is the context, therefore, for any discussion on European social policy. Any progress with respect to the latter must take into account the similarities and differences which exist among and sometimes within national systems of welfare coverage and provision, even if these are difficult to measure. For some people, the differences in social policy which exist across the member states of the Union are a good enough reason not to develop a common social policy for Europe. For others, it is these very differences which make it imperative that some progress is made towards the development of a common European social policy.

## 2. EMPLOYMENT, INCENTIVES AND SOCIAL POLICY[2]

The analysis up to now has focused on the identification of welfare state regimes across Europe. This task was necessary in order to highlight both the theoretical and empirical frameworks within which European social policy is formulated and implemented. It is equally important to present the basic economic arguments for and against social policy, in particular, the efficiency-equity debate as it applies to social policymaking in the area of the labour market. The work environment has been the main focus of European social policy in recent years, while the efficiency-equity debate has been the most controversial aspect of social policy in almost all European countries.

While the initial aims of social protection systems across Europe were wide-ranging and differed across countries, two objectives were common to most systems. The first concerned the alleviation of poverty and the support of people without any market resources whatsoever. There was strong support for the view that the poor in society deserved some form of institutional protection. The second objective was the provision of a secure income for workers subject to temporary financial contingencies due to unemployment, sickness or work injuries. In practice, social protection based on participation in the labour market was supported by the development of residual systems of non-contributory protection, covering people with little or no attach-

---

[2] This section is based on Kennelly and O' Shea (1997)

ment to primary labour markets. That said, the foundations of social welfare in market economies were firmly rooted in the labour market. Moreover, although nearly all countries in the European Union have initiated some changes to their social security programmes, the fundamental attachment of the welfare system to the labour market remains intact (Ploug and Kvist, 1996).

Current debates about welfare reform partly reflect how economic circumstances have changed in recent decades, particularly in the sphere of industrial production and labour market outcomes. During the 1970s and 1980s major and prolonged international recessions led to high unemployment in Europe. Unemployment became long-term for many people, thereby placing an immediate strain on systems of social protection which had been developed to deal mainly with short-term contingencies. More and more people came to rely on social assistance for long-term protection, as eligibility for social insurance came to an end, or was not available in the first instance. People in secondary labour markets, engaged in low paid, temporary or part-time work, are usually not eligible for social insurance cover at all. These changes in the labour market, linked to fragmentation and atypical work patterns, have led to gaps appearing between the provisions of the social protection system and the needs of both the employed and the unemployed.

These changes have led many commentators to question the continued viability of the modern welfare state (see Hills (1993) for a good guide to the debate). There are many diagnoses of the crisis besetting welfare states, but it is possible to identify two main areas of concern about efficiency (Esping-Andersen, 1996). First, in a world characterised by increasing international trade, globalisation, and competitiveness, there are fears that countries in Europe have fallen behind competition from Asia and from the US. Both the US and the newly industrialising countries of Asia have far less developed systems of social protection than in Europe. This has led some people to the view that poorer employment growth, and higher levels of unemployment in the European Union, relative to its main competitors, have resulted from an overly generous social protection system.

Second, some economists argue that the welfare state is a fundamental cause of unemployment (Lindbeck, 1995). Overly generous levels of social protection discourage people from looking for work, thereby destroying their incentive to support themselves and their families. Several overlapping arguments have been developed by economists on the way replacement ratios affect unemployment. First of all, high replacement ratios reduce job search activity. This not only increases unemployment duration, but it also leads to an actual or perceived decline in job skills and work habits. Second, the loss of skills by unemployed workers means that they are no longer regarded as adequate replacements for the employed labour force. Both of these theories imply that the long-term unemployed do not exert sufficient downward pressure on wages growth as required by a well-functioning labour market. A third theory suggests that income support systems serve as a wage floor below which wages cannot fall.

The real wage flexibility in the United States where wage floors are not a problem is widely cited as the main reason why employment growth has been much higher in the US than in Europe. Lindbeck argues that the disincentive effects of the welfare state grow stronger over time as it takes time for existing habits and social norms to break down. Serious benefit-dependency or "learned helplessness" may, therefore, emerge only in a long-run perspective (Lindbeck, 1995).

The key question is the empirical evidence on the relationship between unemployment and replacement ratios. The OECD has constructed a variable benefit entitlements model which takes into account replacement ratios and benefit duration. It concluded that there is considerable cross-country evidence that relative levels of benefit entitlement affect unemployment rates (OECD, 1997). Both benefit duration and replacement ratios were found to be significant causes of unemployment in another cross-country analysis by Layard *et al*, (1991). Esping-Andersen agrees that there is considerable evidence in favour of the employment effect of wage flexibility. Employment growth in the 1980s was two to three times higher in the US, Britain, Canada, New Zealand and Australia (all regarded as having relatively flexible labour markets) than in the rest of the OECD (Esping-Andersen, 1996a).

However, other studies have reached different conclusions. Atkinson (1993) acknowledges that the welfare state and the taxes necessary to finance it may have adverse consequences for economic performance but warns that the extent of such disincentives should not be exaggerated. He concludes his review of the evidence by stating that there are relatively few situations in which a disincentive effect has been clearly established and that, even where it has been established, the effects have been relatively small in size. McLaughlin (1994) concluded that out-of-work benefits have some impact on the duration of unemployment spells but that the effect is small. An earlier review by Geary concluded that "there are disincentive effects on labour supply associated with income support policies, but that . . . they are not very large" (Geary, 1989).

Overall, the theoretical basis for disincentive effects seems to be stronger than the results of empirical investigations of the presumed relationship (Barr, 1993). Where disincentive effects exist they are likely to be weak and confined to certain well-defined categories of unemployed (Atkinson and Mogensen, 1993). The danger is that in seeking to address the disincentive effect for the few, social protection for the many will be undermined, and ultimately reduced. Social protection arrangements are already under threat because European welfare systems are under financial pressure from high levels of unemployment. The deflationary impact of the Maastricht criteria, which was reinforced by the Stability and Growth Pact agreed at the 1996 Dublin summit, is also likely to constrain the future development of social protection in Europe. In these circumstances, it may be easier, but still wrong, for policymakers to cut benefits, on the basis of a presumed employment-inducing effect, leading to an overall reduction in the budget deficit.

## 4. THE EVOLUTION OF SOCIAL POLICYMAKING IN THE COMMUNITY

The remit of social policy, as defined in this chapter, includes both work and welfare issues. Work-related issues include areas such as labour-market management, labour market regulation, industrial relations and discriminatory practices. Welfare aspects of social policy cover both social protection and the various elements of social services provision in areas like health, housing and social care. If one accepts this broad definition of social policy, then the early attempts to formulate social legislation at Community level were incomplete and narrowly focused. This is not surprising since the primary objective of the Treaty of Rome was to create an economic union based on the free movement of goods, capital, labour and services among the member states. In addition, the original six member states were relatively homogeneous in terms of both economic development and institutional design, apart from the Italian Mezzogiorno. Consequently, disparities in either social conditions or social provision were not a major issue.

In the years following the Treaty of Rome, the main emphasis of social policy was on finding ways to enhance the freedom of movement of workers within the Community. The European Social Fund was used for the purpose of generating employment opportunities through the promotion of employment facilities and support for the geographical and occupational mobility of workers. Retraining and resettlement was the major focus of the fund. The resources devoted to the fund remained minuscule, however, making it difficult to achieve anything like the desired effects, particularly in terms of mobility. As Nevin (1990) points out, while the fund may have been useful, it was manifestly not a policy, and therefore could only be relied upon to make very modest gains in terms of equalising opportunities in the labour market for geographically and occupationally disadvantaged workers.

During the 1970s, the area of social policy which received most attention from the Commission was the improvement of living and working conditions, especially for women. The focus on women included the areas of equal pay, access to employment, training and promotion, and equality in respect of social security. In 1975, the Commission issued its first directive in the area of women's rights, covering the application of the principle of equal pay for men and women. The area of women's rights was to be an enduring success for Community social policy, and was a major catalyst for the progress made in the reduction of inequality in pay between men and women in many countries, including Ireland. That said, gender equality legislation was largely confined to the labour market, and did not embrace non-market equality between men and women (Meehan, 1993).

In the first half of the 1980s support began to emerge for a more regulatory social policy at Community level, particularly from France. Concern about unemployment and social division, the existence of disparities in social protection across the member states of the growing Community, and the feeling that further integration in the political and economic spheres would require a social dimension, lay behind the increased interest in social policy. The appointment of Jacques Delors as President of the Commission in 1985 was the catalyst for a more formal and sustained support for social regulation from the Commission. Delors's (1985) view was that market integration without a social dimension was "doomed to failure". He particularly favoured the concept of a "social space", within which the main social partners could negotiate and agree, through social dialogue, a mutually beneficial approach to economic and social progress.

Opposition to the social dimension remained strong, however, ranging from the view that social policy is undesirable since it undermines efficiency (as discussed in the previous section), to the view that it is unnecessary, since disparities in social provision across member states represents genuine national differences in productivity and economic development (Springer, 1992). While steadfast in their support for the single market, the British government was vocal in its opposition to any form of Community involvement in social policymaking, reflecting the free market ideology of the incumbent Conservative government, and the non-corporatist nature of the industrial relations scene in that country. It should be remembered that the focus of much of domestic policymaking in Britain, at that time, was on the deregulation of the labour market. That being the case, the British were hardly likely to support Community initiatives which they believed would restore both credibility and power to the trade union movement.

The conflict between those who wanted more Community involvement in social policy and those who wanted less came sharply into focus during negotiations on the Social Charter. The charter was originally intended as a Citizens' Charter, but this was changed to a Workers' Charter to allow progress to be made in the negotiations. Many of the proposals contained in the final version are watered-down versions of earlier proposals which were not acceptable to some of the member states, particularly the British (Blackwell, 1990). After protracted debate, the Social

Charter was signed by all the member states, except the United Kingdom, at the end of 1989.

The charter asserted the rights of workers in the following areas: freedom of movement, employment and remuneration, improvement of living and working conditions, social protection, freedom of association and collective bargaining, vocational training, equal treatment for men and women, information, consultation and participation for workers (Social Europe, 1990). In addition, the charter covered the protection of children and adolescents, the elderly and disabled persons. The right of the Community to intervene in any of these areas was, however, subject to the principle of subsidiarity. Member states retained primary responsibility for promoting the rights enumerated in the charter. Member states had, of course, considerable discretion in this regard, given the solemn-declaration status of the charter, which meant that it was non-binding on individual countries.

The British Prime Minister at the time denounced the charter as Marxist in both content and intention. The labelling of the document as Marxist was quite a rhetorical feat given how much the document had been watered-down in a forlorn attempt to get the British to sign it. The employers group, the Union of Industries of the European Communities (UNICE) also objected to the document on the basis that it sought to engage the Commission in areas best left to national competencies. The European Trade Union Confederation (ETUC), although generally welcoming the emphasis on workers' rights, was critical of the legislative ambiguity of the document. There was a gap between some of the objectives contained in the charter and the powers available under existing legislation to carry these out (Watson, 1993). In addition, some of the provisions in the charter already fell within the legislative competency of the Community, but had not received the attention necessary to bring them into force.

Notwithstanding these criticisms, and not surprisingly, the Social Charter formed the basis of the Social Chapter of the Maastricht Treaty. In the lead-up to the treaty, social policy was, however, treated very cautiously and conservatively by almost everyone, including the European Commission. The prize of monetary union was much too great for it to be threatened by a failure to agree a comprehensive integration package, including action on social policy. The ongoing hostility of the British to any form of a European social dimension meant that further compromise was inevitable. In the end, British opposition forced the Social Chapter outside of the main body of the treaty, leaving many unanswered questions about the legal status of the provisions of the chapter.

British opposition also succeeded, once again, in diluting the content of the chapter. As Falkner (1996) relates: "what should have been changes to Articles 117-122 of the EEC Treaty were, in a last minute compromise, put into a Protocol annexed to the new treaty," without restoring any of the more innovative aspects of the proposals, which had previously been resisted by the British. In the same way as the Social Charter had been watered-down to suit the British, who, in the event, did not sign, so also was the protocol diluted in an effort to keep the British on board. Once again, this strategy failed, as the British invoked an opt-out clause which meant that they were not subject to the provisions of the Social Chapter, unless by choice.

There are three important issues arising from the provisions of the chapter. The first issue of significance is the extension of Community competencies to a wider range of social policy areas than had previously been attempted. These include working conditions, information and consultation of workers, equality between the sexes with respect to labour market opportunities, and the integration of people excluded from labour markets. The second important development is the acceptance of majority voting for a much wider range of issues. The European Union is now empowered to legislate by qualified majority vote in the following areas: health and safety, working conditions, equality between men and women in the workplace, information and consultation of workers, and the integration of excluded social groups into the labour force. While a number of important areas continue to require unanimity in decision-making, most notably the areas of social security, redundancy procedures and the funding of job creation, and some items remain off-limits entirely, most notably pay, the rights of association, and the right of workers to resort to strikes, important flexibility has been attained with respect to the decision-making process in the Council.

The third major development is the introduction of new patterns of corporatist decision-making. Falkner (1996) outlines three layers of participation for the social partners. First, a member state may hand over joint responsibility to employers and workers for the implementation of directives agreed under the Maastricht protocol. Second, the Commission has now a legal obligation to consult both sides of industry before submitting proposals in the policy field. Third, the social partners may initiate negotiations to reach agreement on social issues, independently of the member states, which may then be turned into EU law by the Council. Rhodes (1992) refers to the move towards social partnership at European level as "the breach in the employers' defences that the unions have been looking for".

The issue of the significance of the Social Agreement contained in the Protocol to the Maastricht Treaty is still not resolved. For some people, Maastricht contains "the potential to be a watershed in the evolution of the EU's social policy role" (Hall, 1994; Falkner, 1996). Others are more circumspect. Streeck (1995) notes the continued opposition of employers to a supranational system of negotiation. Kosonen (1994) also points to the limits placed on Community intervention in social policy by the principle of subsidiarity. Under the terms of new Article 3B of the Maastricht

Treaty on subsidiarity, the EU is authorised to act only when its objectives can be better achieved by action taken at Community level than by the action of the member states. Subsidiarity thus sets limits on social regulation at Community level. Hantrais (1995) supports this view, suggesting that by the formal adoption of subsidiarity into the treaty, "member states seemed to be confirming their continued reluctance to develop an overarching social policy which might impinge on national sovereignty".

## 5. POLICY POST-MAASTRICHT

The publication of the White Paper on European Social Policy (European Commission, 1994) was an attempt to signal the place of social Europe in the overall process of integration. The White Paper is much more explicit on the goals and objectives of European social policy than the Green Paper that preceded it. It is a prescriptive document, detailing a number of specific proposals for future progress on social issues, and is heavily influenced by the White Paper on Growth, Competitiveness and Employment (European Commission, 1993). The context for both documents is the competitiveness of the Union in an increasingly globalised economy (Kuper, 1994). The critical issue is the balance between social protection, competitiveness and employment creation. The overriding concern of the Commission is to improve job creation through greater flexibility in the labour market. Social policy is expected to play a key role in achieving a more participative society primarily through the market economy, but also through developments in the social economy.

The emphasis on employment, within the overall framework of the monetary union project, means that conventional social policy issues are underemphasised in the White Paper. There is no attempt to harmonise social policy across the Community. The emphasis is on minimum standards, reflecting the view that low social standards should not be used as an instrument of unfair economic competition. The social dumping argument is an old one, and reflects the concern that economies with low real wages and low social protection may have a competitive advantage over economies with higher wages and higher levels of social protection (Adnett, 1995). The main instruments for the implementation of a minimum-standards approach are co-operation, co-ordination and information. There is no support in the White Paper for a wide-ranging programme of legislative reform. Co-ordination rather than explicit harmonisation of legislation is the preferred approach. If convergence is to happen it will be through voluntary means.

The reluctance of the White Paper to sanction a new wide-ranging programme of social legislation meant that it was inevitable that the Social Action Programme that followed it would also be conservative in its approach to Community intervention in the social field. There are two further reasons for the slow-down in social action in recent years. First, the social partners are now more closely involved in the formulation of any new legislative measures. The new Action Programme, through structures like the Forum on Social Policy, is also more participative than previous programmes, and reflects a move towards wider consultation on the form and direction of social policy. This inevitably slows down the process of decision-making in the hope of making the implementation process easier later on, should agreement be reached between workers and employers. Second, the Commission is now paying much more attention to the application of existing European legislation at national level. The emphasis is now on the full implementation of proposals already agreed under existing legislation. This strategy has yielded two significant agreements — the agreement on parental leave reached in 1995, and the agreement on part-time workers reached in 1997.

The Amsterdam Treaty does not significantly deepen the policy competence of the EU in the field of social policy. The treaty is noteworthy, however, for the decision of the new Labour government of the United Kingdom to opt in to the agreement on social policy which was attached by protocol to the Maastricht Treaty. The concentration of social policy is, however, once again, mainly confined to the labour market, due to concerns about high levels of unemployment across Europe. Measures for the harmonisation of social protection across Europe are again absent from the treaty. Similarly, wide-ranging measures to deal with social exclusion are also missing, although, significantly, the competence on combating social exclusion now comes under qualified majority voting. This change should speed up decision-making in this area.

What is surprising is that the Amsterdam Treaty does not formally acknowledge the negotiated consensus approach to economic and social decision-making which is a feature of many countries in the EU. The Netherlands and Ireland are good examples of the rise of competitive corporatism in Europe in recent years, with beneficial effects on economic growth and industrial harmony. While there is some legitimate concern that social partnership has not led to major advances for European workers in terms of pay, or a better social wage, incorporating increased expenditure on pensions, health care and education, corporatism in Europe has ensured an enduring role for trade unions in a single currency Europe. While, for some people, this has been a largely defensive role (Teague, 1998), the fact remains that Europe has provided a forum for union issues at a time when the trade union movement was under threat in some of the member states. Opposition to organised labour remains, of course, which is why more progress has not been made in formalising social agreements within EU treaties. The recent failure to formalise a social dialogue within the Amsterdam Treaty is particularly damaging for vulnerable social groups who, very often, face a double exclusion, that of being outside the formal political process and national partnership arrangements.

## 6. AN ASSESSMENT OF CURRENT POLICY

Any assessment of current EU social policy must begin with a statement of what it is we expect social policy to achieve. Marshall (1975) defined social policy as the use of "political power to supersede, supplement, or modify operations of the market system in order to achieve results which the economic system would not achieve on its own". Based on this definition, there is a social policy in the European Union. Achievements in the areas of labour mobility and health and safety, the existence of an embryonic collective bargaining system, together with various market-making regulations are evidence of a supranational exercise of political power designed primarily to improve the operation of the market system. Yet, despite these successes, it is clear that social policy in the EU is not anywhere near as developed as social policy within individual member states. The three main treaties are largely characterised by a liberal economic philosophy (Majone, 1993); social policy remains the poor relation of economic, monetary and political union. Intervention in the social sphere, where it has developed, is mainly a consequence of practical problem-solving stemming from market integration. Indeed, the renewed concentration on employment creation may, in a perverse way, further weaken the resolve of the Community to initiate a common European policy on social issues. European labour markets are already considered to be inflexible and, therefore, a barrier to employment, making it unlikely that any improvements in social protection will be sanctioned at a broad European level.

There is no role for the redistribution of income in the social policy of the European Union. Transfers, where they occur, are confined to inter-regional flows, based on the operation of the

Structural Funds. The emphasis is on place rather than people. Funds are used to deal with differences in economic development across regions, without reference to the economic security of individuals within these regions. Redistribution of income is left to the member states who retain control over national systems of social protection. As a consequence, a crucial and defining component of social policy, redistribution of income, remains outside the sphere of influence of the EU.

If one looks beyond an activist social policy, into the regulatory spheres of both the Commission and the European Court of Justice (ECJ), a different picture emerges, albeit one still limited largely to work-related issues. Pierson and Leibfried (1995) argue that decisions emanating from the ECJ have seriously eroded the sovereignty of national welfare states. The pro-integration sympathies of the ECJ have led to the widening of Community competence, despite national objections to Community encroachment into labour-market areas. The broadening of ECJ decisions to include freedom of services may, in the future, have even more significance for the evolution of Community social policy. The extension of freedom of movement to both consumers and producers of services in areas like health care, education, and insurance, may eventually lead to the harmonisation of national policies in these important welfare-related areas.

Majone (1993) makes a good argument for limiting EU social policy to the regulatory domain. Taking a pragmatic approach, Majone first of all cites the practical issue of the small size of the current EU budget at 1.3 per cent of EU GDP. Quite simply, the Union does not have, and will not have in the foreseeable future, the financial resources required by the modern welfare state. In these circumstances, regulation is the most cost-effective approach to social policymaking in the EU. Regulatory costs are low, while their impact resonates throughout the Community, forcing employers, employees, consumers and producers to take cognisance of their impact. According to Majone, regulation is as far as member states are prepared to go, may be as far as they can go at present, given the heterogeneous nature of the communities that make up the Union.

Heterogeneity of both social structures and provision is the key constraint in developing an elaborate common approach to social policy in the Community. The existing diversity of national welfare states, which is linked to differences in economic development among member states, makes harmonisation very difficult. There are two other reasons why the domain of social policy is likely to be limited to market issues. First, the fragmentation of political institutions, allied to the multi-faceted nature of decision-making at EU level, makes it easier to sustain non-decisions than to agree on models for social progress (Leibfried and Pierson, 1995). Second, the absence of social democratic hegemony makes it less likely that a balanced social corporatism will develop, thereby undermining the possibility of an extension of social rights into areas opposed by capital. In this regard, Caporaso (1996) argues that whereas new transnational spaces have been created for capital beyond the boundaries of the state, opposing forces of organised labour are not always as prevalent, and if they are present, they are not as organised or as strong as capital.

## 7. FUTURE DIRECTIONS

Such pessimism should not stop us speculating on potential scenarios for the future development of social policymaking within the Union. There is no doubt that the most likely scenario is the continuation of the current market-based, work-centred, regulatory model of social progress. The strong support for flexibility and competitiveness apparent in recent Commission documents reinforces the view that social policy is likely to remain residual to economic and monetary concerns. While the Commission will continue to make progress in the setting of minimum standards of social protection, both as a necessary counterfoil to the problem of social dumping, and as a symbol of social solidarity across the Community, it is unlikely to go beyond this minimalist approach. Indeed, how far it will get in reaching this objective will depend on the evolution of social corporatism within the Community, and the relative strengths of labour and capital in the social partnership process. Interference in the labour market is always strongly resisted by employers, as witnessed by the continuing opposition to minimum wage proposals in this country and in Great Britain, and the difficulty some employers have in accepting the 48 hours maximum working week directive.

Variations to the minimum standards model have, however, been put forward as a means of encouraging convergence in social policy. One approach which has received much comment is the "social snake" scheme (Dispersyn *et al*, 1992; Begg and Nectoux, 1995). Under this scheme, agreed minimum social standards would be raised gradually towards the levels prevailing in countries with the most generous provision. Redistribution is implicit under the snake scheme, since countries with the least developed systems of social provision could not be allowed to fall further behind, should other countries decide to increase their coverage. In such circumstances, countries lagging behind would receive a transfer of resources to allow them catch up with countries upgrading their coverage. The problem with this scheme, of course, is that it implies redistribution from "upgrading" countries to member states with weak provision, thus involving a type of double-taxation for people living in the "upgrading" countries. It may also involve a moral hazard aspect, since countries with the least developed social systems may not upgrade voluntarily, waiting instead for financial leverage from other member states as part of the "social snake" process.

Another proposal, put forward by Pieters and Vansteenkiste (1993), is the so-called "Thirteenth State", a scheme to create a system of social protection at supranational level, primarily for migrant workers. The Thirteenth State would aim to supplement rather than supplant national systems of protection. The latter would operate alongside the new transnational system. The value of the Thirteenth State is that it would provide formal recognition of the social dimension associated with the freedom of movement of workers in the Community. It would eliminate much of the complexity currently associated with labour mobility in the Union, by providing social insurance cover for migrant workers. For all the merits of a transnational social insurance system, many practical problems would have to be overcome before the scheme could be introduced. Begg and Nectoux (1995) list the difficulties with the scheme as follows: the danger of cherry-picking, meaning the likelihood that the scheme would be pitched at better-off clients; double contribution issues for employees; differentiated contribution problems for employers; ultimate underwriting responsibilities for the scheme; and finally, the merits of the scheme over purely private arrangements.

There have been other proposals, at various times, suggesting a pan-European approach to welfare policies involving redistribution of income from people in richer countries to people in poorer countries. Indeed, a proposal for a European-wide system of unemployment insurance was suggested as far back as the MacDougall (1977) report. The problem with the latter proposal is that serious redistribution questions arise if it were to be implemented. The reality at present is that solidarity is not developed enough to support income transfers across countries. A more recent and more radical proposal by Lipietz (1996) is for the creation of an alternative social Europe based on four key functional areas: common labour market rules; fiscal harmonisation; Keynesian demand-management; and social equity. The EU would have to gain significant new federal powers if this plan were ever to be implemented. It is unlikely, however, that the member states would ever accept the transfer of huge areas of economic and social decision-making from national governments to the European level as envisaged in the plan.

One way around this issue would be to change the focus of the redistribution objective away from income maintenance towards the concept of social quality (Berghman, 1997). The key element in formulating a new approach is the interconnectedness between participation as a economic strategy (which is consistent with the recent White Paper) and participation as a social philosophy; an approach that would both incorporate and integrate the values of efficiency, equity, solidarity and quality of life. The intellectual basis for this model can be found in the work of Sen (1992, 1993), and his characterisation of living as a combination of "beings and doings". These "beings and doings" are referred to by Sen as "functionings", and range from elementary ones such as being adequately nourished, being in good health, etc., to more complex functionings such as achieving self-respect, or being socially integrated.

Achievement with respect to "functionings" is influenced by "capabilities", reflecting the alternative combinations of functionings that a person can achieve. This implies that we should examine a person's potential, as well as their actual achievements. Using this approach, a person's position can be judged positively in terms of their level of achievement, or negatively, in terms of the shortfall *vis-à-vis* what the person could have maximally achieved. For some objectives at least, social arrangements should be organised so as to equalise the shortfall in the attainments of different individuals (Sen, 1992).

Nowhere is the distinction between performance and potential more important than in the labour market, given the importance of work in affecting the broad range of individual "functionings". Marshall (1950) argued that citizenship should be understood as a set of rights enjoyed equally by every member of society. Perhaps it is now appropriate to revise the concept of social citizenship as entailing a right to lifelong learning and training, leading to meaningful participation in society (Esping-Andersen, 1996b). This approach can be justified on several grounds, but it is primarily an equity-enhancing measure. Given the increasing divisions between households where one, or more members, have secure well-paying jobs and households subject to income insecurity, or having to rely on non-market income, the inclusion of training and education in the social welfare "package" is an attempt to equalise individual choice sets (Le Grand, 1991; Cohen, 1993). Downward wage pressure in the labour market is mainly directed at the unskilled. Lifelong learning and social investment strategies offer a positive-sum solution to the trade-off between jobs and equality, and can be designed to optimise the self-reliant capacities of individuals. The key to progress, therefore, may be the replacement of the guarantee of social protection with a new guarantee of social participation.

While an emphasis on lifelong learning and training may be a necessary condition for making the connection between participation as an economic strategy and participation as a social philosophy, it is not a sufficient condition. Concern about incentives and participation levels have led to calls in recent years for a more radical overhaul of the welfare state in the form of a basic income scheme to replace both social insurance and social assistance (Parker, 1989; Atkinson, 1992; Callan *et al*, 1994). The attraction of basic income is the freedom it would give to individuals to take up whatever work is available consistent with their own preferences, abilities and potential. The safety-net income provides a base on which to build, while eliminating both "poverty traps" and "unemployment traps". The basic income scheme would be consistent with the development of the economy away from a situation where the norm is full-time work for an entire working life. It would facilitate atypical work patterns in the sense of people working for part of each week, and of people leaving the paid labour force for part of their lives (Atkinson, 1992).

The big problem with basic income concerns the cost of introducing schemes that would provide an adequate income for recipients. One way to reduce national costs would be for the European Commission to support the introduction of a Community basic income scheme through the co-financing of national schemes. The EU's intervention in this area would be worthwhile for four main reasons. First, it would facilitate greater personal choice at the level of the individual, in keeping with the principle of subsidiarity. Second, a basic income scheme would eliminate both poverty and unemployment traps, leading to a more competitive and flexible labour market. Third, an intervention of this sort would be novel, involving the Commission in an area not already covered by existing welfare state provision, thus adding value to existing national systems of welfare coverage. Fourth, and most important, a basic income approach would be an innovative response to the new work and welfare problems currently besetting national welfare states, which have not so far been resolved by domestic policymaking. Thus, participation-enhancing and potential-attaining models may be the key to a more expanded role for the EU in social policymaking in the future.

## 8. CONCLUSION

There is nothing in recent treaties to make one optimistic that social policy will become a major issue in the ongoing process of integration. This is a cause of some concern, since it is social policy that has traditionally served to bridge the gap between winners and losers in the capitalist economic system. Currently, it is adherence to monetary indicators which determines commitment to the European project. There is an urgent need to develop and highlight the role of people in the integration process as a counter-balance to the current emphasis on economic issues. Income, work, training/education, and social care are the four person-specific pillars of social policy. For all the current emphasis on employment, these issues can never be fully developed as long as economic and monetary objectives continue to have priority over social ones. It is time to give more weight to social Europe in the integration process. Until this happens, the concept of European solidarity, currently observed only in rhetoric form, will remain elusive.

## REFERENCES

Adnett, N. (1995): "Social Dumping and European Economic Integration", *Journal of European Social Policy*, Vol. 5, No. 1, pp. 1-12.

Alber, J. (1988): "Continuation and Change in the Idea of Welfare State", *Policy and Society*, Vol. 16, No. 4, pp. 451-68.

Alber, J. (1995): "A Framework for the Comparative Study of Social Services", *Journal of European Social Policy*, Vol. 5, No. 2, pp. 131-49.

Anttonen, A. and Sipila, J. (1996): "European Social Care Services: Is it Possible to Identify Models?" *Journal of European Social Policy*, Vol. 6, No. 2, pp. 87-100.

Atkinson, A.B. (1992): "Social Policy, Economic Organisation and the Search for a Third Way", in Ferge, Z. and Kolberg, J.E. (eds.) *Social Policy in a Changing Europe*, Frankfurt am Main, Campus Verlag.

Atkinson, A. (1993): "Conclusion", in Atkinson, A. and Mogensen, G.V. (eds.), *Welfare and Work Incentives — A North European Perspective*, Oxford: Clarendon Press.

Atkinson, A. and Mogensen, G.V. (eds.) (1993): *Welfare and Work Incentives — A North European Perspective*, Oxford: Clarendon Press.

Barr, N. (1993): *The Economics of the Welfare State*, London: Weidenfeld and Nicolson.

Begg, I. and Nectoux, F. (1995): "Social Protection and Economic Union", *Journal of European Social Policy*, Vol. 4, pp. 285-302.

Berghman, J. (1997): "Social Protection and Social Quality in Europe" in Beck, W. et al (eds.), *The Social Quality of Europe*. The Hague: Kluwer Law International, pp. 221-236.

Blackwell, J. (1990): "The EC Social Charter and the Labour Market in Ireland", in Foley, A. and Mulreany, M. (eds.), *The Single European Market and the Irish Economy*. Dublin: Institute of Public Administration, pp. 350-81.

Callan, T., O'Donoghue, C. and O'Neill, C. (1994), *An Analysis of Basic Income Schemes for Ireland*, Dublin: The Economic and Social Research Institute.

Caporaso, J.A. (1996): "The European Union and Forms of State: Westphalian, Regulatory or Post-Modern", *Journal of Common Market Studies*, Vol. 34, No. 1, pp. 29-52.

Cohen, G.A. (1993): "Equality of what? On Welfare, Goods and Capabilities", in Nussbaum, M. and Sen, A. (eds.), *The Quality of Life*, Oxford: Clarendon Press.

Cousins, M. (1997): "Ireland's Place in the Worlds of Welfare Capitalism", *Journal of European Social Policy*, Vol. 7, No. 3, pp. 223-35.

Delors, J. (1985): "Preface" in Vandamme, J. (ed.), *New Dimensions in European Social Policy*, London: Croom Helm.

Dispersyn, M., Van der Vost, P., de Falleur, M., Guillaume, M., Hecq, C., Lange, B. and Meulders, D. (1992): "La Construction d'un Serpent Social Éuropeen: Étude de Faisabilité", *Revue Belge de Securité Sociale*, Vol. 36.

Esping-Andersen, G. (1990): *The Three Worlds of Welfare Capitalism*, Cambridge: Politics Press.

Esping-Andersen, G. (1996a): "After the Golden Age? Welfare State Dilemmas in a Global Economy", in Esping-Andersen, G. (eds.), *Welfare States in Transition: National Adaptations in Global Economies*, London: Sage Publications.

Esping-Andersen, G. (1996b): "Positive-Sum Solutions in a World of Trade-Offs?", in Esping-Andersen, G. (eds.), *Welfare States in Transition: National Adaptations in Global Economies*, London: Sage Publications.

European Commission (1993): *Growth, Competitiveness, Employment: The Challenges and Ways Forward into the 21st Century*, White Paper, Luxembourg: Office for Official Publications of the European Communities.

European Commission (1994): *European Social Policy: A Way Forward for the Union*, White Paper, Luxembourg: Directorate General for Employment, Industrial Relations and Social Affairs.

Falkner, G. (1996): "The Maastricht Protocol on Social Policy: Theory and Practice", *Journal of European Social Policy*, Vol. 1, pp. 1-16.

Ferrera, M. (1996): "The Southern Model of Welfare in Social Europe", *Journal of European Social Policy*, Vol. 6, No. 1, pp. 17-37.

Geary, P.T. (1989): "The Measurement and Alleviation of Poverty: A Review of Some Issues", *The Economic and Social Review*, Vol. 20, No. 4.

Hall, M. (1994): "Industrial Relations and the Social Dimension of European Integration: before and after Maastricht", in Hyman, R. and Ferner, A. (eds.), *New Frontiers in Europoean Industrial Relations*, Oxford: Blackwell.

Hantrais, L. (1995): *Social Policy in the European Union*, London: Macmillan.

Hills, J. (1993): *The Future of Welfare: A Guide to the Debate*, York: Joseph Rowntree Foundation.

Jarre, B.D. (1991): "Subsidiarity in Social Services Provision in Germany", *Social Policy and Administration* Vol. 25, No. 3, pp. 211-7.

Jones, C. (1985): *Patterns of Social Policy: An Introduction to Comparative Analysis,* London, Tavistock.

Katrougalos, G.S. (1996): "The South European Welfare Model: The Greek State, In Search of an Identity", *Journal of European Social Policy* Vol. 6, No. 1, pp. 39-59.

Kemeny, J. (1995): "Theories of Power in the Three Worlds of Welfare Capitalism", *Journal of European Social Policy*, Vol. 5, No. 2, pp. 87-96.

Kennelly, B. and O'Shea, E. (1997): "Efficiency, Values and Social Welfare Policy", *Administration*, Vol. 45, No. 2, pp. 3-20.

Kosonen, P. (1994): *European Integration: A Welfare State Perspective*, Helsinki: University of Helsinki, Sociology of Law Series.

Kuper, B.O. (1994): "The Green and White Papers of the European Union: The Apparent Goal of Reduced Social Benefits", *Journal of European Social Policy*, Vol. 5, No. 2, pp. 129-37.

Layard, R., S. Nickell and Jackman, R. (1991): *Unemployment: Macroeconomic Performance and the Labour Market,* Oxford: Oxford University Press.

Le Grand, J. (1991): *Equity and Choice*, London: Harper-Collins.

Leibfried, S. (1992): "Towards a European Welfare State? On Integrating Poverty Regimes into the European Community", in Farge, Z. and Kolberg, J.E. (eds.), *Social Policy in a Changing Europe*, Boulder, Colorado: Westview Press.

Leibfried, S. (1993): "Towards a European Welfare State?" in Jones, C. (ed.), *New Perspectives on the Welfare State in Europe*, London: Routledge.

Leibfried, S. (1994): "The Social Dimension of the European Union: En Route to Positively Joint Sovereignty?" *Journal of European Social Policy*, Vol. 4, No. 4, pp. 239-62.

Leibfried, S. and Pierson, P. (1995): "Semisovereign Welfare States: Social Policy in a Multitiered Europe" in Leibfried, S. and Pierson, P. (eds.), *European Social Policy: Between Fragmentation and Implementation*, Washington DC: The Brookings Institution.

Lindbeck, A. (1995): "Hazardous Welfare-State Dynamics", *American Economic Review*, Vol. 85, No. 2, pp. 9-15.

Lipietz, A. (1996): "Social Europe, the Post-Maastricht Challenge", *Review of International Political Economy*, Vol. 3, No. 3, pp 369-79.

McLaughlin, E. (1994): "Employment, Unemployment and Social Security", in Glyn, A. and Miliband, D. (eds.), *Paying for Inequality*, London: Rivers Oram Press.

Majone, G. (1993): "The European Community Between Social Policy and Social Regulation", *Journal of Common Market Studies*, Vol. 31, No. 2, pp. 153-70.

Marshall, T.H. (1950): *Citizenship and Social Class*, Cambridge: Cambridge University Press.

Marshall, T. H. (1975): *Social Policy*, London, Hutchinson.

MacDougall Report (1997*): Report of the Study Group on the Role of Public Finance in European Integration*, Vol. 1: General Report; Vol. 2: Individual Contributions and Working Papers, Brussels: Commission of the European Communities.

Meehan, E. (1993): *Citizenship and the European Community*, London: Sage Publications.

Mishra, R. (1993): "Typologies of the Welfare State Comparative Analyses: The 'Liberal' Welfare State", Paper presented at the Conference: Comparative Research on Welfare States in Transition, Oxford, September 9-12.

Nevin, E. (1990): *The Economics of Europe*, London: Macmillan.

O'Connor, J.S. (1993): "Gender, Class and Citizenship in the Comparative Analysis of Welfare States: Theoretical and Methodological Issues", *British Journal of Sociology*, Vol. 44, No. 3, pp. 501-19.

OECD (1997): *Implementing the OECD Jobs Strategy: Member Countries' Experience*, Paris: OECD.

Parker, H. (1989): *Instead of the Dole: An Enquiry into the Integration of the Tax and Benefit Systems*, London: Routledge.

Pierson, P. and Leibfried, S. (1995): "Multitiered Institutions and the Making of Social Policy", in Leibfried, S. and Pierson, P. (eds.), *European Social Policy: Between Fragmentation and Integration*, Washington D.C.: The Brookings Institution.

Pieters, D. and Vansteenkiste, S. (1993): "The Thirteenth State: Towards a European Community Social Insurance Scheme for Intra-Community Migrants", mimeo, Leuven: University of Leuven.

Ploug, N. and Kvist, J.(1996): *Social Security in Europe: Development or Dismantlement?*, The Hague: Kluwer Law International.

Rhodes, M. (1992): "The Future of the Social Dimension: Labour Market Regulations in post-1992 Europe", *Journal of Common Market Studies*, Vol. 30, pp. 23-51.

Sen, A. (1992): *Inequality Re-examined*, Oxford: Clarendon Press.

Sen, A. (1993): "Capability and Well-Being", in Nussbaum, M. and Sen, A. (eds.), *The Quality of Life*, Oxford: Clarendon Press.

Social Europe (1990): "The Community Charter of the Fundamental Social Rights of Workers", Chapter 2, *Social Europe* 1/90. Luxembourg: Office for Official Publications of the European Communities.

Springer, B. (1992): *The Social Dimension of 1992: Europe Faces a New EC*, New York: Praeger.

Streeck, W. (1995): "From Market Making to State Building? Reflections on the Political Economy of European Social Policy", in Zeibfried, S. and Pierson, P.

(eds.), *European Social Policy: Between Fragmentation and Integration*, Washington DC: The Brookings Institution.

Taylor-Gooby, P. (1991): "Welfare State Regimes and Welfare Citizenship", *Journal of European Social Policy*, Vol. 1, No. 2 pp. 93-105.

Teague, P. (1998): "Monetary Union and Social Europe", *Journal of European Social Policy*, Vol. 8, No. 2 pp 117-37.

Van Kersbergen, K. (1995): *Social Capitalism. A Study of Christian Democracy and the Welfare State*, London: Routledge.

Titmuss, R. (1974): *Social Policy: An Introduction*, London: Allen and Unwin.

Watson, P. (1993): "Social Policy after Maastricht", *Common Market Law Review*, Vol. 30.

# Special Districts: Federalism as Soap Opera[1]

*Brendan O'Flaherty*

## 1. Introduction

The European Union currently presents itself neither as a federal state, nor as a loose confederation of individual member states, but primarily as an Economic Community. Within the Community, relationships between the European Commission, the various governments, and the regions are determined by the principle of subsidiarity. Subsidiarity is sometimes interpreted to mean that every function should be assigned to the lowest appropriate level of government. Stated in this manner, the notion is both tautological — since "appropriate" can mean anything — and misleading since it presumes the existence of a hierarchy of governments in which some are lower than others. People thinking about the European future ought not confine their thoughts to such hierarchies.

Some people, to be sure, still think of a federal system as an orderly arrangement. A bunch of municipalities make up a county, a bunch of counties make up a province, a bunch of provinces make up a nation, a bunch of nations make up a union.

[1] This paper has grown out of a series of conversations with Alessandra Casella, to whom I am also indebted for many comments, suggestions and improvements. Parts of this work were completed while I was visiting the National University of Ireland, Galway (NUI, Galway). I am also indebted to seminar participants at NUI, Galway and Columbia.

The analogy is a tree: each branch divides neatly into several off-shoots, and each twig has a unique path back to the stump. As in a postal address or in a traditionally organised extended family, each unit fits uniquely into another unit one step up in the hierarchy. The "subsidiary" part of "subsidiarity" gets you thinking like this.

There is an alternative view — one, I will argue, that is likely to be more useful to Europe in the long run. In this view, a federal system is not a traditional family tree; it's a soap opera. Everyone has step-parents and step-siblings; kids are raised by aunts and grandparents; somebody's cousin is going to marry grandpa's ex-wife; and mom is on the couch with the gas metre reader. Special districts are the key to this alternative view of how a federal system could operate. "Special district" is an American term; loosely speaking, it refers to a unit of government that is organised for a single function, and separate from other units of government. This is not a very satisfactory definition, and I will try to improve it in section 4 below. At this point, it's easier to point to examples: regional school districts, joint sewer meetings, port authorities, housing authorities, turnpike authorities, and bridge commissions, for instance. It is the prevalence of organisations like these that spurs the view of federalism as a soap opera.

In this chapter I will ask why these organisations exist. Why can't whatever job they do be done just as well within the traditional hierarchy? Why can't governments write contracts to get these jobs done instead? And if special districts are so great, why do we have any remnants of the traditional hierarchy at all? Only by answering these questions can we see what role special districts should play in the emerging European federal system. Several groups of scholars have recently envisioned organisations like these as a key part of this system. Casella and Frey (1992: p. 644) find "functional federalism" the natural implication of both public choice theory in political economy and neo-classical public finance: "Each agent will belong to different groups, depending on the issue: a group for cultural affairs, and one for transportation, one for school programmes and one for social security, one for health care and one for telecommunications." Dewatripont *et al* (1995) also advocate things like special districts under the banner of "flexible integration", but their agents are countries rather than Casella and Frey's individuals.

I will try to place special districts within the context of the modern economic theory of organisation. To understand this theory, you have to understand "non-contractible uncertainty" — events that are unknown when a contract has to be written, and which, even when they happen, cannot form the basis of a contingency in the contract. So the first section of this chapter is background on non-contractible uncertainty and the modern economic theory of organisation. The next several sections apply this theory to political organisations in general and federalism in particular. Section 4 is about special districts and what they do well, and section 5 is about the limitations of special districts as a form of organisation. Section 6 concludes by discussing what special districts can and cannot do in a European federal system, and when they can do it.

## 2. CONTRACTS, ORGANISATIONS, AND UNCERTAINTY

Special districts and traditional local governments are both organisations, and so to think about them we need to use the tools of modern organisation theory (Williamson (1975, 1985) and Milgrom and Roberts (1992) are good references for this theory). Coase (1937) started the theory with a very simple but very powerful insight: there is no need for organisations if people can write contracts complete enough to cover every possible contingency.

To see why, think of the hallmarks of an organisation, as opposed to a group of people who just happen to be doing similar things — a crowd at a beach or at a football game, for instance.

These hallmarks are bosses — people who have discretion to tell other people what to do — vague job descriptions, and some degree of permanence. Contracts that were well enough written could eliminate all of these hallmarks. Instead of waiting around for a boss to tell you what to do, you could have negotiated an explicit contract about what you would do. Instead of vagueness, your job description would be precise. Instead of permanence, the people working in a particular place would be whoever happened to have contracts for that day.

Coase's insight, then, implies that to find out why organisations exist and take the forms that they do, you have to look at what sort of things cannot be written into contracts. You can write a contract with a milkman to deliver a quart of milk to your doorstep every Tuesday and Friday, and so you do not need to make the milkman a part of any organisation you belong to; but loving your children and showing them good examples are not easy to write contracts for, and so these activities are usually done by family members, not contractors. So the modern study of organisations starts by examining the reasons why various kinds of potentially desirable contracts cannot be written.

Of the several major categories of reasons that have been found, I will concentrate on the one called "non-contractible uncertainty". (Perhaps this category is large enough to encompass all possible reasons for contractual incompleteness, but this is a taxonomic question that need not detain me.) Uncertainty by itself is not enough to keep contracts from being written: if you don't know when it will snow, you can write a contract for snow-shovelling whenever it snows. Since the courts can find out whether it has snowed or not — the event is "verifiable" — they can easily decide whether the parties are complying with the contract.

The problem arises when courts can't determine whether an uncertain event has occurred or not. I might, for instance, want to write a contract that says that I will pay you if I find your new book interesting and enjoyable, or see that you are working hard at your job. But these events are not verifiable — without taking brain-core samples, the courts can't tell whether I really liked your book or not, and without extensive testing of glycogen depletion in your muscles they cannot tell whether you were working hard — and so no enforceable contract can make anything contingent upon them. There is scope for some form of organisation.

What does this have to do with governments and federalism? Think of constitutions as contracts. If the future contained no non-contractible uncertainty, constitutions could be complete. Whoever framed the constitutions could — and would want to — specify what would happen in each conceivable contingency. Then there would be no need for future elections or for officials with discretion (except possibly for the courts). History would just be the playing out of a script already written, and every government official just an actor mouthing lines written by the framers long ago. (This argument is developed at some length by Laffont and Tirole (1993)

So non-contractible uncertainty is responsible for the discretionary, decision-making institutions of governments that we observe — officials who have to use their judgement, voters who get to judge these officials, elections of all sorts. Thus to think about what those institutions and organisations should look like, we should think about how to resolve non-contractible uncertainty well.

## 3. GOOD MECHANISMS

What does it mean to resolve non-contractible uncertainty well? Let's start with a simple example where it's obvious that non-contractible uncertainty is not being resolved well. Suppose Abbott and Costello live in an isolated place and share a car. Some mornings Abbott gets up and feels like walking to work; other mornings he feels like driving. He doesn't know beforehand which mode he'll feel like taking and the decision is not related to the weather or the day of the week or anything observable. Mainly it depends on whether he got ready for work soon enough to have time to walk. If he wanted to take the car and it wasn't available, he might have to hurry with his breakfast. He would be a little upset, but it would be no big deal.

Costello, on the other hand, is a photographer who sometimes wants to use the car to photograph particular beautiful scenic spots in a nearby forest. Many days the weather is not good for this activity, and Costello would rather not take pictures. But when the weather is right, the pictures Costello takes are worth hundreds of pounds. Costello is an artist who can't explain what it is that makes the atmosphere right for taking these great pictures, but he knows it when he sees it. Even on days when the atmosphere isn't right, Costello sometimes likes to take a drive in the country.

Notice that this is a situation of non-contractible uncertainty. You can't write a contract that says Costello has the car when atmospheric conditions are good and Abbott has it when atmospheric conditions are bad but it's a good day for dawdling over breakfast. The courts could not enforce a contract like this. Somebody has to have discretionary control over the car.

Suppose Abbott has control over the car — maybe he leaves for work early in the morning before Costello can see what the atmosphere will be like. This is a way of resolving non-contractible uncertainty, but it is clearly a bad one. Abbot gets the car for trivial gains, and Costello loses it when it would be very valuable. Both of them could be better off if Costello had control, and paid Abbott something for the privilege. Abbott would have to walk all the time, but this is no big loss, and the money he receives would more than make up for it. Costello would have the car for all his good photo opportunities, and so he would be better off even after he paid Abbott.

This example lets us see what it means to have a mechanism that resolves non-contractible uncertainty well. A mechanism resolves non-contractible uncertainty well if there is no combination of an alternative mechanism and a set of side-payments that makes everyone better off. This is just the standard definition of Pareto optimality (*ex ante*), or of efficiency. Equivalently, if all benefits and losses involved have monetary equivalents, a mechanism resolves uncertainty well if it gives expected total benefits at least as great as those given by any other mechanism. As the Abbott and Costello example shows, this definition has bite — some mechanisms are not efficient.

Different kinds of mechanisms are efficient for different kinds of issues. Consider the issue of which sock (left or right) I put on first in the morning. I care about this issue (though not a whole lot), and, as far as I know, nobody else cares at all. So the efficient mechanism gives me total control over this decision. (This is sometimes called liberty.) It would be inefficient to let anybody else make this decision for me, or to have the matter decided by a majority vote of any group.

On the other hand, for an issue about which a lot of people have about the same level of concern, and nobody has a lot more, majority rule is the efficient mechanism. If a group of us are going to take a 300-kilometre trip together, majority rule is the best way of deciding whether to go by bus or train, provided that *ex ante* we think of both bus and train travel as being about the same, all things considered. Why? Suppose all we know is that x people want to go by train; we might know their names too but since everybody is about the same (before they make up their minds about travel mode anyway) there is no use for this information. Since we don't know about any differences between bus and train *ex ante*, the expected total benefits of going by train for these people are the same (as far as we know) as the expected net benefits that any x people would get by going by bus, if that's what they wanted. If more people want to go by bus than want to go by train, then the expected net benefits of going by bus are greater than the expected net benefits of going by train. So when this happens the mechanism should say to go by bus. Similarly, if more people want train than bus, the mechanism should say go by train. Majority rule is the only mechanism that gives both of these commands, and so it must be the only efficient mechanism.

This argument for when majority rule is efficient explains a great deal about where we might expect to see democratic mechanisms springing up in economic life. Hansmann (1988), for instance, emphasises that co-operative organisation was most likely to arise in those areas — law firms, farming cooperatives, academic departments — where participants were all about the same. Hansmann's argument just has to be clarified slightly. In what way do participants have to be just about the same? In their stake in some non-contractible, uncertain issues.

Of course, efficient resolution of non-contractible uncertainty does not require that it always be resolved either by dictatorship (like my sock issue) or by majority rule. All sorts of different majority rule mechanisms can be efficient when people's stakes differ, but no one individual has a stake bigger than all the rest together. In efficient mechanisms, bigger stakes imply greater weight. Thus, for instance, corporations ("investor co-operatives," as Hansmann calls them) are governed by elections in which investors with bigger stakes in profits get more votes. "One-share-one-vote" is efficient in this context.

Even within the same group of people, all issues need not be resolved by the same mechanism. A group of us travelling together may decide our mode of transportation by majority rule, but continue to let each individual be a dictator with respect to the order in which he or she dons socks. This is the simplest example of, and simplest argument for, federalism. Making different decisions with different mechanisms is better than making them all the same way.

### 4. FEDERALISM

Notice that this argument for federalism is quite different from the traditional Tiebout (1956) argument. That argument concerns service levels — what is produced, rather than how production is decided. It says that having a variety of local governments is good because it promotes a variety of local public goods bundles, and having a variety of local public goods bundles is good because it allows consumers with different tastes to sort themselves out among jurisdictions in such a manner that everyone is enjoying close to an optimal public good bundle. Some people like holiday celebrations and don't care much about education; others want good street-lighting and lax animal control; still others care mostly about libraries and little about police. The more different towns are around, and the more different packages they offer, the more people can be satisfied.

The Tiebout argument, however, is not really about organisation; it's about services. There's no reason why a single organisation can't produce a variety of different outputs. Ford manufactures Escorts as well as Chryslers; grocery stores sell beef as well as yoghurt; universities offer courses in both literature and physics. A single government could very easily set up different hamlets with different service mixes. New York City in fact works in something like this fashion: the major civic celebrations in the West Village are the Gay Pride and Halloween parades while the South Shore of Staten Island celebrates its Little League baseball teams; Bayside in Queens gets better leaf collection while Midtown Manhattan (where there are hardly any trees) gets its streets swept more often. The Tiebout argument doesn't explain (or even try to explain) the *organisations* we see; it's only about their outputs.

In organisational terms, then, federalism is about establishing different mechanisms to resolve different kinds of issues. Which sets of mechanisms are best depends on how the stakes in various kinds of issues are distributed. For instance, consider a region in which the population lives in several different towns. The towns are separated from each other by mountains and rivers. Most roads in each town are used only by local townspeople. However there is a single main road that leads into and out of the region. Everyone in the region, no matter where he or she comes from, uses this road. What organisations should be set up to decide how to maintain the roads? Assuming contracts cannot be written well enough to resolve all road maintenance issues, local road issues should be handled by a mechanism involving only the people of the specific town, and main road issues should be handled by a mechanism involving everyone. If everyone's stake in the roads is more or less the same, then voters in each town should vote on road maintenance in that town, and everyone in the region should vote on the main road. On the other hand, if people travelled around the region enough that residents of each town had large enough stakes in maintaining local roads in all the other towns, a purely regional government would be optimal; local governments would be a bad idea. Everybody doesn't have to be equally likely to use every road for this result; but it is necessary that no one have a stake in any road that is much smaller than anyone else's.

There are also intermediate cases. Suppose that people in each town have stakes three times larger in the maintenance of their local roads than outsiders do. Then the optimal mechanism for each town's road maintenance questions is weighted majority rule where insiders have three votes each and outsiders have one. But we don't see elections like this. However, the way I have been using to describe weighted majority rule mechanisms is only one possible way of describing them; other descriptions turn out to be closer to the mechanisms we actually observe. Suppose, for instance, that person A has four votes, person B has three votes, person C has two votes, and persons D and E have one vote each. You can describe this as weighted majority rule where six votes are required. A proposal wins if and only if it has support from at least one of the following sets of voters:

{A, B}, {A, C}, {A, D, E}, {B, C, D}, or {B, C, E}

Alternatively, consider the following committee system. A, B, and C are a committee. If a majority of this committee are for a proposal and A is part of that majority, it wins automatically. Similarly if a majority including A is opposed, it loses automatically. When A is not part of the committee majority, the matter is resolved by majority vote (one-man-one-vote) of all five voters. Under this committee system, a proposal is approved if and only if it has support from at least one of the following sets of voters:

{A, B}, {A, C}, {A, D, E}, {B, C, D}, or {B, C, E}

But this is the exact same rule for approval as weighted majority rule. So the committee system is equivalent to weighted majority rule in the sense that it always gives the same results.

Mechanisms like this are common — one level of government circumscribes the actions of another, and one group of voters is given discretion over something, but another larger group can sometimes step in. In New Jersey law, for instance, municipalities can erect traffic lights only after receiving permission from the state government, and can vacate streets only with the approval of a majority of abutting property owners. These are the kind of mechanisms that are optimal in the intermediate cases, when some people have smaller stakes than others, but those small stakes are not inconsequential.

Notice that all these results depend on non-contractible issues, not on issues per se. To see this, go back to the first case, with two layers of government, and suppose that the responsibilities of whoever maintained the main road could be very well described and written in a contract that the courts could enforce. Then the towns could just negotiate a contract with a road-maintaining company (or one of their number) and manage without a higher level of government. Is this done? Of course it is. Many, many different local governments buy firetrucks from the same few companies, and all governments buy pencils (you can hardly qualify as a government unless you have pencils), but there is no over-arching "firetruck-making government" or "pencil-making government". Good enough contracts can be written for the purchase of firetrucks and pencils; continuing oversight, discretion, and control aren't needed.

The firetruck example also demonstrates that economies of scale are not a reason for higher-level governments. Since a single efficient-sized plant can meet the firetruck-manufacturing needs of several medium-sized countries, we would expect to see a consolidation of countries under the aegis of firetruck manufacturers if economies of scale dictated how governments were set up. Economies of scale are a consideration for determining government outputs, not government organisation. Cork City and Galway City should have firetrucks that look about the same, but the decisions on how they are deployed should be made separately.

## 5. SPECIAL DISTRICTS

So far "special districts" have not appeared in the analysis. I have shown circumstances under which multiple layers of government would be optimal, but I haven't said whether one of those layers should be called a special district. To do this, I have to tell you what a special district is. As I mentioned in the introduction, no sensible definition has been promulgated, and I will not offer a new one here. I will argue instead that being a special district is not a yes-or-no proposition, like being wet or dry, that there are varying degrees of "special-districtness," just as there are varying degrees of age and youth, or health and ill-health, and all that we can sensibly is indicate what constitutes more of this quality and what constitutes more.

Let me start with some US definitions that are ultimately unsatisfactory, but put us on the right track. Special districts are not "units of general local government". "Units of general local government" are defined (for most federal statutory purposes) as entities with taxing, police and general corporate powers. "Police powers" is a term of art: it refers not just to the power to dress guys up in uniforms and give them painted cars with sirens and red lights on top, but also to a legal power to take actions necessary to "protect public health, safety, morals and general welfare". In the US, police powers give municipalities the right to adopt zoning codes, regulate topless bars and prohibit public expectoration, *inter alia*. Thus one possible definition of a special district is a unit of government that lacks either police or taxing powers.

But this definition seems too broad. It makes every local government in Ireland a special district, since none of them have full US-style police powers. As stated, it won't do, but it does suggest something interesting: special districts have grants of power less broad than other forms of local government. This suggestion, however, can be taken too far, as it is in the popular definition of special districts — units of local government that perform only one function. This definition is too narrow: the Port Authority of New York and New Jersey is often cited as the archetypal special district, but fails to qualify under this definition since it operates a seaport, several airports, two tunnels, four bridges, a subway line, two office buildings, a bus terminal, a trade promotion unit, a language school, and, until recently, an economic analysis office.

These are the problems you encounter when you try to make being a special district a yes-or-no proposition. If we are more realistic and seek only to rank entities in terms of "special-districtness", then we can see a fundamental proposition: the more narrowly circumscribed the issues a mechanism resolves, the more it is a special district. But this proposition by itself is not enough. Like being healthy (and unlike being old), being a special district has several dimensions. Not being a general local government is only one of those dimensions. The Galway post office has narrowly circumscribed responsibilities, and so does the New York Road Runners Club, but no one would think of either as a special district. So we need to consider another dimension as well, one which separates government departments from private associations.

The distinction is difficult; special districts are in the middle in this dimension. To distinguish special districts from government departments, I would say that an organisation is more of a special district the more independent it is of entities with police powers — that is, the more it can decide without specific approval of entities with police powers. To distinguish special districts from private associations, I would say the opposite — an organisation is more of a special district the less independent it is of entities with police powers. Putting these two dimensions together, we see why it is hard to delineate what special districts are: they are inter-mediate cases on this dimension.

Fortunately, though, design is easier than definition. Designing good ways to resolve non-contractible uncertainty forces you to decide where an entity will be placed on each dimension, but it doesn't require you to label how much the thing you come with is a special district. Thus, to return to the road example, where the main-road maintenance organisation fits on the spectrum between special districts and units of general local government depends on how other services are organised. If sewers and police are region-wide non-contractible issues too, then there's no reason why decisions about them should not be made by the same mechanism as road maintenance issues. But if the main road is the only thing the towns have in common (and not in common with other towns outside the region), then road maintenance should be organised as a special district.

This principle of matching mechanisms to people's stakes is more than geographical. While people's stakes are often tied to geography, and this coincidence made the road example easy to construct, sometimes they are not, and when they are not, special districts are best organised along non-geographical lines. Within a town, for instance, some people tend to be a lot more concerned about how the library is operating than others are. So the library gets to be a "special district" by the establishment of a library board, and issues like when to open the library on Sundays and whether to purchase *Satanic Verses* get resolved by a mechanism different from the mechanism that decides bar closing times and police staffing levels.

## 6. LIMITS

What are the limits to special district organisation? Why shouldn't every possible issue have its own mechanism? To explain the limits, I need to go back to a tale of Jersey City politics in the early 1900s. Corruption was always an issue in Jersey City, and one day the authorities investigating it called on a man whose name appeared on the payroll as a "confidential aide" to the mayor. Just what was it that he did, they demanded to know. "If I told you what I did," he replied, "it wouldn't be confidential." Non-contractible uncertainty is a lot like this confidential aide. If you could specify what issues might come up, those issues would not be non-contractible uncertainty — the constitution could say precisely how they should be handled when they came up, and no mechanism for resolving them would be necessary. So an assignment of issues to mechanisms must be vague and subject to litigation. The constitution may say that local road issues are the towns' responsibility and main road issues are the region's, but what sort of issue is a tree that falls on an intersection or a local road that main road drivers use for U-turns or the size of signs that mark local roads?

Vagueness also implies that errors are unavoidable. Shotguns can't hit bull's-eyes. Inevitably, some issues will be decided by the wrong mechanism. The more different mechanisms there are for resolving issues, the greater these problems become. A proliferation of special districts imposes two kinds of costs. First is the simple transaction cost of figuring out the appropriate venue for each issue and paying for the litigation that will arise whenever one party is unhappy with a decision and some ambiguity over venue remains. Second are the costs that arise from having issues decided by seriously wrong mechanisms.

To illustrate this second type of costs and show how a proliferation of special districts increases it, consider a road with houses along one side. People use the section in front of their own houses a bit more than the rest of the road, but the difference is not big. To illustrate the problems of ambiguity and mistakes, suppose that the only two mechanisms that the language can describe are majority rule for all issues and home rule — each person is a dictator for the section of road directly in front of her property. But the property listing used to assign issues is seriously deficient; many sections of the road are assigned to the wrong owner because of clerical errors. It is easy to see that simple majority rule, while unambitious and clearly not optimal in a world of precise language and inerrant property listings, will do better in the world we have described than a more ambitious system of special districts. Language and imagination, then, are the limits on special district creation — and they are real limits.

## 7. CONCLUSION

The arguments in favour of using special districts extensively are strong. Different mechanisms should be used for different kinds of issues: sometimes large groups, sometimes small groups, sometimes simple majorities, sometimes complex veto and committee structures, sometimes constituencies defined by geography, sometimes constituencies defined by interest or history. Who has what stakes in a set of issues should determine how they are resolved, not any preset rule. Special districts — the embodiment of this idea that one size doesn't fit all — are powerful tools for the construction of European federalism.

But like all powerful tools special districts should be used carefully and sparingly; they often have side-effects their inventors didn't dream of. This advice is particularly applicable to the European Union at this time. Both limits on the creation of useful special districts seem to be especially strong now: language, because there is no universally practised and patiently honed European mode of expression; and imagination, because the novelty of European integration makes the future even more difficult to apprehend than it usually is. While setting up multiple mechanisms for multiple problems is generally a good practice to follow, now is one of the worst times for doing so. Fifty years from now will be a lot better. The real trick is to prevent ossification before then.

## References

Casella, A. and Frey, B. (1992): "Federalism and Clubs: Towards an Economic Theory of Overlapping Jurisdictions", *European Economic Review*, 36, 639-46.

Coase, R. (1937): "The Nature of the Firm", *Economica*, 4, 386-405.

Dewatripont, M., Giavazzi, F., von Hagen, J., Harden, I., Perrson, T., Roland, G., Rosenthal, H., Sapir, A. and Tabellini, G. (1995): *Flexible Integration: Toward a More Effective and Democratic Europe*, London: Centre for Economic Policy Research.

Hansmann, H. (1988): "Ownership of the Firm", *Journal of Law*, Economics and Organisation, 4, 267-304.

Laffont, J.J. and Tirole, J. (1993): *A Theory of Incentives in Procurement and Regulation*, Cambridge, MA: MIT Press.

Milgrom, P. and Roberts, J. (1992): *Economics, Organization, and Management*, Englewood Cliffs, NJ: Prentice Hall.

Tiebout, C. (1956): "A Pure Theory of Local Expenditures", *Journal of Political Economy*, 64, 416-24.

Williamson, O. (1975*): Markets and Hierarchies: Analysis and Antitrust Implications*, New York: Free Press.

Williamson, O. (1985): *The Economic Institutions of Capitalism*, New York: Free Press.

# INDEX